THE CIRCUS

LURE AND LEGEND

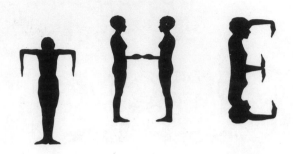

Compiled and Edited by

CIRCUS

LURE AND LEGEND

Mildred Sandison Fenner

and

Wolcott Fenner

Prentice-Hall, Inc., Englewood Cliffs, New Jersey

To
Glenn Alan
Mitchell
Craig
and
Kristin

Design by Janet Anderson

The Circus: Lure and Legend
compiled and edited by Mildred Sandison Fenner and Wolcott Fenner
© 1970 by Mildred Sandison Fenner and Wolcott Fenner
ISBN 0-13-134551-6
Library of Congress Catalog Card Number: 72-109109
Printed in the United States of America   T
Prentice-Hall International, Inc., London
Prentice-Hall of Australia, Pty. Ltd., Sydney
Prentice-Hall of Canada, Ltd., Toronto
Prentice-Hall of India Private Ltd., New Delhi
Prentice-Hall of Japan, Inc., Tokyo

FOREWORD

There are, in this nation, precious few organizations or activities which can rightfully claim the title "American institutions." Ringling Bros.-Barnum & Bailey Circus is uniquely one of them.

For ten decades The Greatest Show on Earth has brought laughter and thrills to "children of all ages." It is, indeed, an American institution in every sense of that phrase.

During its first 100 years many writers have been inspired to set down their thoughts about the special magic that is the circus. Some approached their task with humor, others with sentiment. Together their contributions compose a valid and distinguished body of Americana. This book includes some of the best that has been written about our circus and other circuses that have been noteworthy in history.

Mildred and Wolcott Fenner are steeped in history of the circus. Mildred Fenner, a professional editor, has long studied circus history and lore. Wolcott Fenner, from his position of many years with our organization, has had excellent opportunity to observe the actual workings of the spangled world. The selections they have chosen reflect this world.

Irvin Feld, President, Ringling Bros.-Barnum & Bailey
Combined Shows, Inc.

Acknowledgments and Credits

Among the many people to whom we are indebted, we mention
especially the following, whose cooperation and help made this volume
possible: Irvin Feld, Monica Chase, Maxine Dalton, Marjorie Schleifer,
John Schleifer, Gilbert Smith, Rosalie Sandison Wood, Henry Ringling
North, Paul Caldwell, Robert Parkinson, Tom Scaperlanda, and
Marvine Stockton.

All colored circus posters used were obtained from the Circus
World Museum, Baraboo, Wisconsin, through the cooperation of
Robert Parkinson. Ringling Bros. Barnum & Bailey Combined Shows,
Inc., supplied all color prints of performers. The National Gallery of
Art, Washington, D.C., furnished transparencies and granted permission
for use of the paintings by Picasso, Logan, and Brown. Charles Hammond
gave us the transparency for his painting; Tom Scaperlanda, San
Antonio, Texas, for his circus room. Credits to cartoonists appear
with the cartoons.

All black-and-white prints, except for those listed below, came from
the fabulous collection of Paul Caldwell, Roanoke, Virginia:
The Circus Maximus—*Courtesy, the Bettmann Archive*
Dan Rice—*Courtesy, Harvard Theatre Collection (Fogg Art Museum)*
Tom Thumb's Wedding—*Currier and Ives' lithograph furnished by
American Antiquarian Society*
The Wallendas; Clyde Beatty—*Courtesy, Circus World Museum,
Baraboo, Wisconsin*

King Charles Troupe; Sheila and Barry Sloan; Unus;
Pio Nock; Konyot's Chimps; the Felds and
Hofheinzes—*Courtesy, Ringling Bros.-Barnum & Bailey
Combined Shows, Inc.*
The British royal family—*The Central Press Photos, Ltd., 6 and 7
Gough Square, Fleet St., London EC4, obtained
through the cooperation of Cyril B. Mills*
Soviet circus on ice—*From* SOVIET LIFE MAGAZINE, *March 1965; used
by permission of Managing Editor Nikolai Zhiltsoz*
Soviet audience—*From* PACE MAGAZINE, *March 1968; used by permission
of Robert J. Fleming*
Mrs. Lyndon Johnson; Mrs. Richard Nixon—*Courtesy, Harry Goodman*
Circus stamp—*Philatelic Section, U.S. Post Office Department*

The illustrations of Astley's Riding School and Ricketts Circus are
from *The Circus, Its Origin and Growth Prior to 1835* by Isaac J.
Greenwood (The Dunlap Society, New York, 1898), made available
by Paul Caldwell. It was through Mr. Caldwell also that we were able
to get a xeroxed copy of the difficult-to-locate *Life Story of the Ringling
Brothers* by Alf T. Ringling, published in 1900.

Authors and publishers of selections included (credit lines appear
with each selection) were exceptionally cooperative, as was Marvine
Stockton of the Copyright Office of the Library of Congress.

*Mildred and Wolcott Fenner
Washington, D.C.*

Contents

PART ONE

THE CIRCUS OVER THE YEARS

THE CIRCUS MAXIMUS

Earl Chapin May

It was circus day in Pagan Rome. Pompey was financing a free show for the Roman populace.

Less than a decade had elapsed since this same populace had accorded him one of the most spectacular triumphs ever bestowed on a returning conqueror, with a pageant requiring more than an hour to pass a given point. But the blue-blooded general was not satisfied to be one of a Triumvirate. He planned to rule all Roman subjects without the help of Crassus and Julius Caesar.

Pompey proposed to perfect his popularity by giving a show so stupendous that even his triumphal procession of 61 B.C. would be overshadowed. Hence he had boldly announced, on Rome's walls and pillars:

FIVE DAYS OF PERFORMANCES!
IN THE CIRCUS MAXIMUS!!
FREE, TO ALL AND EVERYONE!

He had positively promised, rain or shine, the sanguinary slaughter of:

500—FIERCE NUMIDIAN LIONS—500!
and
20—PONDEROUS PACHYDERMS—20!
Performances To Be Interspersed With Chariot Racing Plus Equestrian and Acrobatic Feats of Great Daring and Dexterity!

The noble Roman was a showman. He knew what his public wanted. He knew what he wanted, also. He wanted plenty of publicity.

So, at high noon of the opening day, precisely as promised by press agents, a grand, free, glittering street parade wound its golden, glorious way from the Capitol past the Forum to a mammoth structure between the Palatine and Aventine Hills. Rome's rutted thoroughfares and seven hills were jammed with free show customers.

Surrounded by his armored bodyguard of praetorians, Pompey the Great was prominently placed in his impressive pageant. Wearing his toga of Tyrian purple he rode in a richly plated chariot drawn by four spirited horses from Cappadocia. White-clad lictors carried *fasces* denoting Roman law and dignity. Red and gold tableau wagons drawn by mules and elephants bore images of gods and deified members of the Imperial Family. Haughty centurions rode at the head of their marching companies. Behind these came colleges of priests and other notables; horses and horsemen by the score; myraids of attractions assembled to amaze the multitude.

Men, women, and children in holiday finery cheered from the streets or from handy windows, then rushed around corners to have just one more vista before Pompey's parade entered the Circus Maximus to be vociferously greeted by 150,000 eager commoners as the grand entrée went once around the hippodrome.

While Caesar and Crassus bit their envious nails, Pompey with his satellites settled in seats especially reserved for them on a canopied gallery near the main entrance above the chariot stables. The spectators were already packed on unshaded tiers of stone or wood in the roofless, oblong circus.

At a signal from this soldier-showman a white flag was thrown onto a sanded racecourse. Trumpets blared. The big show began.

Well-trained athletes boxed and wrestled. Sprinters and long-distance runners contested for applause and material prizes. Lions and elephants fought—and died. So did many hired strong men and many more condemned criminals whose only chance against a charging lion was one well-aimed thrust with a stylus.

Fresh blood was covered with fresh, clean sand. More trumpets blared. The tense throng yelled. Pompey's circus program was fast and snappy. The great man deigned to summon and commend his equestrian director for putting the show together so effectively. The director had thus far kept his head. If the show made good he might keep it indefinitely.

As the sun swung westward through a blue Italian sky a deep-lunged circus orator proclaimed the coming of *desultores*—equestrians peerless in their performances! As these stars of the Circus Maximus raced around the long, high *spina* which divided the course from end to end, each rider leaped repeatedly from one bare-backed horse to another. The populace, having a first good taste of bread and circuses, loudly approved this expert horsemanship. Still more loudly did it endorse a colorful Roman standing race in which each contestant rode two horses simultaneously, one foot on each horse as they sped side by side.

A long-necked, spotted quadruped from Africa made its premier Italian circus appearance. But though Pompey's press department had enthusiastically heralded this rare "Camelopard," the poor giraffe did not create a good impression. It was too quickly pulled down and killed by imported tigers. Yet it bled freely, just as advertised.

A race between tame elephants went much better. So did seven clumsy laps around the *spina* by African camels "Imported At Great Expense of Time and Money."

But chariot races created the wildest excitement. Spectators ceased purchasing cakes, wine and currant delicacies from circus attachés to argue heatedly about the merits of the many entries, for there were fifteen events on the day's racing card. In each event six four-horse chariots dashed around the long *spina* seven times, each chariot carrying white, red, blue, or green stable colors, while each driver yelled, plied the whip, and did his best to lock wheels with and wreck his rivals.

Patricians and plebeians wagered vast numbers of *sesterces* on the outcome. Spills were rewarded by shouts and groans. Dead drivers and horses were dragged away and replaced by fresh actors. The show must go on, as per a circus tradition tracing back seven hundred years to Romulus.

Five days of this "Circus of a Century," and Pompey was solidly in the hearts of the populace, which had learned to expect bread from the public granaries and circuses from politicians. Politicians, in seeking new attractions, added rope dancing, classical posturing, and ground-and-lofty acrobatics. Blood lust was catered to by gladitorial butcherings.

During the eightieth year of the Christian era, Titus dedicated the Roman Colosseum which was heavily advertised as the *World's Greatest Amphitheatre.* Though Pompey's successors had enlarged the Circus Maximus in marble (until it was three stories high, 1,875 feet long, 625 feet wide, and accommodated 250,000 spectators simultaneously) the new Coliseum promptly became popular because its elliptical form gave each of its 50,000 seats a clear view of sensational performances.

Thousands of wild-eyed racing fans continued to attend the Circus Maximus and watched as charioteers urged fleet horses around the *spina*. But when a popularity-seeking, spendthrift emperor threw a thousand Christians to lions and tigers during one day's Colosseum festivities; when he staged a mimic battle in which thousands of soldiers and sailors participated bloodily; when gladiators fought to the death by gory dozens; when cages of wild animals magically rose from the earth and sank into it again; while beneath an enormous red and white canopy the air was regularly sprayed with perfume—*that* was a show fit for a Roman capital.

Only Maccus, principal clown of a nearby theatre, protested at the appalling paucity of comedy.

Behind advancing Roman legions other amphitheatres arose at Verona, Capua, and Pompeii in Italy; in Sicily, Spain, France, and far-off Briton—nearly a hundred show places all told. Wild animal duels, daring equestrianism, chariot races, and gladiatorial combats closely followed the Roman eagles.

Then Western Culture met Northern Barbarism. The Roman Empire began to totter. Rome was sacked by brutal invaders. Emperors and nobles no longer gave shows. The Circus Maximus, Coliseum, and their provincial prototypes became stone quarries for later builders.

"Circus" was lost to common language and replaced by local substitutes.

Yet, through the Dark Ages, adventurous groups of animal trainers, riders, and acrobats wandered about Europe, Asia, and Africa, sleeping in vans or under hedges, entertaining yokels at rural markets or appearing before royalty by command. King Alfred was treated to a "Wilde Beaste Showe" augmented by mummers and mountebanks. William the Conqueror brought from France a troupe "performing feats of great strength and agility."

Maccus' descendants became court jesters. King Edward III employed and enjoyed a troup of rope-dancers, tumblers, and contortionists. Queen Elizabeth was royally entertained by acrobats and somersaulters. William Shakespeare made the stage-fool popular. The Spirit of the Circus Maximus survived in these humble troupers.

From *The Circus from Rome to Ringling*. Duffield and Green, Inc., New York, 1932.

THE MODERN
CIRCUS BEGINS

All throughout Europe for centuries, jugglers, acrobats, magicians, and zanies (clowns) roamed from town to town and castle to castle, performing at fairs and on feast days, but not until 1770 in England did the circus as we know it begin. It began, as circuses should, with horses—horses on a circular track—and a young English cavalry sergeant named Philip Astley.

Astley was already a hero at the age of nineteen for charging and breaking the French line during the Seven Years' War. For this feat he was made a sergeant major. He was tall, handsome, and a daring rider. One day in 1770 the city of London was littered with handbills announcing "Activity on Horseback by Mr. Astley, Sergeant-Major in His Majesty's Light Dragoons."

His trick riding performance included galloping full tilt around the ring, with one foot on the saddle and the other on the horse's head while he brandished a broadsword, and then riding balanced upside down atop the saddle. Gradually he added to his show: a human pyramid of acrobats, dancing dogs, wire walkers, a clown, and even a freak of sorts—a demure French lady whose golden hair was so long it trailed to the ground.

So the modern circus was born. The standard Astley used for the size of the circus ring, forty-two feet in diameter, is still followed by many outfits all over the world. In 1782 one of his best riders, Charles Hughes, set up a rival show in London. Among Hughes' employees was a young man named John Bill Ricketts,

who decided it was time the circus came to the New World.

In America in the late eighteenth century a few entertainers roamed the countryside with high-wire acts or trained animals, just as they had for centuries in Europe. The first lion to reach this country came in 1770, and a year later Americans saw a camel, but it took a master showman like Ricketts to present a real circus.

In a new country where cities and towns were isolated by distance and by almost impassable mud roads, people depended on horses not only for entertainment and pleasure but also for transportation. They admired fine horses and fine riders, so when Ricketts set up what he advertised as an English-type riding school in Philadelphia, horse lovers flocked to see him. It was no wonder that George Washington was at Ricketts' grand opening in what was then the nation's capital, on April 3, 1793.

Raised on a Virginia plantation, the President was an expert horseman himself. He watched Ricketts, astride his trick horse Cornplanter, jump over obstacles massed side by side, circle the ring with a boy standing on his shoulders, leap through a hoop twelve feet above the ground, do a juggling act, and dance in the saddle as his mount galloped around the ring.

Washington had a white charger named Jack that he had ridden as commander in chief in the Revolutionary War. When Jack was twenty-eight years old and had long since been put out to pasture, Ricketts made an offer to pay $150 to the President to display Jack in a stall at the circus. Washington accepted. Thus the Father of his Country made a deal with the Father of the American Circus, and the new venture got its first side show.

Ricketts' circus did so well that he built a new home for it in Philadelphia, a white amphitheatre with tall, slender columns in front. On top of the conical roof he put a weathervane shaped like the Roman god Mercury, the messenger. In the autumn of 1794, Ricketts took his show on a wagon tour, traveling as far north as New York and Boston and as far south as Baltimore. In 1797, when the President retired, Ricketts put on a special program for him.

On December 17, 1799, three days after Washington died, disaster struck the nation's first circus. Fire destroyed the Philadelphia amphitheatre. Ricketts gave up in despair and sailed for England; on the voyage the ship was lost with everyone aboard.

From *Great Days of the Circus* (American Heritage Junior Library). © 1962 by American Heritage Publishing Co., Inc. Reprinted by permission.

THE GREAT P. T. BARNUM

Irving Wallace

Barnum, who always considered himself a promoter and "a museum man" rather than "a circus man," had achieved his greatest success before his entry into the circus. Only the last twenty years of his long life were devoted to canvas and sawdust. . . .

Barnum's only previous experience with a traveling circus had been in his impoverished youth when he had traveled through the South with Aaron Turner, who had given the primitive entertainment its big top. Now, at the invitation of William Cameron Coup, a former roustabout and side-show manager, and Dan Castello, an ex-clown, Barnum prepared to thrill his old public with the biggest outdoor circus in history. Although lost in the brilliant glare of his senior partner's great name, the natty, bearded Coup was the prime mover of the new enterprise. . . .

On April 10, 1871, the "great show enterprise" of Barnum, Coup, and Castello opened in Brooklyn beneath three acres of canvas tent. Ten thousand spectators peered through the flickering gaslight at the animals, the freaks, the side-show curios, the parade, and the circus acts themselves. Then, the circus went on the road, from New England through the Midwest to California. . . .

Barnum liked to say that he made the circus bigger and bigger over Coup's frightened protests. . . . Coup's version, corroborated by impartial witnesses, was the opposite. . . . It was he who added to "Barnum's Great Traveling World's Fair," as the circus was soon called, such expensive attractions as "the lightning ticket seller," Ben Lusbie, who could dispose of six

thousand fifty-cent pasteboards in one hour; the daring aeronaut Washington H. Donaldson, of Maine, who made semi-weekly balloon ascensions (until, accompanied by a Chicago reporter, he disappeared in a storm over Lake Michigan); a rare giraffe, a half-ton seal, an Italian goat that rode a horse bareback. . . .

Furthermore, it was Coup who overcame the horrified objections of both Barnum and the railroad companies to putting the circus on flatcars. . . . He was also credited with inventing a more efficient system for loading and unloading the trains, inaugurating half-rate excursions that brought in spectators from outlying districts, installing the tent's center pole, and conceiving a two-ring circus to replace the old one-ring affair. . . . In its second season, the circus grossed almost a million dollars in six months. . . .

P. T. Barnum's Great Roman Hippodrome—with Coup the general manager and Castello the director of amusements—was opened to the public in April 1874. For the first performance, the ten thousand seats were filled. A grand procession of triumphal cars, carrying one thousand performers in representation of historical monarchs and rulers the world over circled the arena. Then followed chariot races, in the Ben Hur manner, around an oval track one fifth of a mile long. Then came the tightrope walkers, the Japanese acrobats, the monkey races, the clowns.

The huge Hippodrome show, later taken on the road, was a success in every way. But now Barnum and Coup, whose health was impaired by overwork, had a falling out. . . . Castello had

Condensed from *The Fabulous Showman*. © 1959 by Irving Wallace.
Reprinted by permission of Alfred A. Knopf, Inc.

already sold out his interest to Barnum, and now Coup did the same . . . .

Suddenly, in 1880, Barnum realized that he was being seriously challenged for the first time. A circus known as International Allied Shows, which had bought out Sanger's Royal British Menagerie, was making effective inroads on audiences throughout the nation. . . .

Of the three men who owned Allied Shows, one was the managerial genius, as Barnum would soon learn, and he was the thirty-three-year-old James A. Bailey. What brought Barnum into direct contact with Bailey was an elephant. On March 10, 1880, in Philadelphia, a female elephant in the Allied Shows named Hebe gave birth to a baby christened Columbia. This was the first instance of an elephant being born in captivity. The publicity was nationwide. Barnum was excited by it and he was determined to own the baby elephant. But he made the mistake of regarding Allied Shows as a smaller competitor who could be bought off at a price, rather than as a full-fledged rival. When Hebe's offspring was two months old, Barnum dashed off a telegram to Cooper, Bailey, and Hutchinson offering $100,000 for Hebe and her child. Barnum was shocked when Bailey wired back a refusal to sell and audaciously advised him to look to his laurels. At once, on twelve sheets, Bailey reproduced an enlarged reproduction of Barnum's telegram, and captioned his advertising: "What Barnum Thinks of the Baby Elephant."

Barnum knew that he had met his match at last, but he took it goodnaturedly and sensibly. If he could not eliminate them, he would join them. "I found that I had at last met foemen 'worthy of my steel,'" Barnum admitted, "and [was] pleased to find comparatively young men with a business talent and energy approximating to my own, I met them in friendly council and after days of negotiation we decided to join our shows in one mammoth combination." . . .

A half-dozen years [later], Cooper sold out for a large sum. Then Hutchinson, who had once made his living peddling Barnum's autobiography on a percentage basis, also withdrew

for a price. At last, for better or for worse, it was Barnum and Bailey.

Like Barnum, the short, thin, nervous Bailey, who wore spectacles, mustache, and goatee, and a professional air, had lifted himself to success by his own bootstraps. Like Barnum, he . . . pleaded the highest morality for the show. . . . At this point, the resemblance between the two partners ended. . . .

For a showman, Bailey was extremely retiring. In complete contrast to Barnum, he avoided personal publicity and exaggeration. When celebrities or reporters were on hand, he hid in his personal quarters. He objected to use of his portrait in advertising. He found letter-writing a chore, and maintained almost all his correspondence by wire, often dispatching fifty telegrams in a single day. He wore a perpetual derby hat to screen his growing baldness, and possessed a dozen nervous mannerisms, such as chewing rubber bands and twirling a silver dollar between his fingers. He was too sensitive to fire performers personally, and always delegated the task to an assistant. He meted out justice as sternly to animals as to human beings. When an ill-tempered eight-foot elephant named Mandarin killed one of his keepers in London, Bailey calmly crated the beast for the voyage back to New York. But in mid-ocean, Bailey weighted Mandarin's crate with pig iron and pushed it into the sea.

Logistics were Bailey's specialty. Fred Bradna, a German who became Bailey's equestrian director, wrote in *The Big Top*: "While I was in the army at Dieuze, the German military staff sent its quartermaster general to travel with Bailey and learn how to move masses of men, animal, and equipment by railroad car. His techniques for loading and unloading trains and laying out lots are still, with modern modifications, in use today."

Except for a two-year period when Bailey withdrew from the partnership in protest against Barnum's egotism, the pair remained successful and congenial partners until Barnum's death. At no time was Barnum ever jealous of the younger man. He respected Bailey for his brilliance and originality, and continually begged the press to credit Bailey for the success of the circus.

Barnum's single great achievement as a circus proprietor, the climax of his sawdust-and-tanbark career, was his brilliant acquisition of an elephant, the internationally famous Jumbo. [See Barnum's account, page 34 of this volume.]

In his first season of thirty-one weeks, spent in New York and on tour throughout America, Jumbo drew receipts totaling one million seven hundred and fifty dollars. For three and a half years, ridden by an estimated million children, gulping down endless quantities of peanuts and candy, he enriched the lives of America's young and the pocketbooks of the circus.

On the evening of September 15, 1885, Jumbo and his tiny [elephant] companion, Tom Thumb, had finished their performance in St. Thomas, Ontario, Canada. The show's thirty-one other elephants had already been loaded on the waiting train when, at nine o'clock, Matthew Scott led Jumbo and Tom Thumb to their private car. As they crossed the freight yard, the threesome marched along an unused spur line of the Grand Trunk Railway. Suddenly there was the rising clang of an approaching locomotive. An unscheduled special freight train rounded the bend, and from five hundred yards away its glaring headlights held on the terrified Jumbo. The train, closing the gap at breakneck speed, tried to jam to a halt, but too late. Scott leaped aside in time as the locomotive hit Tom Thumb a glancing blow, breaking his left hind leg, and tossing him aside to safety. Then the engine plowed head-on into Jumbo's towering body. . . .

Taxidermists applied their skills to the mammoth carcass. Jumbo's teeth and bones proved that he was still growing before his death. His stomach gave up a small mint of English coins. His skeleton was presented to the Museum of Natural History in New York. But his hide, which in itself weighed 1,538 pounds, was settled on a shaped frame of hard wood, and thus Jumbo continued to serve the circus until, at last, he was turned over to the Barnum Museum at Tufts College in Medford, Massachusetts. . . .

Just as Barnum always sought, but never found, a singer to equal Jenny Lind, he persisted in trying to locate another elephant to match the box-office appeal of Jumbo. . . . After three years of effort and an expenditure of $250,000, by the showman's estimate, a sacred white elephant named Toung Taloung was secured in Mandalay, through permission of King Theebaw of Siam. Shipped from Rangoon to London, and thence to New York, it arrived aboard the steamer *Lydian Monarch* on March 28, 1884, its appearance celebrated by three prize-winning poems, one written by Joaquin Miller.

Barnum had been advertising the sacred elephant as of purest milk-white hue. But when he went on the steamer, followed by the press, to observe his purchase, he found Toung Taloung's complexion a dirty gray except for a few light pink spots and pink eyes. . . . Because the elephant was not white, Barnum went to great lengths to get Siamese experts to authenticate it. Meanwhile, his leading circus rival, the gray-haired, self-centered Adam Forepaugh, began to exploit and exhibit a pure white elephant named Light of Asia. . . .

While Forepaugh disarmed the reporters with drinks, a sober journalist from the *Philadelphia Press*, Alexander C. Kenealy, sneaked toward the white elephant with a soaked sponge. He rubbed the creature's flank, and the removal of the coating of white paint revealed the animal's natural gray beneath. Instead of publishing his expose, Kenealy sold it to Barnum, who advertised Forepaugh's deception wherever Americans could read. Despite the expose, Forepaugh's white-coated elephant outdrew Barnum's genuine gray one. When Forepaugh died in 1890, his circus was taken over by Bailey.

ENTER THE RINGLING BROTHERS

Alf T. Ringling

Darkness hung over the old Mississippi, and in the uncertain light of a few early lamps near the boat-landing at McGregor, Iowa, a score or more of boys were dimly visible, running along the water's edge, skipping pebbles over the black surface of the river, and stopping at intervals to peer anxiously down the stream.

Huddled close together on the wet sand not far distant were five boys, barefooted and with eyes sleeping yet alert as they vainly tried to pierce the southern darkness. It was a great day in the lives of these boys, who for two weeks had read and reread the crude posters which announced that on this particular morning a circus was coming to town—not the great tented institution of today which steams into town on its long trains, for this was in the 1860's—but a boat show which announced its approach by glaring rosin torches and a river calliope.

Finally in the distance a few dim lights appeared, growing larger and more brilliant as they drew nearer. A cry of delight went up from scores of lusty throats, and a moment later there burst out upon the morning air the weird notes of the river calliope.

Down the one main street of McGregor a good portion of the town's population came in response to the call of the calliope, swelling the crowd that watched on shore the coming of the circus boat. The torches threw fantastic shadows that danced on the banks, and lighted by the tongues of flame the animals and the hustling deck-hands, with faces reflecting the light, and the water surrounding the boat transformed into liquid fire, made a picture spectacular and thrilling.

To the five Ringling brothers the circus boat, with its barge of tent-wagons and chariots along-side, seemed like the triumphant achievement of a great genius, who had arisen out of the waters which hitherto had been inhabited by nothing more mysterious than a catfish. With rapt attention they watched the one big elephant of the show majestically tread down the gang-plank to the shore. Their youthful fancy clad the great beast with all the wisdom of Socrates, and the two trained donkeys that sniffed the air from the side of the boat seemed like wise conjurers in grotesque disguise.

By the time the dawn had faded the torches into a dull red flare, the show was unloaded and much of it on the show-ground. The sight of the spectacle had so affected the brothers that they had stood riveted to the spot, clasping each other's hands in speechless ecstasy. When the last wagon had rolled slowly up the bank to the street, Al, with a sigh of relaxation, turned to Otto and said:

"What would you say if we had a show like that?"

"Well," replied Otto, with a coolness that surprised his brothers, "I would say to the big man with the loud voice, who bossed the fellows unloading the big bandwagon, not to swear like he did."

"And I know what I'd say," said John, just turned four, as the boys trudged homeward; "I'd say, 'Ice-cream seven times a day.'"

"Let's have a circus!" chimed in Charlie Ringling, with all the enthusiasm of his six years.

"Yes," echoed Alfred, the next elder. "Let's —when we grow to be big."

The three youngest rattled along in this manner, naming according to their youthful fancy the things they would like to have and the things they would like to do if they had a circus. One would be an autocratic ringmaster, giving commands to everybody; the other would be a clown, who would be funnier than the monkeys, and the third would eat pie and barber-pole candy in the lion's den. Al and Otto, both in their teens, treated these effervescent outbursts of childhood with the patronizing airs that invariably belong to older brothers; but they were both thinking along the same lines, devising ways and means, with the judgment that belonged to their advanced years.

Al related the story a missionary had told his Sunday-school class about the surprise of a native on an island where he had planted a peach-stone that grew into a big fruit-bearing tree.

"Goodie!" cried Charlie, gleefully; "we'll plant the kind of a stone that raises circuses, and when it grows big we'll pick the baby elephants, Shetland ponies, and trick monkeys off of it. And how will that be for getting a circus?"

"That'll be very bad," said Otto. "You don't catch the peach story at all. It took years for it to grow big, but it started from a little worthless peach-stone, like we fellows must always throw away after we've eaten the juicy cover that it comes in. It took a long time for the peachtree to grow, and it's a long way from right here where we are to the circus we'd like to have."

"Who ever heard of picking elephants off of a tree?" said Al. "If we're ever to have a circus, we've got to get it by starting small, and having it grow like the peach-stone did."

Whether any of the brothers, previous to this morning, had ever thought of owning a circus even they themselves do not know. It seems likely that they had, though the early morning hour when the boat show came to McGregor is remembered by them as the time they first talked of their youthful ambition among themselves and found it to be a mutually expressed desire.

[During the next few years, the boys, starting with a panorama show, presented a penny circus featuring a billy goat, made their first tent with $8.37 worth of white sheeting, added a horse to their menagerie and charged five cents, organized the Classic and Comic Concert Company, went on tour, and reorganized as Ringling Brothers' Carnival of Fun. Eventually the five young showmen, with around a thousand dollars saved, were ready to start the circus about which they had dreamed since that early morning in McGregor.]

A correspondence was begun with "Old Yankee" Robinson. During the summer before, while the boys were traveling with various circuses, Al Ringling had traveled with the then famous showman, and he earnestly urged the advisability of leasing Old Yankee's name.

Yankee Robinson, about this time a victim of misfortune, had been forced to retire from business with nothing but his name, which to the circus-going public had been a great one. The boys wanted this name as soon as they should organize their show, to recommend it to the public. The old showman, who had taken a liking to Al Ringling, readily consented to any kind of a partnership the boys desired. Perhaps he was in that stage of desperation where men grasp at straws; or it may be that he saw with prophetic eye the bright future awaiting the pluck and energy of the Ringling boys.

Late in March the young men arrived in Baraboo, Wisconsin [where the family now lived], and with energy and zeal began the work of building their small circus.

From *Life Story of the Ringling Brothers*. 1900.

JOHN RINGLING NORTH

John Kobler

Of all the marvels, human and animal, which populate the Ringling Brothers' circus none can match John Ringling North, the man who runs it [1948] in sheer, brassy flamboyance. It is the considered judgment of a large following of friends and enemies that the sustained private performance given by North, a former stock-and-bond salesman who hacked his way through a financial jungle to become president and majority stockholder of Ringling Bros.—Barnum & Bailey Combined Shows, Inc., is easily as spectacular as any that takes place under the Big Top of The Greatest Show on Earth.

At forty-six, "Mr. John," as his 1,450 employees address him, is a glittering anachronism whose social and professional activities evoke the tradition of such rococo sports as "Diamond Jim" Brady, "Bet a Million" Gates and his own prodigious uncle, the late John Ringling.

He is one of the last few men left in America to maintain private Pullman cars. The *Jomar* —its first owner, John Ringling, named it in honor of himself and his wife Mable—is a silver-painted pleasure dome, 82 feet long in which North lives both on the road and in winter circus headquarters at Sarasota, Florida.

North seldom wakens before 3 o'clock in the afternoon. From fall to spring, when the *Jomar* rests on a railroad siding at the 200-acre winter quarters in Sarasota, nobody dares venture within footfall of the call until Charles, the valet, telephones the executive office a few hundred feet distant to announce the president's levee. The staff brightens. Presently the president

strides into view. He is broad and stocky, with crinkly black hair and strong, flashing teeth. . . .

Upon settling down to his desk, he tussles with high-level circus problems. The details are supervised by North's younger brother Henry, the circus's vice president, a man as mild and self-effacing as John is aggressive. Toward late afternoon North has a stableboy saddle his favorite mount, a stallion named Stonewall's Pride, and takes a lathering gallop around the grounds.

Like the night-blooming cereus, North does not come fully alive until after dark. When not entertaining on the *Jomar*, he usually turns up with a bevy of fellow-celebrants in the John Ringling Hotel's M'Toto Room (named after the circus's lady gorilla). A cocktail lounge with dance band, the M'Toto Room closes it doors to the public at 1 A.M. To North this is practically high noon, and he steps behind the bar to mix drinks himself, a practice sorely trying to the hotel's accountants. . . .

At about 4 A.M., the martini hour on his drinking program, he sometimes diverts his audience with a repertory of special skills developed at Yale and in the circus. He tap dances, plays the saxophone and cornet, juggles lighted torches and sings songs of his own composition. . . .

His playboyishness has been wrongly taken as a symptom of debility by North's many adversaries to their subsequent discomfort. No tougher, craftier showman ever headed the Ringling Brothers enterprise. . . .

The president's chair in the circus corporation is a spot North coveted from tenderest youth and attained only against the furious opposition of every other branch of the prolific, quarrelsome Ringling clan, which still considers him a "gilly" (outsider). North was a precocious tot in Baraboo, Wisconsin, the circus's early winter headquarters, when the five Ringling brothers were banking their first millions. He had been born to their only sister, Ida, and Henry Whitestone North, a gentle, uncompetitive soul who earned a modest livelihood as a lumber merchant. He died when John and Henry were youngsters, and although they remember him with affection, it is their uncles, especially Uncle John, the most dominating and expansive personality among them, who exerted the deepest-felt influences in their lives. . . .

As a circus employee he could never convince Uncle John that he was worth more than $35 a week. . . . North quit the circus in disgust to become a customer's man, vowing never to return except as top dog. But he maintained close and amiable relations with Uncle John, a course which proved fortunate for both his own ambitions and the interests of the rest of the family. For in the next decade the mighty Ringling empire was shaken to it foundations. In 1929, John Ringling, by then the only surviving brother, made his last merger. The circumstances were somewhat unfortunate. Then, as today, it was vital to the circus to open its season in New York's Madison Square Garden, not only because of the big box office, but also the national publicity. That year, however, Ringling nonchalantly let the usual discussion of an April lease on the arena hang fire and another corporation owning five small circuses booked the arena for April. Ringling bought the circuses—and the lease on the Garden—for $1.7 million, borrowing the money from a loan company on his personal note. Then the Florida real-estate bubble burst. Wall Street blew up, and Ringling's enormous assets were frozen tight. In 1932 he had to default a small part of the interest on his borrowings. To protect

their loan his creditors pounced on the circus, installing as manager an oldtime carnival promoter, Sam Gumpertz. Although they kept Ringling on as president for the value of his name, with a token salary of $5,000 a year, he never again had a voice in circus affairs.

Nor was this the only grief to beset him. His second wife, whom he had divorced, was trying to collect $50,000 he owed her; the government was preparing to claim $13 million in tax arrears (Uncle John had always regarded taxation as unconstitutional), and he was embroiled in approximately 100 other lawsuits. Finally he suffered the first of a succession of heart attacks which incapacitated him for decisive action. He could have bailed himself out of a good deal of debt simply by selling a handful of his paintings by Rubens or Ca' d'Zan [his mansion home] but these he had dedicated as monuments to his own memory and nothing could persuade him to touch them.

In this dilemma John North . . . obtained his uncle's power of attorney and hustled around town scraping together the next interest payment on Ringling's $1.7 million loan. It amounted to about $50,000 and it was due within a month. Borrowing a few thousand here from a college crony, a few thousand there from some wealthy circus buff, and selling 300 cases of Uncle John's rarest bourbon whisky, he managed to raise half of it. Two days' grace remained. A loan shark offered him the balance at 42% interest. In desperation he accepted it. "Thank you, Johnny," was his ailing uncle's only comment when informed that the circus was, for the moment, saved. When North later revealed the interest terms, the old gentleman nearly fell out of bed. "Just like a boy who's never had any real money of his own," he scolded, and he brooded about it to his dying day.

Pneumonia carried Ringling off in 1936 at the age of 70. His estate, when untangled, was appraised at $23.5 million, but the day he died cash on hand totaled $300. His will produced some disagreeable surprises for every individual named on it. Ca' d'Zan and the art collection (valued at $11 million) went to the state of Florida. Half of the remainder of the estate, including 30% of the circus stock, was set up as a trust fund, the income to go to the state for maintenance of the Ringling museums. John and Henry Ringling North were to share the other half with their mother. They were also named executors and trustees. But in a codicil dated a year after the will, Mrs. North's benefits were reduced to an annual income of $5,000, the boys cut off without a penny.

Family antagonisms exploded into one of the bitterest battles of the century. Each camp voted about a third of the stock, each disliked and distrusted the others, each was certain it held a sacred mandate to rule the circus. On one side were Uncle Charles's heirs—his widow Edith and son Robert; on the other, Uncle Alf T.'s heir—his daughter-in-law Aubrey. In the middle stood the Norths.

Robert Ringling fired the first shot with a suit to oust North as executor. He missed. The issue was, in any event, somewhat academic, because Gumpertz and the creditors were still running the circus. North argued they were running it into bankruptcy. At length the Ringlings buried their hatchets long enough to lend North an ear, and when he proposed to try to raise enough money to get the circus out of hock, providing they would then vote him president, they reluctantly agreed.

Shortly after, North sauntered into the Manufacturers Trust of New York and coolly requested a loan of a million dollars. The only collateral he could offer was the frozen Ringling assets and his assurance that he knew how to operate a circus. It is striking evidence of his powers of salesmanship that North, until then distinguished chiefly as an ornament of Manhattan nightlife, got the loan. . . .

The circus flourished in North's hands. He cleaned up the bank debt, paid dividends to the stockholders, and socked away more than a million dollars. But he continued to be a thorn in the Ringlings' collective side and his bumptious insistence that he alone had saved the day did not alleviate their pain. At the stockholders meeting the year the war started, he moved that they either offer the circus gratis to the government as a morale-builder or retire it for the duration. One worry on his mind was the fire hazard. In Cleveland the season before a fire had broken out in the menagerie tent; 51 animals were burned to death. North shuddered whenever he thought of it. All the tents could be flame-proofed, but the process required chemicals which could not be obtained for private use during the war. Nevertheless, the other stockholders voted to carry on and North tendered his resignation. It was accepted with alacrity.

Under its new management (president: Robert Ringling; vice president: James Haley, who became Aubrey Ringling's second husband in 1943) the circus got as far as the 1944 season and Hartford. The fire there, the worst in circus history, almost wrecked the corporation for good. In addition to fixing huge damage assessments, the courts sentenced Haley and five employees to a year's imprisonment. Robert Ringling happened to have been absent the day of the fire and he incurred no prison penalty.

Out of this shambles North, ever watchfully waiting in exile, mapped strategy that ultimately brought him out on top again. . . . When the smoke of battle had cleared, Haley was president, North was vice president, Robert Ringling strictly *emeritus*.

In 1947 the Haleys withdrew from the corporation altogether, relinquishing their stock to North for $475,000. Thus, after an implacable 10-year campaign, the *enfant terrible* of circusdom had 51% of the stock and with it the power to elect himself president perpetually. "That's all I wanted," said he brightly.

Condensed from "Close-up: John Ringling North" *Life*, August 8, 1948. Used by permission.

THE FELD BROTHERS

They started out as youngsters, selling "rattle-snake oil" for $1 a bottle at the Bean Soup picnic, a carnival affair, near Shade Gap, Pa.

This year [1968] more than 30 years later, the two brothers from Hagerstown, Maryland, will gross more than $20 million from such diverse enterprises as the Ringling Bros.–Barnum & Bailey Circus, one-night stands by leading entertainers, and even bloodless bullfights.

That's show biz, and Israel and Irvin Feld, a pair of latterday pitchmen, love every minute of it—the thrills, glamour, excitement, and the money.

Contrary to what people might think, plenty of money still can be made with the circus, the brothers' No. 1 venture, especially now that the tents have been taken down and all the shows are played inside. The Felds won't say how much the circus earns; they don't have to because it is a privately-held corporation. Irvin, who generally acts as spokesman (while Israel and his wife Shirley count the house), says only that the circus generates "a pretty profit."

Business is so good that next year there will be two editions of the Ringling Bros.–Barnum & Bailey Circus. This will mean doubling the number of cities the enterprise hits on its 10½-month tour and, hopefully, doubling both gross and profit.

The Feld brothers and their flamboyant partner, Roy M. Hofheinz of Houston, say the circus now misses 92 cities in the U.S. which have enclosed arenas with seating capacities of between 7,500 and 15,000 persons. Right now, the second edition—"you won't be able to tell it from the original," says Irvin—is being readied at winter headquarters in Venice, Fla., for the 1969 season.

Shade Gap, Pennsylvania, is a long way from New York's Madison Square Garden where the circus opened last week. While many brothers decide as youngsters they will go into business with each other, few make it with the verve and success of Israel and Irvin Feld.

Their father, a Russian immigrant, operated a clothing and home furnishing store in western Maryland. During the depression, Israel, now fifty-one, and his brother Irvin, four years younger, made the rounds of nearby, small-town fairs each summer, selling anything "on which we could make a dime."

By the time Irvin graduated from high school in 1938, they had accumulated enough dimes to launch their life-long business partnership by opening a wholesale drug and sundries establishment in Washington, D.C., the city they have called home ever since.

Drugs and sundries were moderately profitable. To the Feld brothers though, the operation wasn't show business, and to get back nearer their first love, they added a store to sell phonograph records. With the Felds, one thing always leads to another, so by 1944 they were cutting their own records.

Their fourth record, "Guitar Boogie" by the Arthur Smith combo, sold a million copies, and proved to be a forerunner of the currently popular "soul music" variations of rhythm and blues. The Felds, whose retail outlet was in an all-Negro neighborhood, take credit for being among the first to see that this type of music would catch on with more affluent white teenagers.

By 1949, drugs and sundries had disappeared from the Feld business empire, and the brothers were selling records at their four Super Music City stores in the Washington area. It was soon time to branch out again.

The opportunity came when an old friend, dance band leader Vaughn Monroe, suggested having his orchestra play a concert of popular music inside Washington's Constitution Hall, an auditorium owned by the staid Daughters of the American Revolution and normally leased for classical concerts by leading artists and orchestras.

But the Felds were persistent. They broke the classical barrier, and Monroe was a smash hit. In fact, that success, the Felds' own experience with young recording stars, plus awareness that cities all over the country were beginning to build municipal auditoriums or civic centers, prompted the brothers to make the plunge into show business on a nationwide scale.

The Felds say competition from big manufacturers forced them out of the record-making business. However, through advance releases on new discs, available to them through industry contacts and their retail outlets, the Felds were able to get a good line on young artists coming up to stardom.

By signing up promising youngsters and using older established stars, the Feld brothers put together what was billed as The Biggest Show of 1952 (to the Felds, everything is "super," "biggest," or "greatest").

They booked the packaged three-hour variety entertainment into auditoriums in Washington, Baltimore, Pittsburgh, Philadelphia, Richmond, Norfolk, and Winston-Salem. Five years later, their Biggest Show of 1957 was playing 80 consecutive one-night stands in cities across the country and in Canada.

The Felds' big break came in 1955 when John Ringling North and his brother, Henry North, turned to them for help in getting the Greatest Show on Earth—as the circus is billed—out of the financial doldrums.

The Felds quickly identified the show's major problem. Playing under the big tent, it had to contend with uncertain weather as well as carry 3,000 employees—paying their salaries and feeding them three times a day. Just to keep the show on the road, the Norths had to gross $175,000 a week.

In 1956, the big top went down for the last time in Pittsburgh. The Felds, as agents, began booking the circus into auditoriums, many of them newly built. They reduced the number of employees from 3,000 to 300, and cut the break-even point to $125,000 a week.

Once the circus included 100 elephants, mostly working animals. Now, it carries only 20 show elephants. Moving the show indoors permits 46 consecutive weeks of performance, from the first week in January to the third week in November.

Moving the circus indoors also brought the brothers into close contact with Hofheinz, a Houston promoter. He operates the county-owned Houston Astrodome, which has by far the largest seating capacity (48,000) of any enclosed arena in the country.

Once a county judge, elected for the first time when only twenty-four years of age, the fifty-seven-year-old Hofheinz is a former Houston mayor. He has built an enterprise consisting of a fifty-six-acre amusement park, to be called Astroworld, a 1,500-room hotel-motel complex, and majority ownership of three Houston-based professional athletic teams.

What would be more natural than the Felds combining forces with Hofheinz to buy the Ringling Bros.—Barnum & Bailey Circus from the Norths? This is what they did last year for a reported price of between $8-million and $10-million. Formal contracts were signed November 11 in the home of the original circus, the Colosseum in Rome. Where else?

The Felds and Hofheinz own 95% of the stock in Ringling Bros.–Barnum & Bailey Combined Shows, Inc., a Delaware corporation that operates the circus. Equity is "fairly evenly split" between the Felds and Hofheinz, brother Irvin says. The other 5% is owned by friends and associates of the three men.

Hofheinz is chairman of the board and leaves day-to-day operations to the two brothers. Irvin is president of the corporation and chief executive officer, Israel is executive vice-president and treasurer.

Last year, the Felds sold their retail record stores. In addition to the circus, they still operate the outdoor Carter Barron Amphithea-ter in Washington on a 25-year lease from the federal government, the Baltimore civic center on a lease from the city, and produce bullfights in Houston's Astrodome.

To make sure the bullfights don't violate American laws or sensibilities, they are bloodless and the bulls are not killed. To avoid slaughter, the Felds have patented a humane banderilla which can be thrown into the hump below the bull's head without piercing the animal's hide.

Clearly, the circus is the Felds' first love. This year, the show will play 52 cities, and Irvin and Israel expect the gross to increase 20% from last year's record of $12.5 million.

From *Business Week*, April 13, 1968. © 1968 McGraw-Hill, Inc., New York. Used by permission.

◆—◆

SEND NO FLOWERS

Jack Lloyd

◆—◆—◆—◆—◆—◆—◆—◆—◆—◆—◆—◆—◆—◆—◆—◆—◆—◆—◆

There is nothing like it in the world. The Greatest Show on Earth. After all these years, they're still calling it that. And maybe it is. But no matter, one thing is certain: The circus is not dead, and those skeptics, those none-believers, who went to the trouble of making funeral arrangements for the circus only a few short years ago have had to withdraw the death notice. Send the circus no flowers; no condolences to the survivors of the Big Top. It is alive and well.

From *Today*, *The Philadelphia Inquirer Magazine*, May 18, 1969. Used by permission.

THE CARAVAN CIRCUSES OF EUROPE
Marc Connelly

After spending a good part of last summer [1967] visiting circuses in half a dozen European countries, I learned that all share a common obsession. It was summed up by Jack C. Bottenheim, a Netherlands textile manufacturer prominent among the 900 lay members of an organization called Friends of the Circus.

"The great days of the European circus are over," said Mr. Bottenheim with the same ruefulness pessimists use in discussing the theater. "Radio, TV, discotheques and other attractions are killing it. The only place where circuses are insured against competition is Russia, where they are state-owned."

Without meaning to contradict Mr. Bottenheim, I must observe that, while there may not be quite as many circuses in Western Europe as there were twenty years ago, the popularity of those I have visited doesn't suggest any pressing cause for mourning.

Mr. Bottenheim, with other Friends of the Circus, drove me off from Amsterdam to Lingen, Germany, to see the flourishing Carl Althoff circus. I was told that the Althoff aggregation had never played outside Germany. Nevertheless, it is called the Californischer National Circus, and the American flag flies across the cover of its souvenir program. The Californischer has a dozen trained polar bears and even more elephants. Other members of the Althoff clan tour Europe with their own equally large outfits. And there are plenty of Althoff youngsters eager to carry on the family tradition. The devotion of Carl's two sons to the training

and exhibition of their elephants and horses and the enthusiastic responses of their large audiences indicate that the Californischer is to no degree moribund.

There are even larger circuses native to Germany. The name Hagenbeck is still magic throughout the land, and the Krone, which calls itself the biggest circus in the world, travels with 400 people and an equal number of animals. The great Knie Cirkus of Switzerland has just had one of the best of its forty-nine uninterrupted years. It excels in animal acts. Besides the beasts one expects, it exhibits trained pumas and black panthers.

I think the smallest tent circus in Europe is one Denmark has been enjoying for twelve years. It is called the Arena. For several seasons the performing personnel has totaled seven. Last summer it was reduced to six because Miss Jytte, the Cirkus Arena's one and only trapeze artist, was having a baby.

Mr. Arne Olsen, Miss Jytte's father and the owner of the circus, gave me a few facts. Each year the company appears in approximately 150 of Denmark's smaller communities. There is always sawdust in the ring because, wherever the circus visits, carpenters save it for Mr. Olsen. Most of the performers are members of the family. "But this year," Mr. Olsen stated, "we have a foreign act imported from Fyn." Mr. Olsen was having a little joke. The island of Fyn is where Hans Christian Andersen was born. The Cirkus Arena's stable consists of five ponies, one donkey, two goats, twelve dogs, and twenty pigeons. When it arrives in a town the performers help the half-dozen backstage crew put up the tent. It can seat 200. So sure is Mr. Olsen of his public that posters are not distributed until all the equipment is in place and the entire company has had a hearty noonday meal.

There are other Danish circuses. The three that can be seen during the summer everywhere between the Skaw and Gedser all give their performances in a single *manège*, as the circus ring is called throughout Europe. The smallest, but by no means insignificant, is the Cirkus Vivi Louis. The two larger are the Benneweis and the Moreno. They are equal in size and share an enormous popularity. The Benneweis is the older and last year had an anniversary along with the city of Copenhagen; the city celebrated its 800th birthday, the circus its 80th. A few years ago the Benneweis offered four additional performers when it appeared in Graasten in Jutland, a summer retreat of the Danish royal family. As usual the evening performance began with a parade of elephants. The additions to the cast consisted of King Frederick on the first elephant, Princess Margrethe, the Heiress Presumptive, on the second, and her two younger sisters, Princess Benedikte and Princess Anne-Marie (the present Queen of Greece), on the third. The warm attachment of the Danes for their rulers expressed itself in a burst of affectionate laughter and applause.

Denmark's biggest circus, visited in Copenhagen by thousands of foreign tourists every year, is the Cirkus Schumann. That the Danes like it, too, is attested by the size of the building, a city block from the Tivoli, which houses it. From May to October it draws on the world for its acts. A Danish friend of mine recalled enjoying the Marx Brothers there forty years ago.

The Schumann family is famous throughout Europe for its equestrian members. Pauline Schumann, the wife of the current head of the family, is perhaps today's most beautiful and accomplished horsewoman. What gives her added distinction is that she is the daughter of Charles Rivel, last year's headliner at the Schumann and in my estimation the world's greatest clown.

Over many years I have seen and enjoyed hundreds of talented clowns including such stars as Marceline, Grock, and the Fratellini brothers, who so endeared themselves to France that they were made officers of the Legion of Honor; and the outstanding contemporary Russian, Oleg Popov.

Like all the great ones, Charlie Rivel has developed his own technique. It allows him to move from point to point with unique leisureliness, creating a kind of hypnosis of audiences. It starts with Charlie's quiet entrance, which is that of a child who has opened a door into a strange room. For a moment he looks about him with mild curiosity, his short, husky body clothed in a sort of red T-shirt which extends to the tops of his outsize shoes. Under a wig that makes him look half bald, Charlie's facial makeup is grotesque but simple. He carries an old kitchen chair in one hand, in the other a guitar. He seems puzzled by the applause of his reception. Something he alone sees on his right attracts him and again like a child he advances toward it, shyly and slowly. He stops at the edge of the ring. For a moment he looks in mild wonderment at the segment of audience he faces. Eventually he decides a polite greeting is in order. He raises the toe of his right shoe and bends his body in a half-bow. As he lifts his head he notices laughter is coming from other people than those immediately in front of him. Still carrying the chair and guitar he moves a few feet to the left. He stops and after another moment of reflection repeats his courteous gesture. It takes at least five minutes and several repetitions of the bow for Charlie to show his good manners to everyone present.

He next has five minutes of frustration trying to seat himself on the chair in order to play his guitar. Gradually he becomes convinced that the chair is purposely thwarting him. Now the oldest of Charlie's three sons arrives and tries to soothe him. Pointing and indicting finger at the chair, Charlie wordlessly relates its willful animosity. His son's assuagement is futile. Inconsolable, Charlie angrily kicks the chair and stubs his toes. His head tilts back and he emits a quiet distillation of all the soul-deep howls that ever came from infantile throats.

Eventually Charlie plays the guitar with fine musicianship. At the end of a single number he leaves the ring. His son announces that a famed opera star will next sing some of the great arias for which she is noted. Charlie reappears in an inspired travesty of a prima donna. . . .

Charlie's story is in the familiar pattern of the entertainer born in the business. Seventy-three years ago, because of the failure of the circus in which they were performing, young Señor and Señora Andréu and the señor's mother came to Cubellas, a minuscule Spanish hamlet, to entertain in the market square. Señor Andréu was a tumbler; his wife was a tightrope walker. Her mother was a guitarist. In Cubellas the mother was playing an accompaniment to a rope act when the handful of spectators saw the daughter totter. The young husband helped her down, already in labor. A little girl's pleas to her reluctant mother enabled the baby to be born in the attic of a neighboring house. He grew up to be Charlie Rivel.

A decade ago a swarm of journalists and photographers descended on Cubellas, asking if anyone could remember the birth, long ago, of a boy to some circus performers. An elderly woman recalled the incident. She said she was the child who had provided the crèche and had often wondered what had become of the baby. The journalists told her they had come to gather material for stories about a great clown who was the next day receiving the highest honor Spain could bestow upon an artist.

The Dutch have several indigenous circuses of which they are justifiably proud, but the one that springs first to mind is unlike any other in the world. It is the Elleboog in Amsterdam, where circus acts are performed exclusively by and mostly for children. It has been flourishing since 1949. In that year the children of postwar Amsterdam were having difficulty adjusting themselves to normal childhood, particularly in underprivileged neighborhoods.

Mrs. Iet Last ter Haar, the wife of a well-known novelist, conceived the idea of a children's circus. Its name was suggested by one of the first children who responded to the idea. She had heard of the Knie (knee) circus of Switzerland and thought Elleboog (elbow) might fit the new experiment.

Today it has its own building, once a factory, in the colorful Old Jordaan area of the city. It is directed by Johannes Pijnacker-Hordijk, a former medical student who chose to cure social ills rather than physical ones. A hundred children between six and fifteen pay the equivalent of fifty cents a month to have their after-school hours filled with the delights of playing circus; later, if apt, they may become real performers. A former Elleboog boy, once a problem child, is today a tightrope walker with one of Europe's biggest circuses.

A staff of four full-time helpers guides the young in scores of activities. Those who like to sew make costumes from donated materials. Some build and paint scenery. Juvenile electricians handle cables, lights and the tape recorder that serves as an orchestra. There is even a menagerie for animal trainers: last summer it consisted of two monkeys, a parrot, some turtles, hamsters, mice, and other examples of wildlife. Pupils interested in more mundane matters run the Cirkus Elleboog's canteen.

Performances glow with the ardor of the children's mimicry. A dozen performing horses have small human legs, but their ten-year-old trainer's manner is professional. Gymnasts perform real tricks. The unicycle riders are truly skillful and the clowns know how to be funny. The sum of their efforts is good enough to attract audiences not only to the Elleboog's home grounds but also to the performances they give on tour. Every summer the Elleboog visits several cities in Germany as well as others all over the Netherlands. So great has been its success that a dozen or more European cities are creating others like it.

If there is a community anywhere living in contentment, unruffled by the anguish of the rest of the world, you can find it in Ireland. It is not locatable in a fixed spot. On Easter Monday it begins an annual migration and until the first Sunday of October it might be seen early any morning traveling from small town to small town north and south between Donegal and Cork and across the land from Wicklow to Galway. It is known wherever there are villages as the James Duffy and Sons Circus.

Three generations ago it was the John Duffy Circus, and half a century ago, when it first used its present name, it went to Donegal and had an adventure John's grandson James likes to talk about.

"In those days," says James in the clear, almost brogueless speech that makes him easily understood as a ringmaster, "Donegal was hell on circus wagons. Then there were only horses to pull them and it could take a week to move a mile if there was mud. My father knew it was chancy to try going there, but he did. After all, there were people in Donegal and he had a decent show to give them. It was in some town near Letterkenny where he picked his first tobbar. What's a tobbar? It's the place where you put up the tent. A gypsy word, I think.

"There he was one night ready to sell tickets and start the show at eight or half-eight maybe. He'd billed the town but at nine nobody had come. At ten he was still waiting. At half-ten the tent was taken down. The next night damned if he didn't have the same experience in another place. The third night they were in Killybegs and he was wondering if the word was out that they had the plague. Once again they were ready to give up when a man who'd been watching them take down the tent stepped over.

" 'You must be very rich fellahs,' he says, 'traveling around with a circus, putting up a tent, then taking it down again and never giving a show.'

" 'What the hell do you mean?' says my father. 'How can we give a show when there's nobody to see it?'

" 'Well,' says the man, 'you've got to give them a chance to come. It's only half-ten and barely dark. Wait a bit. When the pubs are closed and people are through talking at home they'll come.'

"And damned if they didn't begin to gather about eleven and the circus had a grand house. They were late people in Donegal."

Condensed from *Holiday*, January 1968. Used by permission.

PART TWO

Animals and Animal Trainers

JUMBO CREATES A SENSATION
P. T. Barnum

"Jumbo," the largest elephant ever seen, either wild or in captivity, had been for many years one of the chief attractions of the Royal Zoological Gardens, London. I had often looked wistfully on Jumbo, but with no hope of ever getting possession of him, as I knew him to be a great favorite of Queen Victoria, whose children and grandchildren are among the tens of thousands of British juveniles whom Jumbo has carried on his back. I did not suppose he would ever be sold. But one of my agents, who made the tour of Europe in the summer and autumn of 1881 in search of novelties for our big show, was so struck with the extraordinary size of the majestic Jumbo that he ventured to ask my friend, Mr. Bartlett, Superintendent of the Zoological Gardens, if he would sell Jumbo.

The presumption of my agent startled Mr. Bartlett, and at first he replied rather sarcastically in the negative. Further conversation led my agent to think that possibly an offer of $10,000 might be entertained. He cabled me to that effect, to which I replied: "I will give $10,000 for Jumbo, but the Zoo will never sell him." Two days afterwards my offer of $10,000 was accepted.

From that time an excitement prevailed and increased throughout Great Britain which, for a cause so comparatively trivial, has never had a parallel in any civilized country. The newspapers, from the London *Times* down, daily thundered anathemas against the sale, and their columns teemed with communications from statesmen, noblemen, and persons of distinction advising that the bargain should be broken at all risk, and promising that the money would be contributed by the British public to pay any damages which might be awarded to Barnum by the courts. It is said that the Queen and the Prince of Wales both asked that this course should be adopted. I received scores of letters from ladies and children, beseeching me to let Jumbo remain, and to name what damages I required and they should be paid.

All England seemed to run mad about Jumbo; pictures of Jumbo, the life of Jumbo, a pamphlet headed "Jumbo-Barnum," and all sorts of Jumbo stories and poetry, Jumbo Hats, Jumbo Collars, Jumbo Cigars, Jumbo Neckties, Jumbo Fans, Jumbo Polkas were sold by the tens of thousands in the stores and streets of London and other British cities. Meanwhile the London correspondents of the leading American newspapers cabled columns upon the subject, describing the sentimental Jumbo craze which had seized upon Great Britain. These facts stirred up the excitement in the United States, and the American newspapers, and scores of letters sent to me daily urged me not to give up Jumbo.

The editor of the London *Daily Telegraph* cabled me to name a price for which I would cancel the sale, and permit Jumbo to remain in London. I cabled back as follows:

My compliments to Editor Daily Telegraph *and British Nation. Fifty-one millions of American citizens anxiously awaiting Jumbo's ar-*

rival. My forty years' invariable practice of exhibiting the best that money could procure makes Jumbo's presence here imperative. Hundred thousand pounds would be no inducement to cancel purchase.

This dispatch was published in the London *Daily Telegraph* the next morning, and was sent by the London associated press to the principal newspapers throughout Great Britain, which republished it the following day, giving the excitement an immense impetus. Crowds of men, women and children rushed to the Zoo to see dear old Jumbo for the last time, and the receipts at the gates were augmented nearly two thousand dollars per day. A "fellow" or stockholder of the Royal Zoo sued out an injunction in the Chancery Court against the "councillors" of the Zoo and myself to quash the sale. After a hearing, which occupied two days the sale was declared valid, and Jumbo was decided to be my property.

The fateful day arrived when Jumbo was to bid farewell to the Zoo, and then came the tug of war. The unfamiliar street waked in Jumbo's breast the timidity which is so marked a feature of elephant character. He trumpeted with alarm, turned to re-enter the Gardens, and, finding the gate closed, laid down on the pavement. His cries of fright sounded to the uninitiated like cries of grief, and quickly attracted a crowd of sympathizers. British hearts were touched. British tears flowed for the poor beast so unwilling to leave his old home.

My agent, dismayed, cabled me, "Jumbo has laid down in the street and won't get up. What shall we do?"

I replied, "Let him lie there a week if he wants to. It is the best advertisement in the world."

After twenty-four hours the gates of his paradise were reopened and Jumbo allowed to return to his old quarters, while my agents set to work to secure him by strategy. A huge, iron-bound cage was constructed with a door at each end and mounted on broad wheels of enormous strength. This, with the doors open, was backed up against the door entrance to Jumbo's den, and the wheels sunk so that the floor of the cage was on a level with that of the elephant's. A passageway was thus formed through which Jumbo must pass to reach the outer air. After much hesitation, he was persuaded to follow his keeper, Scott, through this cage to take his daily airing. For several days this ruse was repeated. Then, as he entered the cage, the door behind him was swiftly closed, then the door in front of him, and Jumbo was mine.

Meanwhile Jumbo came up in Parliament, where the President of the Board of Trade was questioned in regard to precautions being taken to protect the passengers on shipboard. Mr. [James Russell] Lowell, our American Minister to the Court of St. James, in a speech given at a public banquet in London, playfully remarked, "The only burning question between England and America is Jumbo."

On the morning of his capture, March 25, 1882, the wheels of his cage were dug free of the ground, twenty horses attached, and in comparative silence of the following night, Jumbo was dragged miles to the steamship *Assyrian Monarch* where quarters had been prepared for him by cutting away one of the decks. The Society for the Prevention of Cruelty to Animals hovered over Jumbo to the last, and titled ladies and little children brought to the ship baskets of dainties for Jumbo's consumption during the voyage. After a rough passage he arrived in New York, in good condition, Sunday morning, April 9th, and next day was placed on exhibition in the menagerie department of our great show, where he created such a sensation that in the next two weeks the receipts *in excess of the usual amount* more than repaid us the $30,000 his purchase and removal had cost us.

From *Struggles and Triumphs; Or Forty Years' Recollections of P. T. Barnum.* Beginning with an 1855 edition published by Redfield, updated editions of Barnum's autobiography appeared until 1888.

THEN MAMMA ARRIVED
Courtney Ryley Cooper

We wanted a new elephant, and the order naturally was sent to Carl Hagenbeck, from whom most circus animals were then procured, and who reared, trained and acclimated his beasts at his "Tierpark" on the outskirts of Hamburg, Germany. The answer to the order was an almost tearful letter from Hagenbeck.

Because of his friendship for the owner of the show, he was giving up his greatest prize, Old Mamma, his pet elephant!

She was more than just a mere trained beast, he wrote. The children played with her, and she was all but a nursemaid to them. She did the work about the park; she was gentle and kind and understanding. It was as though Carl Hagenbeck were parting with some dearly beloved relative or a faithful servant, instead of a circus animal. And the show awaited the coming of the new pachyderm with a constantly growing interest. Then Mamma arrived!

The first report came with the sight of a sweating, cussing animal man who plodded wearily to the circus lot, disheveled, disturbed in body and temper. He sought the owner.

"Of all the rotten, no-good bulls I ever seen in my life," he growled, "that new Hagenbeck elephant's the worst! She won't do nothing!"

"But Hagenbeck wrote me—"

"I don't care what he wrote you; I'm talking about what he handed you! That elephant's a lemon! We can't get it to do nothing; it acts like it ain't even got good sense! Come on down and look for yourself."

Harry Tammen—he was the owner—went, and Harry Tammen looked. He retired to his circus car that night disappointed and disgusted. The wonderful elephant about which Carl Hagenbeck had written so enthusiastically either could not or would not do anything that would indicate former training. Only by sheer tugging with "bull-hooks" and pushing with two-by-fours had it been shunted from its car, and then, once on the ground, it trumpeted and squealed and stared blankly at the shouting animal man—but obeyed not a single command. Such was Mamma's arrival at the circus, and such was the daily program. She was literally pushed and pulled to the lot each day and pulled and pushed back to the circus train at night, an aimless, useless old beast that was more of a liability to the circus than an asset. Then Hagenbeck came to America and Tammen met him in St. Louis.

"A fine elephant you sold me!" he blurted. "It hasn't got a brain in its head!"

Hagenbeck almost wept.

"Ach Gott, Harry!" came excitedly. "Dot old Mamma elephant—she iss human! All day long she played with the children, unt ven day gif her a piece of cinnamon cake—ach Gott, she'd get on her knees to thank them! I come along to her unt I say: 'Wie geht's, Mamma?' and—"

"Wait a minute!" A great light was beginning to break in on Harry Tammen. "What would you say?"

"Wie geht's? or Was ist los? Or—"

"That's enough!" came from the circus owner. "You win! We've been trying to talk English to something that doesn't understand any language but German!"

The next day Tammen returned to his circus, and seeking the picket line in the menagerie where the great, hulking elephants were tethered, he approached the supposedly imbecilic Hagenbeck importation.

"Wie geht's, Mamma?" he exclaimed. "Was ist los?"

You've seen a dog welcome his master after long absence—the frenzy of joy, the unbounded happiness? Magnify that dog into a poor, lost, three-ton elephant in a strange land, among strange people, hearing only a strange tongue then suddenly finding a familiar tone of speech —and you have Old Mamma when she caught that sentence in German. She trumpeted, she sank to her knees and rose again, she wrapped her trunk about the little circus owner and tried in her elephantine way to caress him. She squealed and jumped about and pulled at her picket pin; then Tammen called one of the bull tenders.

"Dig up someone around this show who can talk German," he ordered. "We've got to translate everything for a while to this poor old bull. She's in a foreign country—and we've got to teach her English."

And that was the explanation of Old Mamma's apparent imbecility. She had been captured by German-speaking members of a Hagenbeck expedition, trained by a German, kept on a German animal reservation and received her every command in German. She never had heard any other language, and it was not until patient animal men, giving the command first in German and then repeating it in English, had "taught" her the language of her new home that she became of value.

That was many years ago. Today [1923] it is Mamma who leads the elephant herd of the big circus, who tests the bridges before her followers step upon it, who trumpets her orders to the rest of the great pachyderms on parade, who is first to catch the trainer's command in the ring. She is the head of the herd, and she has become Americanized. What's more, she's forgotten German now, in spite of the fact that they say an elephant never forgets.

From *Under the Big Top* by Courtney Ryley Cooper. Little, Brown & Co., Boston, 1923. © Mrs. C. R. Cooper. Used by permission.

LION TAMER

Alfred Court

I am a lion tamer by profession.

My work has brought me great joy, and it has brought me also, many times, close to great danger. For there remains within every wild beast, no matter how thorough his training, a savage spirit that cannot be broken. I have found this to be true through all my experience, and I have worked with many different kinds of animals, from Siberian tigers to black leopards, from Bengal tigers to polar bears, from black-maned lions to the bears of Himalaya. Of the many animals I have trained, I could not select a single one about which I could say, "This animal is tame," for the savage spirit remains, waiting its chance. And it is just this unconquerable spirit in the animals I work with that has provided me with both my greatest joys and my greatest dangers.

It is strange for me to remember now that I was thirty-five years old before I ever set foot inside a lion's cage.

I had known and lived the circus life, however, from the time that I was sixteen. On the day that I first wielded chair and whip within the cage, I had already toured most of Europe and the United States as an acrobat and a performer on the horizontal bars. I had traveled with circuses from Marseilles, my birthplace, to Copenhagen, from Madrid to Cuba. Yet in all the rough-and-tumble of that life, there had been no hint of the career which was to be thrust upon me so suddenly—the career that was to fill my days, and many of my nights, for the rest of my life.

It happened one evening in Nuevo Laredo, a little town in Mexico.

It was in March of 1917. I had given up my horizontal bars and was then director of a small circus that was in the middle of a Mexican tour. We had pitched our big top in Nuevo Laredo, a town where no circus had stopped for fifteen years, and were soon putting up the "House Full" notices. . . .

We reached the intermission without incident, and I was unworried, watching the circus hands erect the lions' cage in the center ring in preparation for the act that was to follow. The audience was filing back to its seats for the second half of the show.

It was at that moment that one of the performers ran up to me. "It's Sam, the tamer. He's dead drunk in his dressing room," he whispered. . . .

I hurried to Sam's wagon, but one glance told me that he would be of very little use for the rest of the night. As I left his dressing room, I saw Sam's young assistant standing by a pile of huge slabs of red meat.

Desperately I turned to him. "You're Sam's boy. You've seen him work. Couldn't you take his place tonight?"

The boy looked straight at me and shook his head firmly. "No, sir!" he said. "Those lions are tricky and they're dangerous. I've only worked for Mr. Sam a month. I wouldn't get into that cage for anything."

I nodded, knowing that it would not be reasonable to expect him to put on a braver face. As I turned to leave, my foot slipped on the pile of raw meat. "What's this doing here?"

"That's the food for the lions. Mr. Sam gives them something to eat after they work."

I stood for a moment staring at the meat and wondering how I could entertain the crowd. Suddenly I had an idea.

"Get that wheelbarrow," I told the boy. "Load it with the meat and follow me."

When we reached the middle of the empty cage, the boy stood holding the wheelbarrow and looked at me, still not understanding.

"The animals," I said, "will be fed here."

He shook his head and continued to hold the wheelbarrow. "No, sir. You can't do that! The lions are used to eating alone. Mr. Sam always feeds them alone. If you feed them all together here, they'll kill each other."

The crowd was becoming more and more restless, and I had to make some decision, though I was far from certain that this was the right one. As the boy did not move, I took the wheelbarrow myself, tipped its load onto the ground in the middle of the cage, and signaled the band to strike up.

When the band had finished the noisy number that introduced the second part of our program, I opened the center cage door and stepped out into the ring. The audience, thinking I was the lion tamer, applauded loudly. I raised my hand for silence and made my announcement.

"Ladies and gentlemen. Our tamer has been detained at the frontier by the American authorities. The lions' performance cannot be given until tomorrow or the following day."

There was a low murmur of protest from the crowd. Raising my voice, I went on: "Nevertheless you are about to witness a sensational spectacle which has never before been exhibited to the public—feeding the lions!"

I left the ring, and the orchestra went into its regular accompaniment to the act. With Sam oblivious in his dressing room, I gave orders for the grill on the tunnel cage to be lifted so that our four big lions could walk into the center cage.

They came in sleepily at first, stretching lazily, one after another. Suddenly one cat saw the pile of meat. In a single bound he reached it, seized a hunk in his jaws and, growling fiercely, went to crouch in a corner. At once the three other lions followed suit and leaped toward their dinner. Two of them seized on a great leg of horse meat and battled fiercely for it, roaring, letting go, and seizing the hunk of meat in turn. They struck out at each other, tearing tufts of hair from their manes at every swipe. One with the meat tightly clamped in his jaws made an incredible leap, almost to the top of the cage. . . .

The center cage shook as if it were nearing collapse as the animals fought and growled over the meat. Five minutes of savage struggle found each with his portion, and the lions settled down to devour their hard-won meal. Then the struggle began all over again—this time for the bones—and I, more than a little shaken, decided that the act was over. But it took us a full fifteen minutes and many rounds of blank cartridges before we were able to drive the lions back to their own cages, where they arrived, finally, with bloody jaws and claw-lacerated flanks.

It was a foolhardy exhibition, the likes of which I had never seen before and will be content never to see again. But to our Indian audience it was an enormously satisfying spectacle, and none of them seemed sorry that the lions had not performed.

That same night I sent a telegram to the owner of the lion act in New York: "Act could not go on. Trainer drunk at time of performance. Send new tamer at once or contract is off."

The next day, when I arrived at the circus about eleven in the morning, I found the tamer, penitent, sitting near the lions' cage.

"I've wired your boss," I said, "to send me another tamer. I'm sorry, but I can't take another chance on you."

He swore by all his gods that he would not get drunk again. But I was unconvinced. That afternoon I received an answer to my telegram that did little to ease my worries. Sam's employer wired that he was unable to send another tamer and suggested keeping careful watch over Sam to see that he did not drink again. This advice did not seem too promising; I had a feeling that it might well be impossible to be vigilant enough in Sam's case. Therefore, as our tamer began his act for that day's performance, I found myself watching with special care. In the back of my mind I was thinking that someone might have to take his place someday and that it was more than probable it might be me! And I must admit that the animals held a definite fascination for me.

The circus was packed that day, for word of the sensational performance the lions had given the evening before had spread all around town. Sam obviously put his heart into the act, and everything went beautifully. The four lions entered the cage easily, going into their regular routine with apparently no memory of the carnage of the day before. One leaped through a hoop; another lay down in the middle of the ring at Sam's feet and opened its great mouth so that the trainer could put his head in between the terrible teeth. Each of the four seemed especially good-tempered and docile as the act progressed to the finale.

The finale featured Nero, a beautiful black-maned animal, the largest and fiercest of the group. After the other three had been herded from the cage, the trainer armed himself with a chair in one hand and a whip in the other. Then he forced Nero back against the bars, cracked his whip over the roaring animal three or four times, and retreated quickly. Nero leaped after him, crossing the ring in two bounds, forcing Sam against the bars. The trainer defended himself against this charge with his chair, which Nero bit, and then forced the lion back again. This piece of business, all part of the act, was repeated two or three times until the chair was completely destroyed. Then Sam drew his revolver and fired it point-blank

at Nero's face. At that moment Sam's assistant opened the tunnel door and the lion darted out, his performance over.

I watched the whole act with particular attention, and as soon as the afternoon performance was over, a chance came for me to observe again and learn a little more. Sam asked for permission to hold an extra rehearsal because one of the lions had refused to stay in his place in the pyramid. The center cage was set up again, and Sam began to work his lions. I watched carefully from outside the cage. The tamer apparently noticed my interest, for he came over and asked if I would like to come in for a moment. He had no idea how pleased I was. . . .

Sam opened the door and handed me one of the wooden chairs.

"Hold this in your hand," he said. "The only dangerous one is Nero. If he should get too close, step two paces back and keep the chair in front of you. He'll bite it and then go back again. He's been taught that as a regular trick." Then he added kindly, "I'm here. I'll keep my eye on things. Don't be afraid."

I was not exactly afraid, but I had to admit that the advice about Nero made me think a little! First we passed in front of the pedestals on which the lions were to form their first pyramid. Peaceably settled on their respective seats, they stared at me in seeming surprise, although only Nero appeared disturbed by my presence. With the chair held firmly in my hand I followed Sam, thinking it the better part of wisdom to let him stay between the lions and me. He walked up to Nero saying, "Nero, be a nice boy," and touched the end of the lion's nose with the butt of his whip. Nero gave a great roar, lashed out with his paw, tore the whip from Sam's hand, and seemed about to leap down from his pedestal. Instinctively I took the prescribed two paces to the rear and braced myself for attack, but Nero paid no attention to me and stayed where he was, his roar shaking the cage.

We stayed about ten minutes longer, and at the end of this time I found enough courage to go up to Caesar, the gentlest of the lions. With Sam's coaching, I stroked his heavy mane. Caesar seemed to like it, and so, I found, did I. At that moment I was certain that lion taming was an occupation that I would enjoy.

From then on, I studied Sam's act with special care. But I was destined to study it for only a short time. A few days later Sam was once again completely drunk at performance time, and I had no choice but to fire him.

I bought the four lions from their New York owner for 4,000 pesos, purchased Sam's costumes and whips from him, and found myself, surprisingly and suddenly, a lion tamer. I had the lions and their equipment; I had the costumes and the whips. At least I looked like a tamer! And I was destined, though I did not fully realize it at the time, to spend a good part of my life learning to play the role that I had now assumed.

That night I undertook my first rehearsal. I gave orders for the center cage to be set up. Meanwhile, I hurried to the performers' dressing room to put on the extravagant cowboy outfit, with its black and silver spangles, that I had purchased from Sam. It fitted me perfectly, and I found that even this small fact offered some encouragement. Dressed like this, I told myself, I should be able to move with enough assurance to make the lions think I was Sam. And so, assuming a confidence I did not quite feel, I strode into the center cage, cracking my whip to give myself courage.

Taking a stance in the middle of the cage, behind the big pyramid which seemed to offer the best available shelter from sudden attack, I told the boy to open the tunnel grill. As the first three lions came in I felt a shiver go through me, but they were almost insulting in the casual way they walked through the door, stretching and yawning and paying no attention at all to my splendidly arrayed form. All three of them walked slowly to the left. I walked, just as slowly, the other way. Caesar, the tamest of the lot, lay down full length and rolled on his back, while the other two began to play together. I had never

seen them in such peaceful attitudes, and as I watched them, it seemed to me that this friendly play could continue indefinitely. Summoning my courage, emboldened by their obvious good spirits, I took two careful steps toward them and cried, "Take your seats!" with all the authority at my command. At my voice all three jumped as if moved by a single spring and set off at a gallop. They raced in front of the pyramid—I moved cautiously behind it—and each came to his own seat, climbed up, and sat down without a sound.

They aren't so terrible, I said to myself, and felt confident enough then to walk a few yards in front of the lions, cracking my whip and calling each one by name. All three followed my every move with their eyes, their glance interested but not ferocious, as though they were wondering, "Is it Sam, or isn't it?"

Secure in Sam's finery, I edged close enough to touch their muzzles with the butt of my whip, as I had seen him do. As I did this and spoke each name, the lions responded with a sound like "Oua-ah" which seemed to express their satisfaction.

Thus encouraged, I stationed myself again behind one of the tall stools, called, "Send me Nero," and waited tensely for the tunnel grill to open, with very little idea of what Nero might do—and even less of my role—if he was in a mood to attack. I decided to take the offensive quickly. He was hardly through the door before I took a step toward him, cracked my whip and shouted, "Take your seat!" He roared in answer, but with a single leap he passed in front of the pyramid and settled himself on his pedestal, still growling. I started to approach him but found to my displeasure that my legs were trembling, and I stopped instead behind a tall stool a few yards away. From this relatively safe position I called his name and showed him the butt of my whip. He answered with an ear-splitting roar. This response, added to what I already knew of Nero's reputation, convinced me that I must keep my eye on him constantly.

I stepped cautiously in front of the stool. Then in my gentlest voice, I began my first conversation with the stubborn pupil.

"Nero, Nero, be a nice boy."

He seemed to understand my friendly, though watchful, intentions for the roaring lessened to a low grumble as he turned his huge head from side to side, blinked his eyes, and gave me altogether too full a view of his fine teeth.

Introduction now completed, I faced all four lions and gave two or three light cracks of my whip. Not one of them moved; their great eyes remained fixed on me. Growing even bolder, but taking the precaution of drawing my revolver, I gave the whip a very sharp crack which echoed in the dark silence around the cage.

At the sound Nero came swiftly down from his perch, and for a moment I thought he was going to leap at me. I started to raise the revolver in my hand, but with a single bound he landed on one of the heavy, medium-sized seats and leaped from there to the top of the pyramid, where he stopped short, roaring with all the power in his lungs.

Far from attacking me, he was, instead, simply beginning the act on his own, without a word from me. Following his lead and trying to recall exactly all of Sam's gestures, I succeeded in placing the other three on the pyramid, which was the first trick in Sam's act. As I gazed with some satisfaction at the four, I was torn between a surprising confidence and the question of what happened next. Again I tried to remember every one of Sam's movements, realizing the animals would stay up there for the rest of the night until I gave the proper commands to get them down again.

I concentrated on remembering the next move. First Sam had stepped to the right to get the three quiet lions down, and then, after they were settled in their original positions, he had moved to the left to get Nero down. I followed this routine, cracking my whip as I ordered them down. "Take your seats," I bellowed, and the three lions slowly returned to their stools. Nero, proud and silent, did not budge. I moved to the left then, placing myself behind him, and called, "Nero, take your seat!" He growled but stayed where he was. I walked in front of him to say cajolingly, "Nero, be a nice boy," and then went back to the left and repeated my order, this time cracking my whip loudly. Nero responded with a more vigorous roar but stayed on his perch.

Puzzled, I went to the bars of the cage to wipe my face, which was streaming with sweat. Johnny, Sam's boy, came up to me.

"If you want Nero down," he said, "I think you have to flick him on the rump."

I had never seen Sam do this except at the end of the act and hesitated to make so direct an attack; but it was obvious that something had to be done, so I took my place again. This time as I gave the order I tried to give Nero a touch of the whip. I missed completely. The second time I missed again. Nero roared continuously. I had never heard him so loud. My calmness deserted me completely. Moving closer—a little too close as it turned out— I let him have the whip hard. With a bound that upset the pyramid, he leaped and crossed the cage at a gallop, while I did the same in the opposite direction. But he took not the slightest notice of me and, with a roar loud enough to bring down the big top, he went over and sat on his stool.

My breath went out of me in one sharp explosive sigh! Then I walked over to pick up the pryamid all the while watching my big boy out of the corner of my eye. And it was then that I saw Nero's enormous paws were trembling. Suddenly the truth came to me. In this profession someone has to be afraid— the lions or the tamer. Far better that it be the lions! I had found the key.

I gave myself another short recess and went back to the bars to catch my breath. Johnny was frankly admiring. "If you always do the act like that, it'll be better than Mr. Sam's," he said.

I shook my head. "At the moment I'm not doing the act, Johnny. The lions are doing it themselves. They're showing me what to do instead of the other way around. And," I added suddenly surprised at the conviction in my tone, "that's enough for tonight."

But the devil, in the person of Johnny, prodded me. "You ought to try to make Sultan jump. He'll jump on his own."

I moved out into the center of the cage again and placed the medium-sized stools at the required distances, for this was a thing I had taken careful note of earlier. At my first command Sultan made his leap, one which carried him in a beautiful arc halfway across the cage. Then he moved quickly around again and returned to his own stool. Again a success! At that moment I felt so fond of these four animals that, had we known one another better, I would have patted each one. I did, however, call each by name, and was considerably surprised to see Caesar step down slowly from his stool, yawn, stretch, and then advance slowly toward me. I stepped back instinctively. If I hadn't he would have lain down at my feet! Then I remembered that this was the moment in the act when Caesar did his trick, and so, when his name was called, he had not waited to be asked twice but had come to me immediately. The lions surely knew the act far better than did their makeshift trainer, despite his borrowed finery.

Cautiously I now stepped near Caesar and, first with the butt of my whip and finally with my hand, stroked his mane and then his head. I had stroked him once before; after all, we were not strangers. At this moment it seemed impossible to me that this good animal could ever rebel. Indeed, as I patted him, he laid his huge lower jaw on the ground, ready for me to open his mouth and put my head inside.

But we hadn't gone so far as that! After stroking him I stepped back as Sam had done and cracked my whip in the air. Caesar got up and returned to his place.

There! That surely was more than enough for a first rehearsal. I told Johnny to open the tunnel grill and watched with satisfaction as the three lions crossed through the door and lay down in their respective cages. But then I saw that Nero, growling loudly, had stayed on his seat. His eyes were fixed on me as though unaware that the grill was open. We stared at each other while I realized, with a sinking heart, that he was waiting, without any doubt, for the command to start his last trick, his specialty.

I was, quite literally, in a cold sweat. I had not anticipated that he would stick so closely to the script. Another glance into his steady eyes, however, and I knew there was no getting around it. Longing to have done with it, I stepped back to grasp the chair firmly in my left hand. Very quickly I planted myself half facing him about ten feet away. Then shouting his name savagely, as Sam had done, and cracking my whip, I awaited results. They came with tremendous speed as Nero leaped at me, jaws wide and roaring, his heavy paws striking at the chair I held.

I recoiled so quickly that he had no time to fasten on it. He came at me again like a meteor, and I was convinced this time that he would not stop. But as soon as my back touched the bars he paused suddenly and headed for his seat. Then he noticed that the grill was still open and, apparently willing to forget the rest of his act, trotted to the door and went on, still growling quietly, to his own cage. The grill dropped down behind him.

I stood in the middle of the ring, chair in one hand, whip in the other, my heart thumping and my whole body streaming with sweat. Then Johnny and the stagehands cheered and applauded, and I shook away my stupor. A small personal success surely—but my first in a career that was to enthrall me for a quarter of a century.

MYTHS DIE HARD

Clyde Beatty

One of the myths that refuses to die is that the animals are fed before each performance, the theory being that a lion or tiger with a bellyful of meat will not be tempted to make a meal of his trainer.

Yes, myths die hard. One of my recent correspondents insists that he has heard "reliably" that my big cats are fed a few minutes before they enter the arena for each performance. If I had the time, I would write to inform him that fifteen to eighteen pounds of meat—depending on the animal's requirements, which are usually determined by its weight—leaves a lion or a tiger drowsy and ready for a nap. If I fed them just before they were due to perform, I might have to carry an alarm clock into the arena with me to wake the dozers.

The most effective reply is what I tell newspapermen who, to draw me out, occasionally put the same question to me. I invite them to drop in when the animals are being fed. I explain that the butcher who looks after the needs of the big cats has instructions to include in each animal's daily meal a slab of meat that runs heavily to bone—usually a rib section—because I have learned from experience, and also from veterinarians, that a lion or a tiger is a happier and a healthier animal if he has a chance to swallow a certain amount of practically pulverized bone with the raw meat on which he subsists. Anyone seeing the big cats grind up those bones also has a chance to see the big powerful teeth that do the grinding. It is an awesome sight, and an un-

forgettable one, and those who have had a chance to witness it will never again ask whether my animals are toothless.

Frequently these same skeptics also want to know whether my lions and tigers have had their claws clipped. I can't give the answer individually to every doubter, but it is easy to do so for the benefit of the press. Whenever an interviewer tosses a controversial question at me to start me talking, I don't mind in the least. If it happens to be the old clipped-claw staple, I walk him over to the cages and, letting him select the animal whose claws he wants to see in all their glory, I make a few gestures designed to put the lion or tiger in a fighting mood. The claws, normally retracted, show up formidably when bared for action. Then, just to remind the animal that I was only fooling, I say something to him designed to get him to quiet down. If the animal happens to be Rajah, one of the most powerful and best-natured tigers I have ever trained, I get him to purr, which is his specialty. Five hundred pounds of purring tiger is quite a sight.

One reporter thinks I throw away my case when I get Rajah to purr. "Okay, so his claws haven't been tampered with!" he exclaimed. "But how do you expect anyone to believe that a tiger that purrs like my pet cat is really dangerous?" Well, he is. No matter how much affection I lavish on him he will never lose his basic primitiveness. . . .

In recent years wild-animal enthusiasts who have bought big-cat cubs as pets have subjected them to the surgery commonly known as declawing—usually at the age of two months. The animal is anesthetized, and while he suffers no serious discomfort, it is a practice of which I strongly disapprove.

Clawless cats—this operation involves the complete removal of the claws from the pads—have been known to undergo unfortunate personality changes. It is as natural for a big cat, especially a youngster, to sharpen its claws on trees or heavy underbrush as it is for it to breathe. I recall a lion cub that had been declawed, a practice which seems to be on the increase, that changed the animal from a happy-go-lucky, cheerful character to a chronically irritable one. Some of the things he did seemed to indicate frustration, and though he couldn't very well try to sharpen claws he didn't possess, he began behaving oddly, somehow suggesting that he sensed he was missing something, although he wasn't sure what. It is one of those phenomena that is difficult to describe satisfactorily. But that the animal's disposition and behavioral pattern had changed was unmistakable.

It is hard to condone a practice as unnatural as declawing. I have never trained an animal that has undergone this operation nor would I consider doing so.

A woman who professes to love tiger cubs offered me a handsome price for one during the spring of 1964. I turned her down for two reasons: I did not want to part with the animal, nor did I approve of her plan to declaw it.

This woman, whose knowledge of wild animals was sadly deficient, apparently believed that declawing would render the animal harmless. She had overlooked the fact that a big cat—a cub or a full-grown one—can do more damage with his teeth than with his claws. . . .

I don't know how many times I have been asked by correspondents whether it is true that unless the trainer resorts to cruel practices, he cannot hope to train a wild animal. Such queries are relatively infrequent today because of the expanding literature of circusdom, which in dealing with animal training focuses attention on the essentiality of the kindly approach by the trainer who is teaching animals—wild or otherwise—to perform.

In the late 1920s and in the 1930s and 1940s, this was not understood except by a scattering of perceptive mammalogists and people who had had circus experience.

I always welcome questions that give me a chance to clear up misconceptions. It is a simple matter to explain that for years I have made a practice of inviting the public to see me break in new animals. Most of these training sessions take place in winter quarters between seasons. There is no better way of getting a lion or a tiger accustomed to an audience than to have people watching from the very beginning of the training period. In fact, getting an animal used to crowds is part of its training—so the bigger the audience when I conduct these big-cat classes the better I like it. People react at these training sessions pretty much as they do under the big top. For instance, they applaud when something happens that appeals to them. They chat with one another as they watch me work, and this steady buzz of conversation is something my animals have to get accustomed to. . . .

I shall always be grateful to the late Raymond L. Ditmars, former curator of mammals and reptiles of the New York Zoological Society, for debunking a charge made by an organization dedicated to fair play for animals, that I employed "cruel practices" in training my lions and tigers (which information, I might add, they had "on good authority," although the authority's name was not given).

It would take dozens of pages to tell all the weird stories that have gained currency over the years about cruel practices to which trainers have allegedly resorted in breaking in animals. There is one that was once common gossip, although it is seldom heard any longer. It had to do with trainers who, in order to get animals to perform, indulged in the quaint practice of jabbing them with sharply pointed steel rods.

Another that once had quite a vogue had to do with trainers who exacted compliance from their trainees by searing them with red-hot irons. Such cock-and-bull stories never completely die out, although in the long history of animal training there is no record of anyone having ever seen a trainer resort to the methods described.

Only a trainer anxious to get himself killed would attempt such cruelties. There are pleasanter ways of committing suicide.

Myths have always fascinated me, and when possible I like to trace them back to their earliest beginnings. As far as I can determine, the story of the red-hot irons originated in the early 1900s when a visitor to the training quarters of the great English trainer Frank C. Bostock saw some irons being heated in a coke fire. The visitor did not contend that he had seen Bostock apply any of these red-hot irons to an animal (which, had he done so, would have burned unpretty holes in the creature's coat in addition to broiling the flesh underneath). All he said was that he had seen these irons heating. With nothing more than this to go on, the overzealous critic accused Bostock of cruel practices. In his book, *The Training of Wild Animals,* Bostock explained: "It is my practice in cold weather to put hot irons into the drinking-water of my animals. This practice is always observed in my show during the winter months. It has the value of taking the chill off the water, and also imparts some of the beneficial qualities of the iron, thus giving an iron tonic and drinkable water at the same time."

I disagree with Bostock's theory about the iron tonic, as I do with a few of his other beliefs about how to keep wild animals healthy, but there is no doubt in my mind that the accusation against him was absurd. Even if his had been a cruel nature (no trainer ever handled his animals more gently or patiently), Frank Bostock had too much sense to poke an animal with a hot iron and then expect it to perform. He knew, as all successful trainers know, that aside from a basic knowledge of animals, the two greatest factors in securing results in our little-understood profession are the kindly approach and a capacity for taking pains, plus a reasonably cheerful disposition, which helps absorb the inevitable disappointments one suffers in teaching certain types of animals that are very slow, deliberate learners.

Not since 1937—and that was twenty-eight years ago—have I had a complaint from any of the organizations dedicated to seeing that animals are decently treated. Which is not surprising, as my big cats—and all the other animals connected with our show—are so well cared for.

I have a great respect for the people who love animals sufficiently to make a career of seeing that they get a square deal. Understandably, the organizations which they represent have made some mistakes, but there is no doubt in my mind that they perform an essential service and deserve the support of the public.

THE LEOPARD MAN'S STORY

Jack London

He had a dreamy, far-away look in his eyes, and his sad, insistent voice, gentle-spoken as a maid's, seemed the placid embodiment of some deep-seated melancholy. He was the Leopard Man, but he did not look it. His business in life was to appear in a cage of performing leopards before vast audiences, and to thrill those audiences by certain exhibitions of nerve for which his employers rewarded him on a scale commensurate with the thrills he produced.

As I say, he did not look it. He was narrow-hipped, narrow-shouldered, and anemic, while he seemed not so much oppressed by gloom as by a sweet and gentle sadness. For an hour I had been trying to get a story out of him, but he appeared to lack imagination. To him there was no romance in his gorgeous career, no deeds of daring, no thrills, nothing but a gray sameness and infinite boredom.

Lions? Oh, yes! he had fought with them. It was nothing. All you had to do was to stay sober. Anybody could whip a lion to a standstill with an ordinary stick. He had fought one for half an hour once. Just hit him on the nose every time he rushed, and when he got artful and rushed with his head down, why, the thing to do was to stick out your leg. When he grabbed at the leg, you drew it back and hit him on the nose again. That was all.

With the far-away look in his eyes and his soft flow of words he showed me his scars. There were many of them, and one recent one where a tigress had reached for his shoulder and gone down to the bone. I could see the neatly mended rents in the coat he had on. His right arm, from the elbow down, looked as though it had gone through a threshing machine, what of the ravage wrought by claws and fangs. But it was nothing, he said, only the old wounds bothered him somewhat when rainy weather came on.

Suddenly his face brightened with a recollection, for he was really as anxious to give me a story as I was to get it.

"I suppose you've heard of the lion-tamer who was hated by another man?" he asked.

He paused and looked pensively at a sick lion in the cage opposite.

"Got the toothache," he explained. "Well the lion-tamer's big play to the audience was putting his head in a lion's mouth. The man who hated him attended every performance in the hope sometime of seeing that lion crunch down. He followed the show about all over the country. The years went by and he grew old, and the lion-tamer grew old, and the lion grew old. And at last one day, sitting in a front seat, he saw what he had waited for. The lion crunched down, and there wasn't any need to call a doctor."

The Leopard Man glanced casually over his fingernails in a manner which would have been critical had it not been so sad.

"Now, that's what I call patience," he continued, "and it's my style. But it was not the style of a fellow I knew. He was a little, thin, sawed-off sword-swallowing and juggling

Frenchman. DeVille, he called himself, and he had a nice wife. She did trapeze work and used to dive from under the roof into a net, turning over once on the way as nice as you please.

"DeVille had a quick temper, as quick as his hand, and his hand was as quick as the paw of a tiger. One day, because the ring-master called him a frog-eater, or something like that and maybe a little worse, he shoved him against the soft pine background he used in his knife-throwing act, so quick the ring-master didn't have time to think, and there before the audience, DeVille kept the air on fire with his knives, sinking them into the wood all around the ring-master so close that they passed through his clothes and most of them bit into his skin.

"The clowns had to pull the knives out to get him loose, for he was pinned fast. So the word went around to watch out for DeVille, and no one dared be more than barely civil to his wife. And she was a sly bit of baggage, too, only all hands were afraid of DeVille.

"But there was one man, Wallace, who was afraid of nothing. He was the lion-tamer, and he had the self-same trick of putting his head into the lion's mouth. He'd put it into the mouths of any of them, though he preferred Augustus, a big, good-natured beast who could always be depended upon.

"As I was saying, Wallace—'King' Wallace we called him—was afraid of nothing alive or dead. He was a king and no mistake. Madame DeVille—"

At an uproar behind us the Leopard Man turned quietly around. It was a divided cage, and a monkey, poking through the bars and around the partition, had had its paw seized by a big gray wolf who was trying to pull it off by main strength. The arm seemed stretching out longer and longer like a thick elastic, and the unfortunate monkey's mates were raising a terrible din. No keeper was at hand, so the Leopard Man stepped over a couple of paces, dealt the wolf a sharp blow on the nose with the light cane he carried, and returned with a sadly apologetic smile to take up his unfinished sentence as though there had been no interruption.

"—looked at King Wallace and King Wallace looked at her, while DeVille looked black. We warned Wallace, but it was no use. He laughed at us, as he laughed at DeVille one day when he shoved DeVille's head into a bucket of paste because he wanted to fight.

"DeVille was in a pretty mess—I helped to scrape him off; but he was cool as a cucumber and made no threats at all. But I saw a glitter in his eyes which I had seen often in the eyes of wild beasts, and I went out of my way to give Wallace a final warning. He laughed, but he did not look so much in Madame DeVille's direction after that.

"Several months passed by. Nothing had happened and I was beginning to think it all a scare over nothing. We were West by that time, showing in 'Frisco. It was during the afternoon performance, and the big tent was filled with women and children, when I went looking for Red Denny, the head canvas-man, who had walked off with my pocket-knife.

"Passing by one of the dressing tents I glanced in through a hole in the canvas to see if I could locate him. He wasn't there, but directly in front of me was King Wallace, in tights, waiting for his turn to go on with his cage of performing lions. He was watching with much amusement a quarrel between a couple of trapeze artists. All the rest of the people in the dressing tent were watching the same thing with the exception of DeVille, whom I noticed staring at Wallace with undisguised hatred. Wallace and the rest were all too busy following the quarrel to notice this or what followed.

"But I saw it through the hole in the canvas. DeVille drew his handkerchief from his pocket, made as though to mop the sweat from his face with it (it was a hot day), and at the same time walked past Wallace's back. He never stopped, but with a flirt of the hand-

48

kerchief kept right on to the doorway, where he turned his head, while passing out, and shot a swift look back. The look troubled me at the time, for not only did I see hatred in it, but I saw triumph as well.

" 'DeVille will bear watching,' I said to myself, and I really breathed easier when I saw him go out the entrance to the circus grounds and board an electric car for downtown. A few minutes later I was in the big tent, where I had overhauled Red Denny. King Wallace was doing his turn and holding the audience spellbound. He was in a particularly vicious mood, and he kept the lions stirred up till they were all snarling, that is, all of them except old Augustus, and he was just too fat and lazy and old to get stirred up over anything.

"Finally Wallace cracked the old lion's knees with his whip and got him into position. Old Augustus, blinking good-naturedly, opened his mouth and in popped Wallace's head. Then the jaws came together, crunch, just like that."

The Leopard Man smiled in a sweetly wistful fashion, and the far-away look came into his eyes.

"And that was the end of King Wallace," he went on in his sad, low voice. "After the excitement cooled down, I watched my chance and bent over and smelled Wallace's head. Then I sneezed."

"It . . . it was . . .?" I queried with halting eagerness.

"Snuff—that DeVille dropped on his hair in the dressing tent. Old Augustus never meant to do it. He only sneezed."

From *Leslie's Magazine,* August, 1903; *The Crime Solvers,* Dell, 1966.

IVAN AND THE THREE BEARS

John McCarten

Accompanied by Vladimir Danielevitch, one of our house linguists, we went over to Madison Square Garden the other morning to have a chat with Ivan Kudriavtzeff, who is the trainer of Gosha, a bear that is one of the stars of the Moscow Circus, currently on tour in the United States. As we strolled to the Garden from our office, Vladimir said that he had heard many tributes to Gosha from Russian circus buffs of his acquaintance. "I have been told that he is the brightest bear ever to perform in Russia, and that he is regarded there as a national hero," Vladimir continued. "In Russia, you know, there are over fifty circuses in operation constantly, and many, many performing bears, which means that if Gosha is as good as they say he is, he is an artist of the highest calibre." When we met Mr. Kudriavtzeff on the floor of the Garden where the single ring employed by the Moscow Circus was being set up, he quickly informed us, through Vladimir (Mr. K. has no English) that not only is Gosha the smartest bear in the world; if he could talk, he would be the greatest actor. Middle-sized, solidly constructed, moon-faced, and most amiable, Mr. K. beamed happily as he discussed Gosha with Vladimir, who gave us a running translation of his remarks as he went along.

"Mr. Kudriavtzeff would like you to know that Gosha can do thirteen tricks as against an average of two or three for an ordinary professional bear," Vladimir said. "He is thirteen years old and weighs about seven hun-

dred pounds, and is so famous that in Russia, Brazil, and Japan he is called an academician, which means that he is regarded as a kind of honorary professor. Before the Japanese would honor him as an academician, they kept examining him to make sure he was a bear, and not a man—or two men—running around in a bearskin."

We requested that Vladimir ask Mr. K. whether he had rehearsed Gosha at the Garden to accustom him to the unfamiliar surroundings.

The question was put, and Mr. K. responded volubly.

"Rehearse Gosha?" said Vladimir, who was getting into the swing of things. "A performer who has appeared in arenas throughout the world and been the leading actor in a French and an Italian movie? Nonsense! All that is required for an artist like this is to let him see the place where he is to entertain. Anywhere, any time, he can juggle, ride a motorbike, drive a small car, do acrobatics, dance, skate, and play the clown. He can hold an audience for a fifteen-minute stretch without becoming exhausted. He is the one and only Gosha."

We suggested that Vladimir calm down a bit and inquire of Mr. K. how he started out in the bear-training business, which we have always thought of as a fairly esoteric pursuit.

We presently learned that our bear man, who is now thirty-five and less than five years away from a Soviet government pension, had had a persuasive way with animals since his early youth, in a small village in the Ural Mountains, and that upon seeing some trained bears in the neighborhood of Sverdlovsk he had become fascinated with the beasts. Eventually, he was taken on as a pupil of Timofei Ivanovich Sedorkin, the dean of Russian bear handlers, and he soon absorbed enough knowledge to become a bear trainer himself. He acquired Gosha, a brown bear from Siberia, when the future great one was only three months old and just a bit of a thing, and, as time went by, expanded his menagerie to include Gosha II, now aged three, and Mishka, aged two. Gosha II and Mishka serve as understudies for the big bear, but they never substitute for him at premières or in the evenings. Like all artists, Mr. K. observed (via Vladimir), Gosha is fond of applause, and particular about the music that accompanies his act.

At this point, Mr. K. proposed that we go downstairs and have a look at Gosha and his stand-ins. With Mishka and Gosha II—a pair of not overly hefty bears—in cages to the left and right of him, Gosha looked monumental in his own barred quarters, which were adequate, though somewhat cramped. Mr. K. immediately began to bombard Gosha with sugar cubes—the bear accepted them ecstatically—and said to Vladimir, who relayed the information to us, that Gosha and the two other bears live on a diet of bread, milk, sugar, grits, and honey. In the old days, when

Gosha was a good deal smaller, Mr. K. used to include a spot of wrestling in his public appearances with the bear, but as Gosha grew increasingly formidable he realized that he himself would have to put on a lot of weight or concede that Gosha was too much for him. He conceded. Just to insure that Gosha doesn't suddenly decide to change his diet from vegetarian to carnivorous, he is always muzzled when he does a show.

While Mr. K. was ingratiating himself with Gosha, and Gosha, in turn, was ingratiating himself with Mr. K., a pretty young woman came into the enclosure where the cages stood, and greeted the three bears and Mr. K. fondly. It developed that she was Mrs. K., and not only the mother of two small children, who are staying in Moscow while the circus is on tour, but also a bear trainer in her own right, being in charge of Gosha II and Mishka at matinee performances.

By way of our interpreter, we asked Mr. K. what he proposes to do when pension time comes around.

"He will probably go right on with Gosha," Vladimir said, after a consultation. "They've been chums so long that it would be hard for them to separate without heartache. They are so close that every year, on Gosha's birthday, Gosha and Mr. Kudriavtzeff have a party at which Gosha is allowed to drink vodka. He drinks like a gentleman."

THE CIRCUS CANINES
Tom Prideaux

A lot is being printed these days about the science of ethology, or animal behavior. Not the least important of its tenets is that animals really do behave like people, and for the same reasons. Birds often sing, not from some chemical urge but, like people, to stake out a piece of territory or just for the the heck of it. Wrens whisper what may be lullabies to their nestlings. Elephants kiss. Seals in the zoo clap their flippers from joy—maybe because they enjoy the show we people put on for them. And quite possibly snakes hiss because they are not enjoying the show at all.

This thought came to mind when I was indulging, after a rough season of watching people perform, in a favorite pastime of watching dogs perform. My admiration was centered on a superb dog act—I've seen it six times this year—presented by an Irish family, the Stephensons, in the Ringling Bros.–Barnum & Bailey show. Its chief artists are 12 poodles, two schnauzers, 16 smooth and wirehaired terriers, and one Dalmatian.

The act opens when a pony trots into the center ring, and with his teeth pulls a blanket from a wooden bed. Hidden under it is a big white poodle, Ruff, who is all personality and little talent, like Jerry Lewis. Wearing striped pajamas, Ruff is supposed to jump from bed and amble off as a sleepy man might, on his hind legs. But not Ruff. He scoots off on all fours, knowing he can get away with murder because, like Jerry, he is the personality kid.

On the other hand, an ideal amalgam of charm and solid merit is embodied in Debbie, a wirehair who turns somersaults as she is jumping rope. Unlike most dogs, who are inclined to dawdle between somersaults, Debbie spins in perfect tempo like a perpetual motion machine. She is the sole female in the entire act, and she is lovely. In her untiring zest she irresistibly recalls Carol Channing.

Dogs, like actors, are often trained to exploit their inherent abilities. Thus, a natural jumper like Debbie is trained for somersaults. The biggest poodle in the act, 60 pounds of black fuzz and muscle named Buller, is a natural walker. Buller's main stunt is to strut upright while a miniature poodle, Moriarity, runs in and out between his legs. The playoff is pure Abbott and Costello. Moreover, Buller has a comic gift that the Stephensons haven't exploited yet. When he gets excited, he blows air from the sides of his jowls, which sounds like a canary chirping. I've never heard of any actor who could do that, but I know dozens who would be more entertaining if they could.

Running a dog act, like managing any theatrical troupe, depends a lot on being aware of the performers' likes and dislikes: enemies have to be kept apart, and chums held in line. Tiffney, a wirehair who rides ponies, hates Kevin, a waif from Arkansas, and bit off part of his tail. Moriarity is in trouble because he hero-worships Poulet, a silver poodle who does a knockout tumbling act and has star quality if

I ever saw it. Moriarity seems to think so too, for he lets his hero Poulet eat all his food.

Dogs, like actors, sometimes go moodily on strike for reasons that are not wholly clear. When the circus was in Oklahoma City, I understand, the Stephensons bought four terrier brothers: Tubb, Tich, Charna, and Spot. The first three were trained to lie down while Poulet leaped over them. One matinee in Butte, Montana, when Poulet was about to begin, all three jumped up as if by a signal, raced from the ring, tore through the audience and out the front entrance. There they fortunately became engrossed in some interesting smells and were easily captured. Since then they have shown no wanderlust and seem perfectly contented.

Strange? Not in show biz.

The fourth brother, Spot, is an example of the way total dependability may compensate for a lack of histrionic finesse. Spot climbs up an 18-foot ladder and jumps perfunctorily into a blanket. I felt that Spot could get more dramatic effect if he hesitated, showed a little fright, and hammed it up a bit before he leaped, just as I used to feel that Gene Autry could have got a little deeper into the emotional truths of his stunts if he hadn't made them look so easy. But when I suggested this to Spot's trainers, they said that Spot was such a reliable, sterling performer they didn't want to mess around with him. I suppose they're right. After all, nobody messed around with Gene Autry.

GARGANTUA

Robert Lewis Taylor

At nineteen, Gargantua, the Ringling Bros.–
Barnum & Bailey male gorilla, is [1951]
an established feature of American show business, as popular as Crosby and as temperamental as Garbo. . . . In the matter of temperament, he is perhaps in a class apart. While
many stars achieve a renown for tearing up
contracts, Gargantua has built an enviable reputation for tearing up keepers. Richard Kroener,
a young German who was the gorilla's first
keeper, acquired a decorative network of scar
tissue during the period of his stewardship,
which ended with his death (from nonviolent
causes) in 1942. His arms and shoulders bore
traces of stitching not unlike that on a football.
The camaraderie between Kroener and Gargantua was one of the most appealing in the
history of stars and their handlers. Kroener
was deathly afraid of Gargantua, and Gargantua, for reasons of his own, had presumably
sworn some kind of secret oath to murder
Kroener. The gorilla made numerous half-
successful attempts. . . .

Gargantua's present keeper, a stocky, black-
haired, boundlessly optimistic Spaniard named
Jose Tomas, is also mangled with painful
regularity, but the mishaps have no effect on
his outlook. He considers that a marginal loss
of blood is an inevitable aspect of his occupation; he figures it into his overall health
program, as insurance companies reckon the
odds on accidents. Beyond doubt, Gargantua
is the most dangerous animal in captivity or
even in the history of captured animals. There

are eleven or twelve other gorillas behind bars
with circuses or zoos at present, all of them
having pretty risky dispositions, but none, according to animal men, has either the dedicated
homicidal bent or the explosive power of
Gargantua. . . .

When Gargantua was still using the rhino's
cage, an elephant herder stepped close to the
bars to get a better look. By a mischance, the
man had a date and was wearing a necktie,
ordinarily not a standard part of the elephant
herder's costume. There was a light breeze
and the tie ends fluttered through the bars. The
gorilla grabbed them, and with a quick, one-
hand heave, smashed the herder's head against
the iron. He was knocked unconscious; fortunately the tie broke, dropping him to the
ground. In a choice fit of spleen, Gargantua
then threw the tie, the man's next-to-best one, a
peach-colored foulard, after him. The knot
was drawn into a ball that felt as hard as flint.
It was a curiosity around the circus for several
weeks, and is still in the possession of John
North, a reminder that one of his stars is no
gorilla to monkey with, as it were.

North's memory actually needs no refreshment about Gargantua, over and above a
discernible scar he bears on his right arm. Not
long after the hapless elephant man had lost his
second-best tie, North attempted to demonstrate to some café-society friends how the
accident took place. "The fellow was standing
about like this," said North, approaching the
cage, "when the gorilla took his sweater and—"

He broke off as Gargantua, in an exceptionally social humor, obligingly caught the sleeve of his jacket, pulled him to the cage, and bit his right arm with good appetite. North's friends, impressed, agreed that it was one of the most conscientious demonstrations in gorilla annals. North has worried off and on about the possibility of Gargantua's getting loose, in the course of a train accident or through some attendant's carelessness. He has given orders that if such an escape takes place the gorilla is to be shot on sight. . . .

Inside the cage, Gargantua represents one of the principal assets of the Ringling circus. Both Roland Butler and Frank Braden of the show's publicity department think that the gorilla excites the liveliest attention of all the Ringling attractions. "He's made good," Butler says. "We bill him above the humans." Certainly, for an immigrant youngster born into a middle-class gorilla family, Gargantua has advanced far. His career is a heart-warming example of the benefits of American democracy. He started from scratch, so to speak. His parents were residents of the Cameroons, a mountainous former German province of West Africa. . . .

Aside from chance encounters in the jungle, the natives leave the gorillas strictly alone on the theory that it's impossible to tell what a mad man or monkey will do next. In November of 1930, Gargantua's parents were killed in such an encounter. The natives who made the kill found, in the mother's arms, a month-old male infant and this they took back to the village. He was a husky baby, larger and more active than the average gorilla offspring of his age. For the next few months he was nursed in a kind of reverse Tarzan manner, by a village woman who had lost a child. Shortly before his first birthday, the captive was presented to a neighboring missionary couple, who presumably looked as though they needed a gorilla. The missionary stuck it out for a year, then threw in the sponge. His work was slipping; even the natives noticed it. Instead of

wrestling with the gospel, he was wrestling with the gorilla, who covered the house like a swarm of ants. On one occasion, the missionary, after hours of sweaty work with an indecisive case, a middle-aged ebony cutter, had been right on the point of getting the man's custom away from the witch doctors—he had promised to put on a pair of coveralls and take the saucer out of his lip—when the youngster pranced in and broke things up. The missionary, and he probably should not be blamed too much, sold the infant gorilla to a freighter captain for $400 and a crate full of nonsectarian hymnals.

The captain brought his new acquisition, together with six champanzees, to New York to sell. He had hoped for a big price for the missionary's pet, but a brutal and mystifying incident on shipboard lessened the gorilla's value. Somebody threw acid in his face, leaving deep, ugly burns over his mouth and down the left side of his chest. Though the captain pressed an energetic inquiry, he never learned the identity of the culprit or the reason for the apparently senseless act of savagery. A Brooklyn woman, Mrs. Gertrude Linz, who made a hobby of raising rabbits, pigeons, and St. Bernard dogs, bought the injured gorilla and six chimpanzees for a total $2500. . . .

In 1936, during a trip Mrs. Linz made to Miami with her peculiar household, Buddy underwent his second torturing experience at the hands of man. A shiftless houseboy, discharged by Mrs. Linz for good cause, concluded that the way to get even was to torment the gorilla. Accordingly, he sneaked back at night and gave him a beaker full of syrup heavily dosed with disinfectant. Buddy lost eighty pounds in five weeks before his appetite began to return. Despite this second setback, he remained tolerably genial. It was not until a short time later, when his owner saw him accidentally crush to death a pet kitten, that she realized he was potentially dangerous. Buddy, at six years of age, weighed four hundred pounds and, of course, had no notion of his strength. Also, as turns out to be the case with all gorillas, he had begun to have unprovoked fits of temper. She decided to cage him. The night before she took this step, however, she had what quite evidently was a narrow escape. It had been her custom each night to let the gorilla have the run of her home. This night she awoke with a feeling of uneasy foreboding; then she felt Buddy's thick fingers groping at her throat. Through a steely exercise of will power, she managed to speak calmly, saying, "Come on, Buddy, let's go get a banana." She repeated this several times, and he released her. Early the following morning she bought a cage from some animal importers and put the gorilla behind bars.

Caged for the first time, Buddy became actively hostile. . . . [Mrs. Linz] opened negotiations with John Ringling North. . . .

North . . . bought Buddy [rechristened Gargantua] from Mrs. Linz for $10,000 for which he also got two chimpanzees and Kroener. The gorilla's first home with the circus, a rhinoceros cage, proved so inadequate that North conceived of the present, glassed-in, air-conditioned quarters. Aside from the reduced danger of mayhem, with its encouraging effect on circus crowds, North believed that the new cage would be more conducive to longevity. In times past, gorillas had rarely achieved adulthood in captivity; in addition to their weak lungs and nervous stomachs, they were vulnerable to several other ailments. . . .

The main compartment of Gargantua's cage, his living room, so to speak, is twenty feet long, seven feet wide, and seven feet high. Soon after he moved in, North and Kroener made several attempts to stock it with comfortable furniture, such as a chair, a fancy swing, benches, and so on. Each time, the gorilla smashed the furniture to pieces; at present, his cage contains a steel trapeze suspended by a long chain, and an ordinary automobile tire, also suspended by chain. The chains are frequently broken. Gargantua's principal form

of exercise is running back and forth and smacking the tire with one hand each time he passes. . . .

In 1940, North had the inspiration to seek a mate for his anthropoid attraction. Studying the gorilla, and reflecting on his quarrelsome ways, North and his colleagues somehow interpreted the twisted snarl on Gargantua's face as an affecting urge to woo. "The boy needs romance," North said. "Gorilla was not made to live alone." By a striking coincidence, a wealthy sportswoman, Mrs. E. Kenneth Hoyt, shortly offered to sell North an eight-year-old female gorilla named Toto, which she had reared from baby-gorillahood. . . .

She sold Toto, and Tomas' contract, to John Ringling North in 1940 for $10,000, the same price paid for Gargantua. North had a carrier identical to Gargantua's built for his new gorilla and stimulated a monster publicity campaign about an impending mating. The possible bride and groom were introduced, in Sarasota, under the auspices of a good-sized press gathering. Some of the finest gorilla writers in the South were on hand. The event gave little promise of a happy marriage. The cages were shoved end to end and the doors arranged so that the animals were separated by only two bars. Then they had a good look at each other. Gargantua, plainly unimpressed, tossed a stalk of celery into the other cage, and Toto threw the usual tantrum of a female pelted with vegetables by a thoughtless suitor. . . .

Since Toto and Tomas joined the circus, the keeper has never had as much as one day's vacation. His charge refuses to be tended by anybody else; she rejects her food, sulks, and acts menacing. Tomas is philosophical about the restrictive nature of his career. "Like penitentiary," he says with a laugh. "I stay here rest d' life." After Kroener's death, in 1942, he was presented the double burden of caring for both Toto and Gargantua, and he spends his time between the two cages and his own wagon, which is always parked nearby. His animals, now fully grown, keep him pretty steadily in transit with food. . . .

They each get about twenty pounds of food a day, which includes half a dozen eggs, three quarts of milk, two bunches of celery, a loaf of bread, two tablespoons of liver extract, half a pint of chocolate syrup, a dozen assorted raw sweet potatoes, carrots, onions, and beets, and a dozen assorted bananas, oranges, apples, and pears. Tomas varies this diet from time to time. Both gorillas like fried chicken pretty well, and Gargantua now tops off his noon meal with an almond chocolate bar. If he doesn't get it, he raises all manner of hell, banging on his bars, slapping the tire around, and screeching low, gorilla curses at his keeper. At mealtime, Tomas usually opens slots in the lower part of their cages and pokes the food in on pans. . . .

Both animals drink from cups, affixed to chains, that Tomas hands through the bars. The staple of their liquid diet is distilled water, but besides that and the milk, they also get Coca-Cola, ginger ale, and Cocomalt. To clean the cages, Tomas has capitalized on the gorilla's chief fear—that of snakes. The keeper has a mock blacksnake tied to the end of a bamboo pole, and at cleaning time he opens the door-way connecting the two compartments, shoves his snake through the feeding hole, and waves it around briskly. Either Toto or Gargantua at this intrusion will scoot without argument into the other compartment. Infrequently, Tomas steps briefly into Toto's cage, mostly for old times' sake. She is undoubtedly fond of him, in her odd, gorilla fashion, and he still regards her as his lovable but slightly wayward pupil. He now understands that her spirit is mercurial, however, and he prepares carefully for his visits. From a box in his wagon he takes a live blacksnake, and coiling it neatly, places it in his shirt pocket. Inside the cage, Tomas seats himself on the trapeze and shouts "Vamos!" in a strong Spanish baritone. The

keeper is a bluff, forthright man and his approach to his charges is brusque and sure, as any successful animal man's must be. His remarks to the gorillas, on all subjects, rest on the word "Vamos." When Tomas yells "Vamos" at Toto or Gargantua, he may mean "Beat it," "Come here," "Cleaning time," or "Here's your food." One or two of the Ringling staff have observed that it must be intensely baffling to the gorillas, but apparently it's just something they have to get used to.

Upon seeing her old pal, Toto shuffles for-ward, looking quizzical and friendly, and either strokes his arm or attempts to put her arm around his shoulders. Tomas stays only a few minutes, watching her eyes steadily. In their green, near-human, unfathomable depths he must detect the first subtle flicker of the swift, perhaps mad change that often means, with the gorilla, the difference between affection and murder. Two years ago, when he was in the cage, Toto came forward with a foolish grin that suddenly wavered, and Tomas whipped out the blacksnake a split second before she started to leap. "Snak, snak!" he screamed. "Vamos!" She shrank back, snarling and whimpering, helplessly confused, poised on the border line between instinct and training.

Tomas has been heard to say that he wouldn't go into Gargantua's cage for all the money in the mint, American or Spanish. . . .

He has strong affection for Toto, the com-panion of his youth, but it is in the male that his real interest lies. He is positive that Gar-gantua, in addition to his muscle, is one of the most brilliant of his species. Sometimes, in the very early mornings, Tomas looks into the giant's eyes and detects an expression of profound, watchful amusement. These are moments of uneasy divination. Has the gorilla, he asks himself, areas of understanding to which we are tragically insensitive? "Might come big atomic war," says Tomas. "Boom, boom —then maybe gorillas paying money to look at humans. Mens smart? Gorillas smart? Vamos!"

From *Center Ring: The People of the Circus* by Robert Lewis Taylor, Doubleday & Co., New York, 1951. Used by permission.

MONKEYS AND THE CIRCUS DOCTOR

Dr. J. Y. Henderson

The monkey is the average spectator's favorite animal. People are impressed by its similarity to themselves. They refer to it as "cute." They enjoy watching monkeys as performers who are always doing something unexpected. They are impressed with a monkey's smartness —with the chimpanzee's especially, because he is by far the brightest.

I am impressed, too, but not in quite the same way.

From the day I first joined the circus, I began realizing that the chimps were going to be a very special problem. It wasn't that they were so hard to handle; they weren't. It was simply that you could never devise a method of handling them that would stick. You could devise methods of treating every other animal and, once devised, that method could be relied on. But not with the chimps. They were simply too smart. The better the method, the less likely it was that they would ever permit it to be used again. They could see through it.

Nellie, a chimpanzee, came down with a bad cough late one night. The keeper called me up at home and I drove out to look at her. He said she had been coughing for about two hours. Her chest sounded normal and clear so I gave her some cough syrup and told the keeper to keep feeding it to her every couple of hours.

But by the time I got back to quarters in the morning, she had a well-developed case of pneumonia. I decided that the only thing that would save her was an injection of penicillin or streptomycin. Injecting a chimp is a special

problem because they have four hands and a very sharp strong set of teeth. They will fight you with all five weapons. I didn't want to struggle with Nellie or have several men hold her down because the strength she would use in fighting would weaken her even further.

I had two of the keepers take her out of the cage and each one held a hand while they took her for a walk down the path. Then each boy stretched her arms up so that she could not bite them. Another man held her feet and I gave her an injection in the hind quarters. Nellie let out a squeal, but it was all over in a couple of seconds. Within a couple of days she was all right. Her recovery was complete. But ever since that time, Nellie has refused to give up both her hands at the same time. If two men want to take her for a walk, she will give one a hand and tuck the other one under her armpit, only releasing it when the other hand has been shaken free and tucked under its armpit.

Thus such a patient taxes a doctor's ingenuity because you need as many different methods of treating as there are times when treatment is necessary.

Besides, chimps cause more trouble than most other monkeys, because chimps are basically meaner. If a bad-natured chimp can possibly grab you with his hands—and his arms are extremely strong—the chances are he won't let you free until he has pulled you up to him and bitten you. His bite is sharp and hard. Of course, it is possible to get friendly with even the mean ones. If you have

From *Circus Doctor* by J. Y. Henderson, D.V.M., as told to Richard Taplinger, 1951. By permission of Little, Brown & Co., Boston.

enough patience and you spend enough time talking to them and playing with them, they will become friendly. My disadvantage is that I don't have the time. Furthermore, whenever they see me they get hurt, and they've learned that very quickly.

The result is that I can't, even now, pass any of the chimps without being bombarded with tin plates, orange peels, bananas, or anything else they happen to have in their cages. I am their sworn enemy; nothing will convince them otherwise.

Monkeys are frail anywhere in our climate. They develop coughs and colds at the slightest provocation, and these develop into pneumonia or TB almost while you watch. Before the days of penicillin and the drugs of that family, a monkey with TB or pneumonia was as good as dead. But now I have very good luck treating them and we lose very few.

Contrary to popular belief, it is not the cold that bothers them but damp weather and drafts. For that reason, we ship all our monkeys in glass cages. When the weather is warm and no wind is blowing, we can throw up the glass in the front and let the fresh air in. If there is any chance at all that the weather isn't good for them, we drop the glass and let just a small amount of air in for ventilation.

The nicest thing about monkeys is that they can take care of themselves pretty well. When the weather is cold we not only keep the cages filled with straw, but we throw in blankets and sacks. The monkeys do the rest. They wrap themselves up in several sacks and roll up in the blankets.

I have never had any tooth trouble in any of the monkeys. I don't know why this is so; I suppose their teeth and their bones generally are extremely hard. Their diet may have something to do with it; they eat fruit and vegetables, codliver oil and vitamins. The only dietary trouble occurs when a monkey eats too many oranges. They can, like babies, develop an allergy to oranges.

It surprised me to learn that monkeys are fine swimmers and divers. We have a big monkey island in winter quarters around which is the hippopotamus pool. The monkeys climb up into the high trees and go diving off into the water. They dive beautifully. They swim well, too. The only trouble we ever had with swimming monkeys was one day when we let the Diana monkeys out for the first time. They had never seen water before and had never been in swimming. Like children, they stayed in the water so long they both developed serious chills and bad coughs.

I went into the cage with them and, taking them one at a time, wrapped them in blankets and rubbed and massaged them, not only to get them dry but to get them warm. They tried their best to bite, and I had more trouble keeping from getting bitten than I did keeping them warm.

These same two Dianas caused us considerable trouble because the female was very weak and timid and the male was extremely rough. This male amused himself chiefly in two ways. One of his exercises was harmless. He would race from one side of the cage to the other, taking a flying leap, hitting the side of the cage feet first and then doing a backward somersault landing back on the floor on all four feet. His other exercise was a little less innocent. He would go racing around the cage at a gallop while the female sat huddled by the bars at the front. Every time he passed her he would either hit her on the head or grab her tail and pull her after him for a few feet.

Somehow or other he once got hold of a broom handle and one day he varied this game by hitting her with the stick. By the time we discovered this game, she was having trouble walking. When I examined her I realized she had a spinal injury. It wasn't serious, but it impaired her activity. At this point we separated them.

This is characteristic of monkeys. If one monkey in a pair or group is timid or weak, that one will be unmercifully set upon by the others.

One year we ordered a shipment of ten rhesus monkeys from a dealer in New York.

The monkeys were all healthy and in good shape when they were shipped, but when they arrived we found nine healthy live monkeys and one dead one. This is not uncommon in monkey shipments. For if one becomes sick or turns out to be a little timid, the group will bite it and beat it to death. In a pair, a strong monkey may eat all the food and the timid monkey will make no attempt at all to eat while it starves to death.

Our chimpanzees are much more subject to ailments than are the orangutans. This is probably because the chimps represent a higher order. Certainly they are more intelligent than the others—but I like the orangs.

I had a little orang who was quartered in a cage next to a chimpanzee. She tried to get friendly with him, but he would have none of her. One day, she put her arms through the bars of the cage and made an attempt to touch him. He grabbed her hand and bit the end of her finger off, including nearly all of the nail, and broke what was left of the finger.

The keeper called me immediately and I treated the wound and put the finger in a cast, hoping that the bone would heal. She was a little annoyed by the cast and bit most of it off. However, she left enough so that the bone stayed in place and eventually healed. It was a little pathetic to watch her after that, because as long as the splint stayed on her finger, whenever anyone would come near her, she would push her arm through the cage and hold the hand up, her eyes wide and her eyebrows arched: "Look. I have a sore finger." This was some years ago and even now, whenever I come near her, she will hold that hand up to me and at the same time cover her eyes with the other hand and turn her head away, for all the world as if she was saying, "O.K. Doc, I know it's going to hurt, but I know it's for my own good."

ANIMALS AIN'T PEOPLE

Connie Clausen

I accepted the fact that the elephant men were elephant happy, but because I seldom had the opportunity to talk to any other animal men in the show it wasn't until the season [her one season with the circus] was half over that I learned the men who worked around the horses were horse happy, the men who took care of the big cats mooned around the cages like stagedoor Johnnies, and that even the loners (who only warmed up to animals everyone else avoided) tended to become misty-eyed if their sullen charges showed any response whatever. In this last group I included the man who talked for hours on end to a completely impassive hippo (who gazed back at him indifferently with her bulging water-logged eyes, and often dove into her tank right in the middle of his best ideas); the gorilla keeper who cared for Gargantua (who would have killed him instantly had he been foolish enough to step into the heavily glassed cage); the reptile fanciers; the camel fans; and the zebraphiles.

Just as dog lovers can seldom understand people who prefer cats and vice versa, I found that a man who is elephant happy can't see horses for dust. Even Doc Henderson, the circus vet, who took care of all the animals, admitted that elephants left him less than enthusiastic, and though he found lions and tigers fascinating he remained, first and foremost, a horse man.

Now why a person is drawn to one animal and not another is as mysterious as why a woman prefers one man above all others. I asked Tony to tell me why he particularly liked and chose to work with elephants and not, say, the monkeys or the giraffe. He said, "Well, an elephant is—an elephant," and stopped. I knew exactly what he meant. In a way, an elephant does defy description or definition. It's like no other creature on earth. There is something about its size and shape that defeats the imagination. That piercing primeval trumpet, that wrinkled, seemingly elastic trunk, and those solid squared-off legs, tiny eyes, and long siren lashes are all strictly elephant, nothing else. Certainly their intelligence, ability to respond to affection, and that hint of jungle violence that lies beneath their apparently easy-going natures made them fascinating. Yet I still didn't know why any of us found them irresistible and only tolerated other animals.

I came close to finding out one day during my usual pre-matinee visit to the elephants. When I went over to give Ruth a Coke I noticed that something seemed to be wrong with her eyes. "What's the matter with Ruth?" I asked Tony. "Her eyes are watering."

Tony paused awhile; then he looked directly at me with an expression of patient sadness, as though he knew he would not be believed, "Ruth is crying," he said.

"Animals don't cry," I protested. Tony didn't answer; he just kept looking at me in that terribly patient way.

Finally I said, "All right then, she's crying. Why?"

"She's crying because she's an elephant, that's why. She knows she's a whole lot smarter than most humans, but she's trapped in that big animal body and she can't get out. So . . . she cries sometimes."

I looked at Ruth, and for an instant I saw her as Tony did. Suddenly it seemed possible that a highly intelligent spirit was vainly struggling to emerge from those ridiculously small eyes and that archaic body.

Perhaps my antipathy to horses was inevitable after my association with Gertrude. Besides, unlike the bull hands, who were walking propagandists for pachyderms, the groom who led Gertrude to and from the ring-stock tent had never said a word to me about anything! Then I made the mistake of asking him a question about horses, like, "Why are they so silly?" and my groom, or rather Gertrude's groom, looked at me as though I had just asked why he was the handsomest man in the show and said, "I didn't know you were interested in horses."

I said, "I'm not really," but he never heard me. He began an account of everything that had happened to him since the day of his birth, "everything" being in some way connected with horses. I met every horse he had ever known, from the first pony on his grandfather's farm. Without exception the horses he had encountered were smart, noble, loyal, loving (at least they all loved him), and about three hundred times nicer than any human being he had ever met or ever hoped to meet. I said, "You mean you never ran into a horse who was, well, a dud?"

He grudgingly conceded that a few were kind of slow-witted, but he quickly added, "They make good horses to hitch to a plow or a float. No temperament."

"That's what I mean, temperament," I said. "Isn't there such a thing as too much temperament? Now take Gertrude here. She seems to me to be a prime example of too much. . . ."

"Oh no, you're wrong. Takes a temperamental, high-strung horse to make a good performer," he said.

The next day he was waiting for me with a new fund of horse stories. I tried to counter-

act them with a few anecdotes about my elephants, but it was useless. I'd say, "You have to admit Ruth is clever. Why yesterday, when it rained, Ruth came over to the dressing tent to pick me up so I wouldn't get my feet wet. Nine Blankets said she walked over there on her own; he didn't even tell her to. Now Gertrude would never think of anything like that. She always looks as though she'd like me to go to the horse tent and pick her up."

Gertrude's groom said, "You've got to remember, Gertrude once starred in the center ring; she's got other things on her mind. Did you know that she can leap through a flaming hoop and is the best. . . ."

I gave up trying to top him after a while. After all, he could think up his next horse story standing on solid ground. I was on Gertrude's back, and since Gertrude was usually warming up for her big moment before the cheering crowds my position wasn't really conducive to quick repartee. One day I did interrupt him long enough to ask his name. He said, "Well, it's John, but around here they call me Horse-meat." He wouldn't tell me why. I finally learned it was because when he found out that the cats were fed horsemeat he broke down and cried like a baby, and always referred to the lions and tigers as a bunch of caged canni-bals, a point of view I was inclined to sympathize with. I also suggested a few times that I thought Gertrude had long since passed the age for a comeback and was more than a little unstrung, but he said righteously, "You have to understand Gertrude." Gertrude was at that moment standing straight up on her hind legs, so all I could do was hold on to the saddle and shout back, "It's enough to have to ride her. I don't have the energy left to under-stand her."

I did get a certain satisfaction, however, when Horsemeat showed up one day with his arm in a sling. Gertrude, "that poor, mis-understood mare," had kicked him the night before. "She was trying to tell me something," Horsemeat explained. "I should have stopped what I was doing and listened to her."

I said, "Yeah, she was probably asking you to come closer, so she could get a better aim." Horsemeat gave me a wounded look and sulked for three days in welcome silence, but it didn't last. Like the elephant men he'd found a captive audience, so I continued to hear about horses. He never sold me on horses, however. I still thought they were flighty, not very bright, and although their liquid eyes and sleek bodies were certainly handsomer than the elephants' I just couldn't get horse happy.

Horsemeat wasn't alone in trying to convert me. There were dozens of horse enthusiasts among the performers, including a rabid group among the North starlets, who wore nothing but riding pants and leather boots, carried crops everywhere (even to the cook tent), and were only content when they were in the saddle. Like Horsemeat these partisans all knew, personally, horses who had saved their masters' lives, horses who could tell time, count to ten, would have won the Kentucky Derby if they hadn't been tripped, and pined away with grief when their masters died. None of them seemed to know any horses who had kicked their masters to death; horses who were slow, stupid, mean, or just plain silly like Gertrude; or if they did they weren't talking.

The big cat devotees—the cage boys who handled the lions, the tigers, the panthers, the cheetahs, the jaguars—who fed them and kept their cages clean were of another breed than the men who worked with other animals. There was a kind of tension, a concealed explosiveness about them so strongly reminiscent of the cats themselves, that seeing them around the lot one knew instantly they were cat men.

They, too, idolized their charges, but with a difference. They bragged about the deadly fierceness of their lions, the stealthly cunning of their panthers, the sinister swiftness of their tigers, like kids boasting of the speed of their hot rods or the superior toughness of their gang over anyone else's. They even kept score of the man-killers, the maimers, the eye-gougers

among the cats, as though the animals were underworld heroes, temporarily imprisoned but still full of fight, ready to strike out at their jailers with every weapon nature gave them. That the boys themselves were often the targets didn't seem to dull their worship. They continued to poke their thin arms through the cage bars, and got their reward if the animal within condescended to be fondled and didn't try to bite off an arm.

I'd grown so accustomed to men behaving as though animals were human (or better than human), that I accepted the cage boys' strange devotion to the cats without question. Then in Ohio somewhere, during a matinee, one of the cage boys was affectionately stroking a tiger that he was certain was his "friend." The tiger, obeying some swift, murderous impulse, attacked him, suddenly, without warning, pulling him in close against the bars with one powerful paw and holding him there until she could get at him with her teeth. The boy screamed so horribly that we heard him over the music of the Big Top band, and everyone ran to the menagerie tent. But before anyone reached him, it was too late. The cage boy was lying on the bloody straw in front of the cage—dead. The tiger leaned quietly against the cage bars, cleaning her fur, her eyes cool, almost bored.

The boy (he was about sixteen) had apparently shielded his face with his hands, because except for a long scratch across one cheek it was unmarked, so that the expression of stunned horror on his features remained even in death. Although I don't think I had ever seen the boy before a strong conviction that I knew him persisted. I could not get that expression out of my mind.

I went through the rest of the show, alternating between a deep pity for the dead boy and anger that his death should have occurred at all. The tiger's attack had been senseless, the boy's taking such a risk even more so. "Why did it happen?" I kept asking myself. I couldn't wait until the night show began to talk to the professor [a bull hand, a former university professor]. I went to the elephant men's top between shows—something I knew I could be fired for doing if I were seen by any of the bosses—and asked one of the hands to call him outside. When he came out I said without any preliminary explanation, "Why was he killed? What did he want from the tiger?"

The Professor knew immediately who and what I was talking about. It was almost as though he'd been waiting for me. He said, "Let me tell you something about men who hang around animals. There are men who know they're men and who know animals are animals. They like animals, respect them, but they don't let the animal forget who's boss. They don't take chances, either. Now the other kind aren't men yet—like that cage boy. He's not sure what he is or who's boss, him or the tiger."

"I still don't understand."

"Look, a skinny kid like that figures if he can control something as big and deadly as a tiger, why hell, he's got it made. The more danger there is for him the bigger man he is. But an animal's an animal. You can't woo a tiger like she's a woman."

"I've seen great devotion," I said, "between some of the men and their animals."

"Think, girl, think! Quit romanticizing. You suppose that poor bastard cage boy would look to a tiger for love if he had a woman to love him, or that Nine Blankets would go around acting like Ruth was his mother if he had a mother that gave a damn about him? You think a man, a real man, would spend his time talking to animals, if he wasn't scared to death of people?"

I said, "Scared? The men hate towners, hate squares, that's all."

"What do you think hate is, you hopeless girl? It's fear! We don't hate the towners as we say. We're afraid of them. Afraid we won't make it with them, that we aren't good enough. That's why we're here, talking to animals that can't talk back."

I suddenly realized that the Professor was saying "we"—including himself. He caught it at the same moment and said, in a funny, almost gentle voice, "I sometimes wonder who is learning the most, you or me." Then the usual sarcasm came back into his tone and he said, "To sum up today's lesson in three words: Animals ain't people! Don't forget it."

THE SEAL WHO BECAME FAMOUS

James Thurber

A seal who lay basking on a large, smooth rock said to himself: all I ever do is swim. None of the other seals can swim any better than I can, he reflected, but, on the other hand, they can all swim just as well. The more he pondered the monotony and uniformity of his life, the more depressed he became. That night he swam away and joined a circus.

Within two years the seal had become a great balancer. He could balance lamps, billiard cues, medicine balls, hassocks, taborets, dollar cigars, and anything else you gave him. When he read in a book a reference to the Great Seal of the United States, he thought it meant him. In the winter of his third year as a performer he went back to the large, smooth rock to visit his friends and family. He gave them the Big Town stuff right away: the latest slang, liquor in a golden flask, zippers, a gardenia in his lapel. He balanced for them everything there was on the rock to balance, which wasn't much. When he had run through his repertory, he asked the other seals if they could do what he had done and all said no. "O.K.," he said, "Let's see you do something I can't do." Since the only thing they could do was swim, they all plunged off the rock into the sea. The circus seal plunged right after them, but he was so hampered by his smart city clothes, including a pair of seventeen-dollar shoes, that he began to founder at once. Since he hadn't been in swimming for three years, he had forgot what to do with his flippers and tail, and he went down for the third time before the other seals could reach him. They gave him a simple but dignified funeral.

Moral: Whom God has equipped with flippers should not monkey around with zippers.

From *Fables for Our Time* by James Thurber. © 1940 by James Thurber. © 1968 by Helen Thurber. Published by Harper & Row, New York. Originally printed in *The New Yorker*.

PART THREE

CLOWNS

UNEASY LIES THE HEAD
THAT PLAYS A CLOWN

Robert C. Benchley

Almost anything is likely to happen to a man these days [1917]. Last night, for instance, I was a clown in Barnum & Bailey's circus. If it isn't one thing, it's another, as the fellow said.

I don't think that I was a very good clown. I get too silly when given a free rein and a whole arena to work in. But it was for only one night, and there were lots of other attractions in the show, and if people didn't like the way I clowned they could look at something else. In fact, I think quite a number of them did avail themselves of that alternative. . . .

I didn't take up clowning because I felt irresistibly drawn to it as a profession, or because of any family tradition. I simply wanted to see what it felt like to be one of a number of cynosures of neighboring eyes, when the neighboring eyes happen to number somewhat over eight thousand. Each year I had watched the clowns tread the sawdust trail around the arena in the execution of their lawful business, and I wondered how it felt to them to have so many people watching them at it. . . .

With motives as purely scientific and disinterested as these, it was not difficult for me to induce the circus authorities to let me dress up as a clown and go on with the rest of the boys. . . .

The question next arose as to what particular pleasantry I could indulge in when I should once get inside the arena with my make-up on. . . .

So an Entertainment Committee meeting was held, consisting of Buck Baker, the Thomas A. Edison of the clowns, and myself. Mr. Baker devotes his time to inventing mechanical devices which, by working the wrong way, will make a success. And when he has got his invention perfected, or imperfected, he whitens up his face and rides it out into the tanbark. If anybody could think of something for me to do, he could.

"Well, I'll tell you," said Mr. Baker, at the first meeting of the committee, "there are several things you might do. There is the jitney bus, for instance. You could get in that, and all you'd have to do would be to jump when the fellow throws the bomb into it and the bus explodes and falls to pieces. You couldn't go wrong, so long as you jump quick and high."

Now, I had seen that act. And, as I remembered it, jumping quick and high were only the fundamentals of procedure for getting home that night in a fairly decent state of preservation. In the first place, the jitney bus was driven at lightning speed around the track, and then, when the bomb was thrown into it, the detonation and general destruction were gigantic. I remembered thinking at the time that a man needn't enlist to do his bit in the way of getting his head blown off, or, in the case of a slacker, a compound fracture. And here I was, being proposed for membership in this Local Chapter of the Suicide Club. I decided right then and there to blackball myself.

"I don't think that that would be a very good thing for me to do," I said modestly.

Condensed from *New York Tribune,* April 22, 1917. Reprinted by permission; © 1917, 1945 Gertrude D. Benchley.

"You see, I know absolutely nothing about the thing. I might spoil the whole act by failing to jump in time. I think that it would be better if I weren't quite so conspicuous, don't you?"

Mr. Baker said that I couldn't possibly spoil the act. It wasn't the act, however, that I was worrying about.

"Or," he continued, "you could sit in with me in the Ford that runs backward. All you have to do is sit tight and hang on to the dummy wheel, and when the back of the automobile drops off and we run over the cop, just hang on and make believe you are driving. I'll be doing the real driving backwards, see?"

I said that I saw. I also said that I was afraid that I might do something wrong, but that excuse was beginning to sound weak, even to me. I suggested that it might be better for a novice not to take part in any such elaborate ensemble, that perhaps there would be less danger in letting me do something alone, such as rake an imaginary garden, or even sit, doing nothing, watching the rest of the performers with a very dejected air. In fact, I could think of all kinds of good stunts, stunts which would be at least inoffensive and which would, in addition, ensure me the probably permanent use of both legs.

My mentor listened politely to all of my craven proposals, and even suggested himself that I might ride the rubber bicycle, a contrivance which goes a certain distance and then gets discouraged and slumps, owing to most of its important bars being made of rubber hose. This sounded like a good idea to me. Falling from a bicycle has its advantages over being projected from an exploding jitney bus, or even riding wildly backward around the ring in a drunken Ford. So I pushed the rubber bicycle idea with enthusiasm. . . .

In Madison Square Garden they dress in large rooms which are divided up into so many square inches of floor space for each man. Whatever room is left over after he has put his trunk down, he is free to stand on. As he

usually sits on his trunk, however, those extra three square inches of floor space are just so much velvet, and he may either use them for a garden or rent them out to a neighbor.

And, incidentally, circus folk are just what circus folk ought to be. There was a time, long ago, when every one supposed that a clown, when he was not clowning, was a merry, smiling sort of person, who tried to make things as pleasant for his friends as he did for the audience. And then some psycho-analyst came along and said that clowns off-stage were very gloomy, that they talked Ibsen, and that a clown, to be really a clown, had to have nine or ten children starving at home so that he could be very dejected just as soon as he came out of the ring. And everyone proceeded to take up with this theory, until it has become almost a truism that a clown is a serious-minded, dreary sort of person in private life.

Such may be the case, but all the clowns that I met struck me as being exceptionally cheery and just what you would want a clown to be. Buck Baker has a chuckle and a collection of personal anecdotes in which Ibsen or Maeterlinck are not once featured, and from Al Ferrell and Harry Rose (one of whom is dragged in a bathtub around the ring by a motorcycle, both being known as the speed kings of cycling comedy), I got several stories with happy endings, a quantity of laughs, and very gracious attention in the matter of getting my make-up off. They may have secret sorrows, but they are not getting any pleasure out of them. They are most all of them athletes and are in it because they like it. You have to be an athlete and you have to like it, to jump quick and high from an exploding jitney bus.

In that one room there were enough nationalities represented to start a peace conference on the spot. German, French, Italian, all blended in together in one conversational chorus. The Spanish clown showed his neutrality by playing a mandolin to a guitar accompaniment while waiting for his act. Over in another corner there was a phonograph helping the neighbors in that section to pass the hours away until it should come time for them to take part in the Greatest Show on Earth, which was then going on below them.

Making up as a clown is easy enough when you have some one there to do it for you. And there is little worry about the fit of the clothes. I did object to the false feet, especially as they laced up the back, but there wasn't much else I could wear. As Ferrell remarked, being in another man's shoes was one thing and being in another man's feet was something else. It wasn't so much that I objected to the unanatomical appearance of the feet, as that they were very large and clumsy, and I still had in mind the fact that I was, later on in the show, to jump quick and high, a maneuver which would be practically impossible with these Gargantuan feet.

For I saw that my participation in this jitney explosion and the perverse Ford escapade were becoming more and more inevitable. At times I would think that I had won my tutor round to my way of thinking, and that I was to be allowed to flock by myself and hoe, or ride the rubber bicycle, but at the end of each suggestion of mine, to which he had apparently assented, he would say:

"Now, remember, all you have to do is hang onto the wheel when we go round the corners, and sit tight, and make believe you are driving, and then, in the other act, just jump out when the rest do, and be sure to jump quick and clear out of the bus when it explodes."

I was all made up, and couldn't very well resign; so I said that I would remember.

Then one of the clowns came in to get dressed, and on meeting me said ominously to Brother Baker:

"Is this the one we give the bumps to tonight?"

I gave two short, sharp laughs and licked my lips, getting my mouth full of grease paint.

"Let's see," said the newcomer, as he tied back his hair so that it wouldn't get into his make-up, "wasn't it that other fellow that came in with us for one night that got his arm broke?"

I omitted the laugh this time, and simply licked my lips, with the same result as before. Then, feeling that I must show that I appreciated the humor of the thing, I said something very flat, which, as I remember it now, made no sense. I was getting so that I didn't give a darn *what* the audience at the circus looked like from the ring. And my mouth was full of grease paint.

Then the Big Spectacular Parade was on and the building resounded with the blare of trumpets and the thunderous tramping of elephants and prancing horses. We went downstairs to watch it.

As you sit in the circus and see these cavalcades disappear between the doors under the end of the arena you imagine a place into which they go which is at least as large as the Garden itself. Anything smaller would seem to be impossible as an anteroom. And yet it is a room about the size of a small hotel lobby, and is apparently in the wildest disorder. Baby carriages, hoops, bells, wheels, everything stacked up against the other in no evident scheme, leaving a narrow pathway for such incidentals as elephants, camels, wild horses, rampant motorcycles, all to pass through on their way to and from the arena. It looks like a big bedroom of a tremendous boy who is planning to enter a gigantic Institute of Technology in the fall.

And yet it is needless to say that everything is in its place and that there is room for everyone. I still don't understand how it can be so, but you'll have to take my word for it that it is. Of course, a man can't loll about in the middle of the passageway as he would in the front hall at home, but no man would probably want to.

I made my debut in a very unostentatious way (as I had always expressed a wish to have it) by trailing along in with a bevy of clowns and seating myself on the edge of a stage in a despondent attitude to watch the proceedings. I was made up to look sad, so there was not even the effort of facial arrangement in this part of my work. And I had plenty of time to observe the audience, which had, at one time, been my chief aim of the evening. My chief aim now was to get out of the Garden in a recognizable condition.

It is, nevertheless, a peculiar sensation to be in a position where five thousand people can look at you if they want to. As a matter of fact, I don't suppose more than four in the audience saw me, and two of those were there to cheer me on and hold my watch. But, whenever the crowd laughed at a stunt that was being executed in my vicinity, I felt that they were laughing at me. I forgot for the time that I was made up as a clown, and I was sure that every one had spotted me and was laughing at something that was wrong about my clothes. Perhaps I had a rip in my coat, or had come out without any necktie. I tried to argue with myself that they were not laughing at me, but at the act, and that, anyway, there could be nothing wrong with my dress, for the reason that there could be nothing particularly right about it either. But the laughter seemed so distinctly personal that I was glad when the whistle blew and I trotted off the field with the rest of the team.

And then I saw active service. The inventive Baker and his cohorts were putting together his eccentric Ford, which runs backward while going forward. As I stood watching, one of the attendants came up to me, not knowing that I was to be Baker's mechanician, and said in an easy, conversational tone:

"That man Baker is going to get smashed up some one of these days."

"Yes?" I asked, with assumed indifference.

"You bet. Why, he doesn't care how he drives that thing. The other night he came whizzing out this door and crashed ker-bung into that post there; see it?"

I saw it, and was just about to sneak out the stage door into Fourth Avenue when the reckless driver in question signalled to me.

"All right," he said. "Hop in, and remember all you have to do is hang on to the wheel."

Well, I hung on to the wheel. Out of the doors we shot, Baker and another clown in the front seat with me, and two others in the false tonneau, all shouting and waving at the audience—except me. I hung onto the wheel, and tried to act as if I thought I was driving the thing backward. . . .

But, as a matter of fact, after the first wild dash into the bright light of the Garden, I might as well have been swirling about in a river all by myself for all the audience I saw, or for all I knew of what my colleagues were doing. Now and then I would see a face shoot by, so I knew that there were still people in the seats, and once in a while I heard a cry from behind, as when the tonneau fell off or the policeman got in the way. But the general impression that I have of the wild ride is one of coming to the surface after a long dive. And then we were back in the anteroom again.

I had hardly straightened my fingers out and found my tongue when I was told that I could get into the police patrol if I wanted to and go to the clown fire. I wasn't too keen about it, for the horses that draw the patrol wagon are a pair that have been dismissed from some firehouse for overspeeding, but there wasn't much that I could do about it. So I climbed in beside the farmer-policeman and twined my arms in and out between the siderails.

"Look out when the bunch of clowns get in at the fire," he said. "A big one will jump right in here and another one will follow him up and kick him in the stomach. Look out that you don't get kicked in the head, that's all."

Again I was catapulated out through the doors, this time behind a pair of wild horses which were evidently twenty minutes late for something. A large patrol wagon is a roomy place for two thin men when it is drawn by a runaway team. I ended the ride in approximately the same position in which I began, but only after having tried almost every other position that a man could try and and on every square inch of seating space in the wagon.

I need not add that I *was* in the way of the large clown, and that I *was* kicked in the head by the other, and that as we tore back into the retiring room I decided that I had all the material I needed for the story. In fact, I had more than enough. I had material enough for two stories and an official investigation.

I climbed out of the patrol into the path of an elephant, and, dodging him as I would dodge a city block, I stepped between a bear cage and a nest of sleeping dogs. "Heads up," came the cry, and suddenly the whole side of the wall in front of me was let down on pulleys. I didn't wait to see what for. Up the narrow stairs I went as fast as my reinforced feet would let me, and made for the little nook where my clothes were hung. I thought it was about time that I made a few notes.

But I wasn't to get out of the jitney bus explosion that easily. At the clown corner I met one of my co-workers.

"Come on down," he said cheerily, "the bus goes on pretty soon."

"I'll be right down," I said. "I just want to jot down a few notes."

It was too late, however. The time had come to go, for the band had changed its tune, and by the music that the band is playing the performers know at what stage the show is, and from that judge their cues.

"Come ahead!" he shouted, and dashed down the stairs.

I pulled my tam-o'shanter close down over my head and followed. An explosion is only an explosion, and, after all, perhaps I might be able to jump quick and high enough.

But as I reached the stairway I realized that I was exempted from service. There, on his ponderous way down, only two steps in front of me, was the Fat Man in pink tights. The stairway to the dressing rooms in the Garden is wide enough only to let an emaciated boy through comfortably, going one way at a time. It was a question whether or not the Fat Man could negotiate the passage himself, to say nothing of my trying to pass him. Down another step he went, and I followed. Heaven knows, I did my best to make the act. I went as far as I could down the stairs. No man could do more.

I heard the gong on the jitney bus clang. Someone yelled my name. But there are no waits in a circus. If you are not there, your act goes on without you. I was counting on that. And by the time my fat benefactor and I had reached the third and fourth steps from the bottom respectively, I had the distinct relief of seeing the whole equipage rattle out at the doors, crash down the track, and finally explode, with all the clowns jumping quick and high. They did it very well, too.

My explanations were accepted, but I felt guilty as I accepted the solicitous suggestions of the rest of the crew in cleaning the white from my face. I wouldn't have got it off, however, if I hadn't accepted their suggestions. In fact, I haven't got it all off yet. My eyes still look pale.

❖❖❖❖❖❖❖❖❖❖❖❖❖❖❖❖❖❖❖❖❖❖❖❖❖

It is meat and drink to me to see a clown.—Shakespeare.

❖❖❖❖❖❖❖❖❖❖❖❖❖❖❖❖❖❖

ETERNAL DROLLERY

Francis Beverly Kelley

Byron wrote, "He who joy would win must share it; happiness was born a twin."

Circus people know this, and no one puts it into more consistent practice than does the clown, or "Joey," as he is dubbed, after the famous English buffoon, Joseph Grimaldi. It would be difficult to estimate how many children and grown-ups annually rock with laughter at the antics of these mimers, and almost any day you can expect to find them loaded into automobiles, on their way to a children's hospital for a charity performance.

There is not half so much tragedy behind the funny make-ups of clowns as people like to believe. By and large, they are a happy lot; but here is a little story to illustrate the eternal drollery of the circus buffoon: Johnny Patterson, famous Irish clown, lay dying in a dressing tent. The physician who attended him tried to cheer him up and, upon leaving, said, "Good night, Patterson. I will see you in the morning."

A smile flickered across the old clown's face. "I know you will, doctor," he replied, "but will I see you?"

The next time you attend a circus, notice that no two clowns have their faces painted alike. That is because, once a Joey decorates his face according to an original design, he is conceded to have a sort of moral copyright on the make-up and no colleague copies it. All in all, the clown's is a noble calling. The world is full of tears, and man by nature is a sorrowing creature. It requires infinitely more to send us into gales of laughter than it does to make us cry. Barnum is said to have remarked that clowns are pegs used to hang circuses on.

From "The Land of Sawdust and Spangles," *The National Geographic Magazine,* October 1931. Used by permission.

ONLY ONE REAL LIFE

Dexter Fellows

The laugh-clown-laugh theme is as old as the story of the melancholic jester and his doctor. It has been told of George L. Fox, one of America's greatest clowns and pantomimists—how he went to a physician to be cured of persistent depression; how the physician, after failing to find a physical cause, recommended amusement of one kind or another, suggesting that his patient "go and see George Fox"; and how the patient lugubriously answered: "I am Fox." Fifty years before, the same story was told of the renowned English clown Joseph Grimaldi and Dr. John Abernethy, and doubtless it was told a hundred years before about some other unhappy Pagliacci.

While every harlequin costume in our brigade of buffoons does not cover a breaking heart, I know of several instances when the crowds roared with laughter at clowns who played their parts under the most agonizing conditions. Frank (Slivers) Oakley, who was as well known at the turn of the century as Charlie Chaplin is today [1936], is an example although, in his case, there was no audience to laugh as he made his final exit alone, penniless: suicide by gas.

I shall never forget the story Slivers told of an old clown who used to work with him. In all the time he was in the business he got only one real laugh and that was when the elephant stepped on his foot and smashed it flat. His scream of pain was answered by an explosion of delight from the audience, and when his fellow-clowns carried him out, groaning and biting his fingers, the laughter and applause for what the spectators thought was part of the act were deafening.

Excerpts from *This Way to the Big Show* by Dexter Fellows & Andrew A. Freeman. The Viking Press, New York, 1936.

A GENTLE, WISTFUL QUALITY

Thomas W. Duncan

Think of the circus as a microcosm; within the oval of the hippodrome track the arena of life is epitomized. But life's externals: the crude dangers, the lofty ventures, man's mastery of the lower animals, man's acrobatic victories. All is fanfare, rodomontade, raw color, sunburst success. It is a celebration of man's material triumphs. Any hint of man's inner nature is lacking. Counterpoint is lacking. Then come the clowns. And the clowns—although most of us never guess it—are supplying the lack. They are gently and obliquely suggesting that this brawny, bespangled, victorious, stentorian fellow called man has also—forgive the phrase—a soul. If he has his triumphs, he has his defeats as well. If sometimes his gaudy projects succeed, oftener they go awry.

With a pantomimic simplicity that would have delighted Constantine Stanislavski, Emmett Kelly enters the ring carrying a broom. He espies a spot of light, tries to sweep it away. The light shifts; he gives chase; always it eludes him. (Have not will o' the wisps eluded us all?) Or he is given a peanut, but when he cracks it he uses a sledge and the peanut is smashed. (Which one of us has not at some time lost everything by overextending himself?) He prepares a garden for planting but eats every seed before the ground is ready. Nothing comes out as it should. And the spectators are convulsed. But are they laughing only at Kelly? He doesn't think so. "By laughing at me they really laugh at themselves, and realizing that they have done this gives them a sort of spiritual second wind for going back into battle."

In the modern circus, remember, the clown works in pantomime, a medium vastly more difficult than the wit employed by the talking clowns of the past. Wit is often mere word-and-idea juggling; even the best wit is of the intellect only; of itself it has nothing to do with art. But clowning in pantomime is very nearly pure art. Its target is the same toward which, so he said, Molière aimed his plays: at the audience's vitals. At their emotions, the heartland of art. Sometimes the pantomime is unalloyed humor; oftener it is sardonicism. And if we are to believe H. W. Fowler, and we had better, because he is usually correct, the aim of the sardonic is self-relief, its province adversity, its method pessimism.

No artist works in a vacuum. For his materials he must look to his own experience. Granting that the clown is an artist, and his humor usually sardonicism, it would seem to follow that, other things equal, the clown who has nibbled many rinds of failure, many dregs of grief, will possess the richest treasure troves of slag to transmute into golden laughter. The clown must be melancholy, which is another way of saying he must be sensitive. Certainly every clown I have known, from little George Halpin to Red Skelton, has had a gentle, wistful quality.

Condensed from "The Counterpoint of the Circus," *Saturday Review,* April 3, 1954. © 1954 The Saturday Review Associates, Inc. Used by permission.

MARK TWAIN ON BEING A CLOWN

Robert Edmund Sherwood

I have ridden in Venetian gondolas to the music of tinkling
mandolins; shaken the hands of Queen Victoria and John L.
Sullivan; and slept under the stars in the Grand Canyon and the
Valley of the Yosemite. I would willingly forego the memory
of them all, could I once again sit outside a circus tent, with the
stars twinkling overhead, and listen to Mark Twain tell of his
experiences as a pilot on a Mississippi River steamboat.

Picture, if you can, a perfect night in June. Now and again the
faint strains of "The Blue Danube Waltz" came to our ears,
which told that the Hasselback Brothers were doing their double
trapeze act; then the music would change to a lively gallop
as Billy Sholes turned backward somersaults on a flying horse,
whose broad back was well resined to prevent slipping.
There I sat entranced, listening to Mark's stories, until the boom
of a gun warned me that Mademoiselle Zazel, the human
projectile, had been catapulted from a cannon into the outstretched
arms of her assistant, hanging from a trapeze forty feet from
her starting point. That was my cue for reappearance [as a
clown] and I tore myself away, only to return at the
first opportunity.

Mark Twain repeatedly confessed to me his ambition to become
a clown. At first I thought he was joking; later I found he
was really in earnest. I ridiculed the idea, and inquired of him why
a man who could write such books as he, wanted to become
a common clown.

"Well, Bob," he replied, "I think it would be a very satisfying
sensation when you come to a ripe old age, to feel and know
that you had made people happy—children especially."

At the time I thought him sentimental; but since I have arrived
at a sedate age, I have come to know he had the true

conception of life—making people happy. I would rather take a hundred hungry, ragged youngsters to the circus, and fill them up on peanuts and lemonade, than attend a big banquet given to royalty.

From *Here We Are Again*, The Bobbs-Merrill Co., 1926. Used by permission.

AN EIGHT-YEAR-OLD CLOWN

Charles Chaplin

When touring the provinces we went to school for the week in each town, which did little to further my education. [He was "past eight years old," a member of the Eight Lancashire Lads troupe on tour before 1900.]

At Christmas time we were engaged to play cats and dogs in a Cinderella pantomime at the London Hippodrome. In those days it was a new theatre, a combination of vaudeville and circus, elaborately decorated and quite sensational. The floor of the ring sank and flooded with water, and elaborate ballets were contrived. Row after row of pretty girls in shining armor would march in and disappear completely under water. As the last line submerged, Marceline, the great French clown, dressed in sloppy evening dress and opera hat, would enter with a fishing rod, sit on a camp stool, open a large jewel case, bait his hook with a diamond necklace, then cast it into the water. After a while he would "chum" with smaller jewelry, throwing in a few bracelets, eventually emptying the whole jewel case. Suddenly he would get a bite and throw himself into paroxysms of comic gyrations, struggling with the rod and eventually pulling out of the water a small trained poodle, who copied everything Marceline did: if he sat down, the dog sat down; if he stood on his head, the dog did likewise.

Marceline's comedy was droll and charming, and London went wild over him. In the kitchen scene I was given a little comedy bit to do with Marceline. I was a cat, and Marceline would back away from a dog and fall over my back while I drank milk. He always complained that I did not arch my back

enough to break his fall. I wore a cat mask which had a look
of surprise, and during the first matinee for children I
went up to the rear end of a dog and began to sniff. When the
audience laughed, I turned and looked surprised at them,
pulling a string which winked a staring eye. After several
sniffs and winks the house manager came bounding backstage,
waving frantically in the wings. But I carried on. After
smelling the dog, I smelled the proscenium, then I lifted my leg.
The audience roared—possibly because the gesture was
uncatlike. Eventually the manager caught my eye and I capered
off to great applause. "Never do that again!" he said breathlessly.
"You'll have the Lord Chamberlain close down the theatre!"

❖◆❖◆❖◆❖◆❖◆❖◆❖◆❖◆❖◆❖◆❖◆❖◆❖◆❖◆❖◆❖◆❖

ON GRIMALDI [1779-1837]

❖◆❖◆❖◆❖◆❖◆❖◆❖◆❖◆❖◆❖◆❖◆❖

I never saw any one to equal him [Grimaldi]—there was such
mind in everything he did. It was said of Garrick, that when he
played a Drunken Man, he was "all over drunk"—Grimaldi was
"all over Clown."

Charles Dibdin the younger (1830)

Grimaldi was a household word; it was the short for fun,
whim, trick and atrocity—that is, clown-atrocity, crimes
that delight us.

The Humorist (1839)

WHAT WITCHERY BUT A CLOWN'S?

Charles Dickens

It is some years now since we first conceived a strong veneration for clowns, and an intense anxiety to know what they did with themselves out of pantomime time, and off the stage. As a child, we were accustomed to pester our relations and friends with questions out of number concerning these gentry; how it was they got such beautiful complexions, and where they lived; and whether they were born clowns, or gradually turned into clowns as they grew up. On these and a thousand other points our curiosity was insatiable.

The delights—the ten thousand million delights of a pantomime—come streaming upon us now, even of the pantomime which came lumbering down in Richardson's wagons at fairtime to the dull little town in which we had the honour to be brought up, and which a long row of small boys, with frills as white as they could be washed, and hands as clean as they would come, were taken to behold the glories of, in fair daylight.

We feel again all the pride of standing in a body on the platform, the observed of all observers in the crowd below, while the junior usher pays away twenty-four ninepences to a stout gentleman under a Gothic arch, with a hoop of variegated lamps swinging over his head. Again we catch a glimpse (too brief, alas!) of the lady with a green parasol in her hand, on the outside stage of the next show but one, who supports herself on one foot, on the back of a majestic horse, blotting-paper colored and white; and once again our eyes open wide with wonder, and our hearts throb with emotion, as we deliver our cardboard check into the very hands of the Harlequin himself.

But what was this—even this—to the glories of the inside, where, amid the smell of sawdust and orange-peel, sweeter far than violets to youthful noses, the first play being over, the lovers united, the ghost appeased, the baron killed, everything made comfortable and pleasant—the pantomime itself began! What mattered it that the stage was three yards wide, and four deep? We never saw it. We had no eyes, ears, or corporeal senses, but for the pantomime. And when its short career was run, and the baron previously slaughtered, coming forward with his hand upon his heart, announced that for that favour Mr. Richardson [John Richardson, who brought his players to the fair] returned his most sincere thanks, and the performance would commence again in a quarter of an hour, what jest could equal the effects of the baron's indignation and surprise, when the clown, unexpectedly peeping from behind the curtain, requested the audience "not to believe it, for it was all gammon!" Who but a clown could have called forth the roar of laughter that succeeded; and what witchery but a clown's could have caused the junior usher himself to declare aloud, as he shook his sides and smote his knee in a moment of irrepressible joy, that that was the very best thing he had ever heard said!

From the introduction to *Memoirs of Joseph Grimaldi,* edited by Dickens, 1838.

A SHARE IN THE WORLD TO COME

One day, when the Prophet Elijah was standing in the market place, a friend of his came up to him and asked:

"Is there anybody in this multitude who will have a share in the World To Come?"

Elijah looked about him and with a sigh he answered: "No."

Then he looked about again and pointed to two men who had just entered the market place and were making their way through the crowds. "Those two men will have a share in the World To Come."

"What is their occupation and what have they done to deserve it?" asked Elijah's friend.

"They are clowns," Elijah replied, "and when they see people troubled in mind or heavy with sorrow, they make them laugh; and when they meet people who quarrel, they make peace between them."

The Talmud: Moed-Taanith, 22a: *The Lore of the Old Testament* by Joseph Gaer, Little, Brown and Company, Boston, 1951. © 1951 by Joseph Gaer.

A RECOLLECTION OF THE 1890's

W. Earl Aumann

The big tent was only about half full when we got there shortly after 1 P.M.—we liked to be early—but the time passed quickly watching the clowns pull their tricks on the hippodrome track in front of the seats.

One clown dressed in a Prince Albert suit and wearing a silk hat (but without clown make up) carried an old fashioned camera on a tripod and would ask people coming in, especially large families, for permission to take their pictures. Quite flattered they would readily agree and the photographer would take infinite pains in posing them, frequently changing their positions and then putting his head under the black cloth again. After about five minutes of that when the family began to get restless, he would quietly pick up the camera and stroll unconcernedly away, leaving the family still posed..

From *The Gondolier,* Venice, Florida, January 7, 1965. Used by permission.

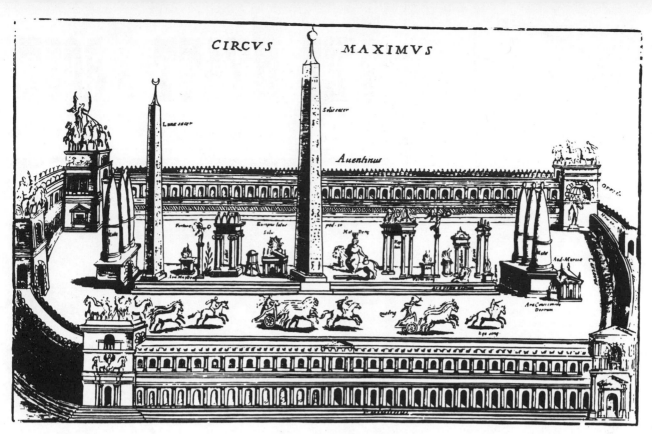

The Circus Maximus of Rome

Advertisement in the *Boston Journal*, 1893

"That guy must have the nerves of a school bus driver."

BIG GEORGE by Virgil Partch, courtesy of Publishers—Hall Syndicate.

"I'll bet he couldn't control a sixth grade classroom."

L. H. Russell in NEA JOURNAL, April 1964

"Annette, I believe we've come to the end of our rope."

Henry R. Martin in SATURDAY REVIEW, June 17, 1967. © Saturday Review, Inc.

THE HYATT FROST.

VOL. XLIX.   VAN AMBURGHVILLE, 1870.   ISSUE—1,000,000.

COMBINED WITH
Lowanda's Brazilian Circus!
HYATT FROST, - Manager.
This Radical Combination
ONE POWERFUL MENAGERIE!
ONE POWERFUL CIRCUS!!
Combined with another Powerful Circus!
VAN AMBURCH!......SEIGRIST!!......LOWANDA!!!
☞ MENAGERIE!—CIRCUS!!—CIRCUS!!! ☜
C. H. FARNSWORTH, General Agent.

Front page announcement in the *Peoria Transcript*, 1870

Mrs. Al Ringling, one-time snake
charmer

Stationery, Ringling Bros. Advance Department, 1896

Ringling Bros. Circus, Baraboo, Wisconsin, 1884

Simpson Ltd. of London celebrates the 200th anniversary of Astley's
Circus, November 18-30, 1968, with a remarkable collection of circusiana

This U.S. postage stamp was issued May 2, 1966, at Delavan, Wisconsin

Ricketts Circus, Philadelphia, 1795

Astley's Riding School, 1770

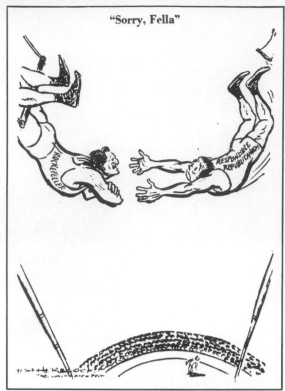

"Sorry Fella" and "The Tightrope Chase," from THE HERBLOCK GALLERY (Simon & Schuster, 1968)

Tom Thumb's wedding, 1863

Dan Rice, 1846

The Ubangis, saucer-lipped side-show attractions of the early 1930's

The Hartford fire, July 6, 1944

Tent entrance

Roustabouts

Cole Bros. circus wagon

The Ringling brothers and
their mustache cups

Barnum & Bailey bill posters

Barnum & Bailey ticket wagon

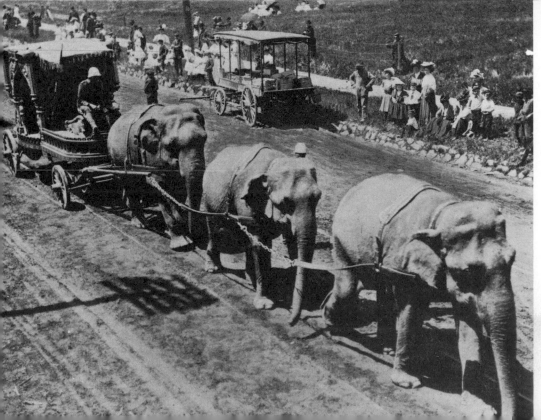

An early circus day parade

Emmett Kelly

Lillian Leitzel and Alfredo Codona

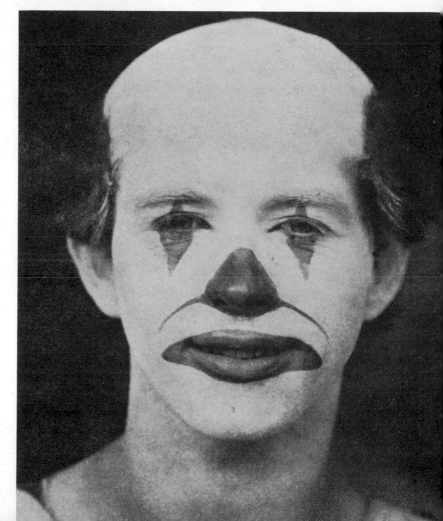

Slivers Oakley

The King Charles Troupe

Five of the famous Wallendas. The "human pyramid" of these high-wire artists long thrilled circus audiences. On the evening of January 30, 1962, the pyramid of seven Wallendas collapsed, killing two of the performers and paralyzing a third. Marshall Smith in *Life*, May 30, 1969, reported that the Wallendas "have gone on with the show and the old master, Karl Wallenda, still performing at 64, is teaching a new generation to follow in his footsteps."

Switzerland's famous clown, Pio Nock, rides his bicycle the hard way

Gargantua

Konyot's chimp

May Wirth, Australian bareback rider

Mabel Stark

Clyde Beatty

Alfred Court

John Ringling North

New first families of the circus—the Felds and the Hofheinzes—with John Ringling North, from whom they purchased Ringling Bros.-Barnum & Bailey Circus in November 1967

The circus "big four," at the Roman Colosseum in November 1967, when papers were signed for the purchase of Ringling Bros.- Barnum & Bailey Circus. Left to right: Israel Feld, Roy Hofheinz, John Ringling North, Irvin Feld

Russian audiences wholeheartedly
enjoy the circus

First Lady at the circus—
Mrs. Richard Nixon

First Lady at the circus—
Mrs. Lyndon Johnson

The British Royal Family and
Bernard N. Mills and Cyril B.
Mills in the stables at Olympic
London, during a private (prev
ously unannounced) visit to a
public performance of Bertram
Mills Circus, 1959

PART FOUR

AERIALISTS
and Other Performers

BLONDIN—PRINCE OF MANILA

Vincent Starrett

It is Niagara with which the name, the Mighty Blondin, Monarch of the Cable, is most intimately associated, and it is probably true that on the day [June 30, 1859] of Blondin's feat all roads led to the giant cataract. Some twenty-five thousand persons had come to see Blondin, the Prince of Manila, as he sometimes called himself [his name was actually Jean Francois Gravelet], stroll across the boiling cauldron of Niagara on a bridge of rope. Bridge, of course, is figurative. It was a single hempen cable that stretched from shore to shore. Its elevation above the water was 160 feet at one side; at the other, 270.

The chasm bridged was 1,100 feet—a dizzy span. At one end—the starting point— lay the United States of America; at the other —the finish—lay the Dominion of Canada. Between and beneath lay the seething river, and all around and about rose endlessly the clouds and pillars of damp vapor from the cataract. A misstep would be followed by almost certain death for the performer.

The French rope-walker was no novice. He had walked many ropes before, in perilous places and at perilous heights. The son of one of Napoleon's own heroes, he had inherited many of his father's qualities. On the voyage to America he had sprung overboard to rescue a drowning man. In spite of his reckless daring, he knew his ability to a hair's breadth and was careful not to venture beyond it.

The Niagara adventure was to be his pièce de résistance, the crowning feat of his career. He was then about thirty-five years of age, slight, agile, but withal nobly whiskered and mustachioed as befitted the leading acrobat of his day. He had no nerves to speak of. His coordination was excellent. If he entertained qualms, he did not display them.

His audience was waiting. Suddenly the air was torn with shouts and cheers. Blondin had appeared at the American end of the rope and was making his preparations. Now he was talking with those about him. He was making ready to step off. He was picking up his balance pole—a fifty-pound burden— and placing his foot upon the rope. And now he was launched in space and had begun his journey toward the British province of Upper Canada. A breathless moment.

Without hestiation, the performer proceeded briskly, almost casually, to the center of the cable. There he seated himself with great composure and glanced complacently about him at the thronging shores. He did not look down, it was reported. That was something he had trained himself never to do. After a few seconds he rose upright, strolled forward for some feet, and again stopped. This time he stretched himself at full length upon the rope, lying upon his back, his balance pole horizontally across his chest. Another moment of suspense; then a feat of appalling rashness. He turned a back somersault upon the rope, came upright upon his feet, and walking rapidly to his landing stage, arrived as coolly as if he had no more than alighted from a bus.

In the pauses of the deafening shouts on either bank of the river, a Canadian band could be heard playing the "Marseillaise."

Thereafter there was an interval of about twenty minutes, at the end of which the performer reappeared at the Canadian end of the rope with a camera and tripod on his back.

Advancing upon the cable to a point some two hundred feet from shore, he lashed his balance pole to the rope, unstrapped his burden, adjusted it in front of him, and took a picture of the crowded shore line. This achieved, he shouldered his machine, unlashed his balance pole, and returned whence he had come, quickly to reappear again with a lumbering chair. When about a third of the distance had been covered, he placed his chair upon the rope, seated himself, and crossing his legs, gazed around him with magnificent unconcern. Coming closer to the American shore, he readjusted his chair and stood upright on it. At this point women began to faint.

When it was all over, Monsieur Blondin, still bland and smiling, came ashore at his original point of departure, and was seen to be in no wise fatigued by his adventure. The entire performance had occupied perhaps an hour. . . .

Later, Blondin offered a large sum of money to any man who would volunteer to cross Niagara on his back. At once a number of ambitious citizens, thirsting for distinction, visited Niagara intending to offer their services; but after being shown the swaying rope across the rushing flood, thoughtfully retired.

There was in Blondin's train, however, a young man named Harry Colcord. Young Mr. Colcord had voyaged on Blondin's back across a number of ropes—never, however, across any such pit or gorge as Niagara. In circuses and opera houses of the day, he had been Blondin's favorite burden—a reliable fellow, thirty-one years old and weighing only 135 pounds.

Blondin, failing to lure a rider outside the profession, made his proposition to Colcord; and Colcord agreed to test his luck. Several times that autumn Blondin carried Colcord across the river on his back, and again in September 1860 the crossing was repeated in the presence of the then Prince of Wales. The rope for this latter journey had been removed to a spot farther down the river, over the famous whirlpool, and newspaper accounts of the adventure featured the emotions of the young man who was later to be Edward VII of England. The yellow journals shrieked: The Prince of Wales Faints!

Edward did not faint, but he was genuinely moved. Before the crossing he said earnestly to Blondin, "For heaven's sake, don't do anything extraordinary because I am here." Blondin replied: "Your Royal Highness, I'll carry yourself across, if you wish!"

The passage was made without incident and was Colcord's last experience with the famous gymnast. The same day, with immense pain to all beholders, and in spite of the Prince's injunction against "anything extraordinary," Blondin crossed the cable on stilts. He did not carry Harry Colcord—that thankful young man watched the rash performance from the sidelines. "Thank God it is all over!" said the Prince of Wales when Blondin stepped safely ashore.

Condensed from *The Saturday Evening Post*, October 26, 1929. Reprinted by permission of *The Saturday Evening Post*. © 1929 Curtis Publishing Co.

IN THE BACK YARD
Henry Ringling North

When I was a little boy May Wirth was queen of the back yard. In his book, Fred Bradna unequivocally states that she was the greatest equestrienne of all time; a true and generous tribute, since May was a rival of Fred's beloved Ella. It is doubtful if there will ever be another like her, for the family discipline that made her great is out of fashion.

When May came to Barnum & Bailey from Australia in 1912, she was sixteen years old, a small, softly rounded girl with lovely, pure features. She wore her hair tied little-girl fashion with a big bow of pink ribbon. May had been an equestrienne under her mother's tutelage since she was five years old and was a star at thirteen. Perhaps her greatest trick was the back-backward somersault. She stood with her back to the horse's head and did a complete somersault with a twist so that she landed facing forward. Though a terrific athlete and one of our brightest stars, she was so sweet and gentle that we all loved her.

Another charmer was Bird Millman, the first American girl to work on the tightwire with no pole or parasol for balance. Dressed in short fluffy skirts, with her long hair piled on top of her small head and a little balloon in her hand, she made a series of birdlike runs on the wire, chirped a couple of popular songs, and danced a hula while a chorus sang "Aloha." Con Colleano, of course, far exceeded her in daring and agility on the tightwire. This dashing if unpredictable fellow of Spanish-Irish-Australian descent wore toreador pants and a flowing white shirt as he danced a dazzling bolero, and wound up his act with a feet-to-feet forward somersault. He was the first man ever to accomplish this most difficult of all tightwire stunts.

Toward the end of this period, we acquired Mabel Stark and her tigers when Uncle John bought the Al G. Barnes Circus. Mabel was an Amazonian lady with masses of yellow-dyed ringlets on her head and a body covered with scars. And no wonder! For her specialty was wrestling with a full-grown Bengal tiger. Without whip or gun or fear in her heart, she worked sixteen of the great cats in the most commanding manner a lady ever had.

Though Mabel was so formidable, she could not have been without feminine wiles, for she had two ardent suitors whom she played off against each other to the delight of the entire circus. One of them was our manager, Fred Worral. Quarter-Pole Worral we called him, because he seemed always to be leaning against a quarter pole with his great paunch impressively decorated with an elk's-tooth watch charm and a skimpy little pipe sticking out from under his handle-bar mustache, the perfect, pompous picture of an old-time circus man.

Also, Andrew the giraffe man, fell in love with Mabel. He must have been seventy-odd; but spring came into his life for the first time. As far as anyone knew, he had never before shown affection for anything but giraffes.

With extraordinary dexterity Mabel kept these suitors separate and unknown to each other, while each lavished gifts upon her and no doubt dreamed of sharing a rose-embowered cottage when Mabel should finally forsake her tigers for domestic bliss. It was an awful shock to both of them when they finally discovered the mutuality of their courtships. Poor Andrew was the worse affected, having waited so long for love. He went to Mabel and demanded his presents back. Hopeless rebellion! Eyes that could quell a Bengal tiger pierced and confounded him. Back he went to the gentle giraffes.

My favorite clown as a boy was Herman Joseph. Herman was Jewish and played the role to the hilt, exaggerating his already adequate nose. He worked in the main show, but his moment of limelight came in the Wild West after show which we still had in those days —twenty-five cents extra. Then he would dress himself up in a cowboy suit calculated to end all cowboy suits, and clown throughout the show with a constantly varied repertoire of gags and impromptu wisecracks. For the finale Herman fired off an ancient blunderbuss that seemed to kick him halfway across the track.

Another clown—not a great one, but a great person—whom I love dearly is Pat Valdo. He came to the Barnum show in 1902, seven years before I was born. He was a tall skinny lad of twenty-one who, like my uncles, had seen one circus in his home town—Binghamton, New York—and became insanely inspired to become part of it. Pat worked up from walk-ons to a good clown spot and married a circus girl. Together they developed a wonderful boomerang act which we used for many years. Pat's executive ability was early noted by my uncle John, who made him assistant equestrian director to Fred Bradna.

When he was over seventy years old my brother and I retired him on a pension, but Pat refused to stay retired. He is still a tall lanky lad with the sawdust oozing out of his ears; and happy as a circus seal doing a great job as general director of The Greatest Show. He is seventy-nine years old [1960].

Bobby Clark was also with us when I was

a boy. He was a good clown who became a great comedian.

There were others almost as great, many others. Merle Evans, the superb bandmaster who for thirty-seven years produced the blare and cacophony, the sweet, soft strains, or the roll of drums that accompanied each act; responding to a couple of hundred cues twice every day and sending the audiences with the brazen clangor of the loudest cornet in show business. There were the Wallendas with their pyramid of people riding a bicycle across a wire at the top of the tent; Charlie Sigrest, a good acrobat, flier, tightwire man, and equestrian, but spreading his talents too thin to be quite great; Clyde Beatty was with us for a while. In the Wild West after show we had Tom Mix, the good cowboy in the white hat who in real life was just that, for he always played himself. We paid him $10,000 a week one season, and he lost it all when he started his own show. He was not quite smart enough for the black hats.

Another great character whom Uncle John brought to America in the twenties was Hugo Zacchini, who had himself fired out of a cannon. Of course, other people had done it before. I think the genesis of the act was in 1870, when some Italian invented a cannon that was supposed to shoot a soldier over the enemy lines. The idea was that he would float down on a parachute and wreak havoc in the rear. Lulu, a man dressed up as a girl, first did it in the circus in 1879. But Zacchini brought the act to dramatic perfection, with a huge cannon actuated by a spring—but lots of noise and smoke—which hurled him in a great arc the whole length of Madison Square Garden into a net. It is very dangerous, for if you do not fall into the net just right you can be badly hurt. To say nothing of the total damage if one misses the net entirely!

There were dozens more with us in the twenties, many of whom might have been greats today but who were overshadowed then by those who were even greater. It is impossible to speak of them all, though I knew and liked them all. But there was one, or rather two in one, whom I have saved—the best and dearest—for the last.

They were Lillian Leitzel and Alfredo Codona, who in the circus firmament belong together like the Gemini. As in the case of all those inseparable pairs of lovers who walk forever side by side through history and myth, many fine writers have told their story. However, having known and loved Leitzel from the time I was five years old, and watched Alfredo at his apogee of greatness swooping as effortlessly as a barn swallow under the luminous peaks of the Big Top, perhaps I can add a fresh touch or two to their portraits.

Leitzel came first—she always came first, for she was the greatest star of them all, personifying in her tiny lambent person the quintessential glamour of the circus. Like most of our other greats, she was a child of the tented arenas; reared, trained, and disciplined from babyhood for her profession. Unlike most of them, she was beautifully educated, knowing the literature and philosophy of five languages, and the language of music as well. Had she chosen, she could have been a fine concert pianist.

She came to America from her native Bohemia with a family trapeze-and-bicycle act, of which her mother was the star. From the age of nine she had been stealing the show from her mother, and when the family act went back to Europe, Leitzel elected to remain. She got her big break in a Hoboken honky-tonk and became a star of vaudeville before she joined the Ringling show in 1915.

At the time I met her, Leitzel was not only our brightest star but our smallest. She was only four feet ten inches tall, and her luxuriant golden hair covered her in glory. In all things but one she was exquisitely formed; with an incredibly narrow waist, lovely legs, and feet so small that she wore a child's size 1½ shoe. Exquisitely dainty and feminine, she had the shoulders of a Notre Dame tackle. This was due to the exigencies of her act.

It consisted of two parts. Wearing silk tights and a diaphanous short-short skirt, Leitzel would go up the web—as the dangling ropes for the aerialists are called—in a series of apparently effortless roll-overs until she reached a pair of Roman rings high above the center ring. There was no net beneath them—Leitzel never used a net. For technique, grace, and style, her performance on the rings was unequaled. Where others labored, she floated; where others assumed grotesquely contorted positions, her body held the grace of a Grecian marble; where others wore the set smile of stress and fear, she laughed as joyously as a little girl playing on a swing.

Though Leitzel's artistry reached its height on the rings, it was the second part of her act which appealed to the Roman-holiday instincts of the crowd. When she had descended from the rings and taken a bow, she grasped another rope and was flown aloft to the top of the tent. Now everything in the whole great arena was stilled. Even the candy butchers were forbidden to hawk their sweets while Leitzel did her final turn.

As a single spot focused on her tiny glittering figure, she slipped her right wrist through a padded loop attached by a swivel to a hanging rope. Then she got up by momentum and hurled her entire body in a full circle over itself. This is called the full-arm plange, or "dislocate," for each time she did it her right shoulder was dislocated and was snapped back by its powerful muscles.

Over and over and over Leitzel went while the drums signaled each turn with a roll and crash and the audience chanted the count: "one—two—three—four . . . twenty-five—twenty-six . . . fifty-one—fifty-two . . . eighty-five—eighty-six . . . Often she did a hundred turns; her record count was two hundred and forty-nine. Incredible endurance! On a blazing August day up there in the peak of the tent, where the temperature was twenty or thirty degrees higher than at ground level, she would still complete the dizzy century of turns. As she spun around, her long hair gradually, artfully loosened from its pins and swung free, following the parabolas her body made like a golden comet's tail.

Sensational as her performance was, it was not what Leitzel did, or even how she did it, that made her so great a star. It was her own self. She could walk out and simply stand there before ten thousand people, and win and own them before ever she made a move. They felt the incandescence of her personality back to the last row of the "blues."

Sometimes we wondered that she was not consumed by the violence of her passions. Oh, she was a violent person! Without doubt, part of her flaming temperament was calculated showmanship. But where artifice ended and Leitzel took over, no one, not even Leitzel, knew. When she flew into one of her terrible rages everyone took cover. I think that even Uncle John was afraid of her. Cursing in all five languages, she often let fly with a right-arm slap that stunned the recipient. On the other hand, she could move in the most sophisticated society with perfect decorum, and talk at ease with kings.

She could be tender, too. There was no artifice in her love of children. There were many youngsters traveling with us in family troupes. They all called her Aunty Leitzel, and adored her. Whenever she went shopping she came back loaded with presents for them, and she was always giving them birthday parties with cake and all the trimmings.

There was no proper schooling for the performers' young families at that time, so every weekday Leitzel kept school in her luxurious dressing tent for the children of the circus. With infinite patience she taught them to read and write, and enjoy the beauty of music and poetry, and to understand noble thoughts. She also had a little trapeze rigged up in her tent, on which she showed the tots who wanted to emulate her the rudiments of her art.

It was because Leitzel first knew Johnny [John Ringling North] and me when we were young that she always loved us. In her blackest mood, when all else failed to move her, Johnny would go into her tent and whisper some secret magic words to her. She would start to laugh and quickly be on her way to the Big Top to charm the audience with her graciousness.

I remember one time when I was at Manlius she came to Syracuse with a little "winter circus" that Fred Bradna had put together. Some of my best friends at the Academy and I got leave to go over to see the matinee. As I entered the auditorium Bradna came up to me looking desperate. "That God-damned Leitzel is having a tantrum," he said. "She claims I hung her rigging wrong, and she won't go on. See if you can do anything with her, Buddy."

So I went to knock on her dressing-room door, and she screamed between lurid oaths that she wanted to be let alone.

"It's me, Buddy North," I yelled.

The door flew open and a radiant Leitzel jumped at me and hung around my neck. After the effervescence of her greeting subsided she admired my uniform and I admired her lack of same, for she was nude to the waist. I asked her how things were going.

The lightning flashed around my head. "That triple-blanked son of a gun Fred Bradna hung my rigging wrong," she yelled.

"He's a dope," I said sympathetically. "But I've brought some friends over from Manlius just to see you, and we feel pretty bad that you aren't going on today."

"What God-damned fool told you I wasn't going on?" Leitzel demanded. Then she added sweetly, "Of course, I am. And you are going to introduce my act."

I was horrified, but I knew better than to refuse. So when the time came I stood on the stage and went through the spiel I'd heard Lew Graham give a hundred times to introduce Leitzel's act. Looking over my shoulder, I can see myself standing there very tall and lanky and young in my cadet uniform, with big frightened blue eyes and a small squeaky voice saying those grandiloquent phrases. The audience loved it. It was, in fact, superb showmanship, which Leitzel knew very well when she made me do it.

Leitzel was married three times, but only once that counted. The first time she was very young. She always claimed she could not remember her first husband's name. Certainly nobody else could. The second time she married Clyde Ingalls, our great side-show manager. On a certain tempestuous night she cut off one of his fingers with a butcher knife. Her third and true husband was Alfredo Codona.

Again I say without fear of contradiction that Codona was the greatest flier of all time. Though he was not the first to do a triple somersault from the flying trapeze to the hands of his catcher, who was his brother, Lalo Codona, he did it better than anyone before or since. Arthur and Antoinette Concello both did the triple later, but they were never able to emulate Alfredo's apparently effortless style. Indeed, that word—style—was the mark of Codona's greatness. Whether in the most difficult feats or a simple pirouette from the catcher back to the bar, his form was as classic as Nijinsky's in ballet. When he caught the bar he seemed merely to touch it weightlessly, and when he flew through the air it was as though he were moving in his natural element. Even if he missed and fell to the net, it was gracefully done.

Indeed, one of Alfredo's most hair-raising stunts was based on the time Lalo missed his catch and he fell into the net far off center, bounced high in the air, and came down through the spreader ropes at the side of the net. They broke his fall, but he hit ground quite hard. He got up and dusted himself off. Then he climbed up again to complete his famous triple amid a perfect tornado of applause.

Frequently after that, Alfredo would do this dangerous trick on purpose. Fred Bradna tells of how he got Codona to do it one time when Uncle John [John Ringling] was in the house. He says that in his agitation Uncle John swallowed his cigar.

Alfredo Codona was of Mexican-German extraction. His father flew in a small one-ring circus in Mexico. He came to us first as a talented young flier, and promptly fell in love with Leitzel, as who did not? She had no time for him then, and he went away and married someone else. He came back to us about 1925 as a full-fledged star. By that time Leitzel was married to Clyde Ingalls, but no bonds of God or man could keep those two fated and fatal people apart. Codona became a fixture in Leitzel's tent, which was furnished with oriental rugs and always adorned with fresh flowers provided by the management. There she taught him, as she taught the circus children, the pleasures of literature and the social graces.

Leitzel got a divorce and she and Alfredo were married in Chicago in 1928. I have a wonderful snapshot of them leaving the show grounds in an open landaulet plastered all over with Just-Married signs. Though Leitzel was well into her thirties that year, she looks like a high-school girl, and a small one at that; while Alfredo looks like the boy next door. They were so radiantly happy that their faces wore, not professional smiles, but broad grins.

Alfredo Codona was nearly as great a star and almost as violently temperamental as his wife. No one could describe their marriage as serenely happy. It was gloriously impassioned. It lasted for three years.

In February 1931 Alfredo was flying at the Winter Garden in Berlin while Leitzel was performing at the Valencia Music Hall in Copenhagen. Frank McClosky, who later became general manager of our circus, was her head rigging man for this winter engagement.

On Friday the thirteenth—so obvious are the coincidences of real-life tragedy—Leitzel was doing the first part of her act on the Roman rings. McClosky was standing beneath her, anxiously watching every move. Something distracted his attention, and in that instant the swivel supporting one of the rings crystallized and snapped. Leitzel plunged headfirst twenty feet to the ground.

McClosky was beside her in a flash—too late a flash. In a moment or two she stood up shaking her golden head. The audience cheered wildly, and Leitzel said, "I'm all right. I can go on."

McClosky would not let her and took her to the hospital. Codona canceled his performance in Berlin and rushed to her. On Saturday she seemed so well and gay that he let her persuade him to go back to Berlin. On Sunday, February 15, 1931, Leitzel died.

Leitzel's death saddened her admirers all over the world. It stunned us who had known and loved her so well. It destroyed Alfredo Codona.

For many months he disappeared into some accursed solitude. Then he came back to fly again with the circus. Never had he been so brilliant. But now his brilliance had the raw edge of recklessness. Even the crowds watching him sensed that the flashing figure doing impossible feats was inviting death. As is his way, Death declined the invitation.

In his frantic effort to escape memory, Alfredo was married again, to Vera Bruce of the Australian equestrian family. He continued his reckless performances, with the inevitable result—not death, but a fall that tore his shoulder ligaments so that he could never fly again.

Now the descent from glory quickened. If he had saved any money, it quickly disappeared and he was forced to take unsuitable jobs—Vera's equestrian director in a one-ring show. That was too bitter to be borne. Then he was part proprietor of a gas station. One wonders if the casual customers were frightened by the bright gleam of hatred in his eyes—hatred or madness.

No one could live with a man who could not live with himself. Vera sued for divorce. A conference was arranged at her lawyer's office.

Alfredo came there very calm and reasonable. He asked the lawyer if he might have a moment alone with his wife. At Vera's nod the attorney went out, closing the door.

On cue, at the click of the latch, Alfredo pulled a forty-five automatic from under his coat. As fast as his finger could pull and release the trigger he fired five shots into Vera Bruce's body—three of them unneeded. The sixth shot pierced his own brain. Thank God, at least he did not miss.

Alfredo Codona was buried beside little Leitzel.

From *The Circus Kings—Our Ringling Family Story* by Henry Ringling North and Alden Hatch. Doubleday & Co., Inc., Garden City, New York, 1960. © Henry R. North and Alden Hatch. Used by permission.

SPLIT SECONDS
Alfredo Codona

The pulse of the big show beats in a multitude of places, just as it does in the human body. A circus, with all it contains, lives or dies by the steadiness of that heartbeat. An education in timing begins for a circus person almost with his first step.

That is not exaggeration. I knew more about timing when I was less than a year old than I did about walking. In fact, I was already in the circus performance. My father carried me into the ring in a closed carpetbag. It was the opening trick of the act to open the bag, lift me out, balance me with one hand, and tumble me about a bit—just to show that there was another circus performer coming along to carry on the name of the Codona family. Even then I knew enough to raise and lower my hands in adjustment with my father's balance when he gripped both my legs in his hand and raised me aloft. By the time I was four years old I was doing hand stands, back bends, flip-flops, and even backward and forward somersaults. . . .

The circus lives by split seconds. My job [1930] with the Ringling Brothers–Barnum & Bailey Circus hinges upon the fact that I can be depended upon twice daily, rain or shine, to turn a triple somersault from a trapeze into the waiting hands of my brother Lalo. My speed, when I leave my trapeze for the triple, has been accurately measured; I am traveling at a rate of sixty-two miles an hour. At that speed I must turn completely over three times, in a space not more than seven feet square,

and break out of my revolutions at precisely the instant that will land me in the hands of Lalo, who, hanging to his trapeze by his hocks, has swung forward to meet me.

Once I was four inches off. My head struck Lalo in the chin, knocking him unconscious from his trapeze. Naturally, I also fell, landing face down in the safety net. Lalo, still unconscious, fell like so much lead, and struck on top of me, the full force of his fall exerting itself upon the small of my back. I went to the hospital for a two weeks' stay; three ribs had been broken on one side of my back and two on the other, in addition to other injuries. Yet the accident which had caused this had resulted from the fact that I had misgauged my time in leaving the bar by less than a hundredth of a second.

The difficulty about mastering circus time—when to pull yourself higher in a somersault or break out, to pirouette, to leave a flying bar, to take your leap to the back of a ring horse, or even to do the simple swings on the comparatively childish ladder acts—is the fact that there are no rules, no guidebooks, and no precision instruments by which to learn. A child, in studying music, gains a knowledge of time from a metronome ticking beside the piano; a musician has his master's baton as a guide. But there is nothing for the performer save a finely developed sixth sense, which can neither be explained nor passed on. You simply learn when to let go, and until that finesse is developed, the most agile, most muscularly active person in the world is a failure as a performer.

Naturally, the development of this sixth sense begins with childhood—usually with a parent as a master. That training starts with an elaborate system of bending, both for suppleness and for a primary knowledge of time, just as a child's first exercises on the piano must consist of whole notes, which must be mastered before progress can be made to halves, quarters, and eighths. There is a time to bending, just as there is to a double somersault. When that is mastered, with the parent "patting" for the pupil, as the calling of directions is termed, then the pupil may advance to a handstand, or to roll-overs and flip-flops, and slowly to somersaults. It sounds much easier in description than it really is; hours of practice, days of practice, weeks and months of it must follow in order that coordination shall be established and a certain clocklike regularity of action become second nature. To a child it seems he must swing, swing, swing on a trapeze for a dozen eternities before his master will even allow him to drop into the net. For even in swinging on a trapeze, there is a split second when the coordinated propulsion of the body will accomplish more for even a weakling, if applied at the proper instant, than for the strongest man in the world who does not know timing. There are a great many men stronger than myself, yet I require only two full swings of my trapeze to gain the terrific speed and height necessary for my triple somersault.

The high-school work of acrobatic practice concerns the "mechanic," with the master holding the ropes and to a certain extent guiding his pupil through the air. The mechanic is the life belt of the circus; a performer rarely ceases to use one in his practice. A wide band of leather, it fits about the waist, and from a ring on each side ropes run through lofty pulleys to the hands of the "patter." Primarily it is for safety; the performer knows that he cannot seriously injure himself in a fall, thus giving him confidence to attempt new tricks. But if the man who holds those safety ropes does not know the

exact instant at which to apply leverage and when to release it, the performer can practice forever without success.

There is even breathing to be considered. I am fortunate enough to have for my wife Lillian Leitzel, who for years has been a feature of the Ringling–Barnum Circus. Perhaps you have seen her—a tiny woman with a wealth of hair, who literally rolls herself up a rope to the top of the tent, and, following her work on the Roman rings, suspends herself by one arm and then turns in giant, wheel-like gyrations. She has in certain instances made more than two hundred turns at a performance. It requires muscle—a great deal of it. Of course it requires endurance, and a certain sense of fatalism, in as much as no bandage ever has been devised that can protect her arm from the constant danger of blood poisoning from rope burns.

But more than this, it requires a knowledge of breathing as expert as that of any opera star. The gauging of weight and time for the application of her strength in these turns is so finely attuned that a breath at the wrong place might end the act. She must inhale swiftly on the buoyant upswing—but not too soon. She must exhale the instant that the fine hairline of gravity resistance has been passed; nor can she continue that exhalation too long. That's one reason why actors watch their work more closely in high altitudes: the necessary difference in breathing may mean the difference between a difficult catch and a bad fall.

I may have given the impression that timing is only essential to the more difficult acts. That is not true. Time, time, time! It pounds through the life of the circus like a blood flow, and by its beat everything is gauged. Even the simplest acts must have their time; the clowns synchronize their gags to a fraction of a second, that all may begin their work about the ring at the same instant and finish together—for, as a rule, when a clown stands for long moments upon the hippodrome track he is not merely awaiting his turn to be funny. Equestrian acts are in progress in the rings or other acts upon the stages which, at a certain moment, must have a change of horses or some other delay that might slow up the act in the eyes of the audience if there were not an instantaneous diversion. And so, when that change comes, the clowns, with much hulla-baloo, leap into action an instant before the audience realizes that a halt has come to the main act. Attention is switched and held until the instant that the change has been effected. Then the equestrian director's whistle blows again, and the average person in the audience does not even realize that horses have been changed, that sometimes even actors have been changed.

Speaking of equestrianism, another factor enters here. That is the horse. When one enters the ring barn of an equestrian family during the training of a new horse, there is little resem-blance to what one sees in the circus. The ring is there, of course, and the horse and the ring-master. There the similarity ends. Grooms sit about, chins in hands, staring; or, at a command, arise lackadaisically to kick cans about, to rattle a ratchet, or to fire a revolver or a shotgun. The performers themselves merely stand about, while the horse itself may trot about the ring with a five-gallon tin can tied to its tail. The reason for it all is time.

Here is a necessity for synchronization, the time of the performer to the time of the horse; necessarily, neither must vary. Therefore, a good ring horse, or rosin-back, is only one which can be depended upon to hold his pace in exactitude; a variance means trouble. There can be no stamping of feet, no lengthening of a stride or break of gait; and the horse which performs in an equestrian ring must be proof against any interruption that might bring about a break of time. Hence the tin cans and revolvers, news-papers which are thrown before the ring horse in training, white cloths waved in front of his eyes, figures running before him. Every conceivable noise and flying form that might interrupt a circus performance is brought into play when a rosin-back is in training. And a good ring horse, true to his schooling, ceases his peculiar rocking gait only at the command of his trainer—nothing else. The audience may leave, the band halt its

playing, and even the tent blow away—but if he's the right kind of ring horse, he'll keep rock-ing along, around and around that ring, until he is given the command to stop.

About all that an audience ever notices about a rosin-back is that a broadbacked horse appears to have a wonderful ability to keep time to the music. But a circus audience does not see all that it believes it sees under the big top. With rare exceptions nothing in the circus keeps time to the band. The band keeps time to it. Essential as the circus band is—and I believe I would halt my triple somersault in mid-air if the drum should stop rolling—it, nevertheless, is secon-dary. For instance, when the elephants dance their hootchy-kootchy, they are not following the music; they are leading it. The band follows them, matching their movements so close that they are in unison; the elephant pays attention to no one but his trainer. The same is true of dancing horses and all the other animals, and of the acts themselves. None of them is practiced to music; the performances are perfected, and then the music is fitted to them.

Today there is not so much jealousy and bickering in circus life as there once was. But when it does arise, the performer who works in the center ring has an easy system by which he brings grief to other performers whose acts he does not desire to shine. He simply develops a penchant for changing his music, with the result that while the playing of the band is matched to his act, it is not matched to the others. Time is thereby destroyed, and good performers sud-denly become bad ones.

But for all of us there are plenty of difficulties even when things apparently are running at their smoothest. We must work in the dark to a certain degree; we do not know why we let go at a certain instant, or what clocklike arrange-ment of our brain gauges that tiny part of a second which forms the starting time. We only know that a flashing energy shoots through us and on we go, to the double somersault, the triple, to the back of a horse, or to speeding cart wheels along the ground, to the applause of a well-done act, or to the sympathy of an audience as we fall, spin about, fight for a safe landing and then, rope-burned or bruised, go back to our tricks again.

I have had more bumps in my life than the usual performer, for the reason that I have always hated to use a mechanic. In fact, I learned the triple somersault without one. It wasn't pleasant, but I felt that was the only way I ever could master it. There would be plenty of falls, I knew, after I had become proficient; I might as well learn to take them in the beginning, and while doing so learn to guard against the dangers of the net.

For that great spread of knotted rope which stretches across the breadth of a big top during a flying-trapeze act is not the beneficent thing which it appears to be. It is dangerous, a friend indeed if you fall into it properly, but otherwise a lurking enemy, waiting to snap the bones of an arm or a leg—or a neck. Persons have been killed by falls into the net, and even on many tumbles which the audience classes as uneventful, it seems to possess satanic joy in gouging the flesh out of one. A net is made by a succession of spaces between square knots. Those knots can flay one like a whip if the fall is not accurately gauged.

So I practiced my triple into the net, and I believe that it was due to this that I succeeded. The history of the triple somersault is a history of death; as long as there have been circuses, there have been men and women whose sole ambition was to accomplish three full turns in the air. The struggle to master it has lasted more than a century, beginning with the old days of the famous leapers who worked with a springboard, and the triple somersault has killed more persons than all other dangerous circus acts combined.

The reason lies in the terrific speed at which the act must be accomplished. At a propulsion of more than sixty miles an hour, the body is traveling so fast that by the time the second revolution is reached, the space gauges of the brain have ceased to function properly. The body is going faster than it can be controlled, and for a split instant one loses all knowledge of

time, space, distance, or surroundings. Then, in another split instant, as the body begins to fall and slows slightly with the third somersault, that ability to gauge must be regained, so that when the performer breaks out of the third revolution and toward the hands of the catcher, his brain can be clear again. It is a lack of clarity here which causes death; the performer has spun so fast that he has lost all knowledge of where he is, and plunges downward to the net or onward to the mat—if the turn is from a springboard—without being able to protect his body properly in the fall. The impact, therefore, comes not on his back but at the base of the skull, in as much as the natural whirl of the fall almost invariably carries him toward that position; and the net or mat snaps his neck.

What my own end will be, I, of course, do not know. I think I'll die of old age. But other persons have different opinions, among them the manager of a Berlin theater, a cheerful soul who did much to make an engagement happy for me several years ago. He dug into every file that existed, and with a complete list of the scores of deaths resultant from the triple somersault wrote an article for his program, incorporating all the fatalities and exactly how they occurred. Following this, he added:

"Alfredo Codona is now the one living man consistently performing the triple somersault. Sooner or later, of course, he will meet the same fate that has befallen others who have attempted this dangerous feat."

That program had a strange reaction upon me. I fell more times during the Berlin engagement than in all the rest of that year's European trip.

Indeed, there are times when I wonder just how closely psychology and muscle are mingled in the triple. I do know that its fatalistic history had an effect which prevented me from learning the trick in spite of five years of hard work. I couldn't get it; there was always the ingrained feeling that since it had killed so many others, it would kill me too. That interfered with my concentration, and as a result I invariably cast in the middle of it.

"Casting," to the circus performer, is purely a psychological term. It has to do with that part of an instant when the mind seems to let go, to refuse longer to hold to the terrific burden of concentration which has been placed upon it. It is like a sharp knife struck suddenly against a set of tightly drawn strings; the performer sprawls hopelessly, all thought of his trick departed. And, of course, he fails.

The invisible demon of the circus tent, "casting," is always present, working through gravitation, through a headache, through some piece of sharp kidding which has hurt sensitive feelings, through heat and illness and fatigue, for the failure of the act. Sometimes it comes more into the open; it almost visualizes itself into a personality. Through experience I can tell why a certain queer, overtired light appears in Lillian Leitzel's eyes when, her act done, she can cease to be the taut, watchful performer and relax into my wife. It is a peculiar light, like no other expression I ever have seen, and I know without a word what it means.

Forty netless feet from the ground, suspended by one arm which never ceases to pain, owing to the remorseless gouging of the rope from which she hangs, Leitzel has been fighting something more dangerous than height, or loose rigging, or heat, or fatigue. A queer, argumentative streak in her brain has leaped into action, so strong that instead of a mere mental quirk, it seems like an actual voice incessantly pleading:

"Why don't you let go? You're tired; it's foolish to hang onto a rope away up here in the air. The audience won't care; there is plenty more for them to look at. Let go! Let go!"

To loosen her grip would mean death. Or in that instant when, with hands wide open, she poises herself in a hand stand upon the Roman rings, balancing herself upon the web of flesh between her thumbs and index fingers; to relax them would mean a forty-foot plunge to the ground. Or when she swings over, still holding her hands open until that hundredth of an instant when her body lies upon the dividing line between pressure upon the Roman rings and

the effects of gravitation—if in that hundredth of an instant the hands would fail to grip, there would be little left of Lillian Leitzel. But the voice goes remorselessly on:

"Let go! Let go! Why go to all this effort, when you could drop to the ground and rest?"

I know that circus performers are not supposed to know much about psychology. Perhaps not, as it is taught in the textbooks, or in the Freudian philosophy. But we have our own manifestations which perhaps might interest an occasional professor. My conquest of the triple somersault, for instance, was as much mental as it was physical.

As I have mentioned, the long, fatalistic history of the triple deterred me from its accomplishment for years. Then, in 1919, I determined either to accomplish it, get killed, or quit trying. My brother Lalo and I fitted up our rigging in a building in Shreveport, Louisiana, and with my father "patting" for me and aiding me in my timing, we set to work.

It was not long until a psychological effect exerted itself. I had adopted a fatalistic attitude; if this was to be the end of my efforts, very well, then, it would be the end, and there need be no more thought wasted on the subject. So, with that out of the way, my mind cleared itself of extraneous matters and exerted itself fully upon the concentration necessary to the accomplishment of the feat. The next spring, in the Coliseum at Chicago, I went into performance with the triple somersault as a climax of my regular routine.

To repeat, the success of the triple lies principally in the reestablishment of brain coordination following that dazed second in which the body is turning so swiftly that the mind apparently loses control. For an instant I know nothing except that I am turning with increased velocity—a thing which the audience rarely notices is that in the triple the body of the performer during the second revolution is actually more than a foot higher than in the first. This is the height of the speed; I spin as though I had been caught in a whirlwind, and during that second revolution the speed of my body has exceeded the speed of my brain. But once the height has been reached, my brain begins to fight for renewed control.

It is comparable to a swift recovery from unconsciousness. The tent, the music, the roll of the band's drumbeat; hearing, sight, sense of direction, knowledge of surroundings—all have been instantaneously absent. Then, suddenly, I am alive again. I am falling, and spinning as I fall. The sudden deadness of my brain is jerked instantaneously to life. From far away a vague, filmy mirage rushes toward me with the speed of a bullet. The trapeze from which it hangs is cobwebby; the outstretched arms are misshapen and grotesque. I see only one thing clearly—the eyes, growing swiftly larger and more luminous. Closer, closer they rush, until they are staring into mine—the reflected lights of the big top seeming to gleam from them like the glare from enormous headlights. There in the air, I seem to halt. Suddenly the eyes lose their grotesqueness; they become the humorously lighted, normal eyes of my brother, Lalo. I feel the grip of his strong fingers upon the silken taping of my arms; my own hands grip his taped wrists; I hear the applause of the audience; I am swinging safely beneath his trapeze. That is, as a rule. But sometimes we miss.

That is when the strangest of all mental disturbances occurs. Perhaps I miss because my brain, like a tired muscle, has not been able to flex swiftly enough to reassume control. Perhaps that fatigue has exerted itself when I swing off the pedestal, in failing to give the proper command that will send my body high enough; perhaps it was when I left the trapeze for the beginning of my revolutions. Somewhere in the intricacies of the trick, my brain has sideslipped, and as I fall to the net, it continues its vagaries. This, in spite of the fact that it is in partial control; the triple somersault is a great place to study the freaks of the mind. I am plunging downward to the net. My brain is sufficiently alert to know that this fall, unless gauged to the merest fraction of body balance, may result in my death. Therefore, my body turns so that the force of this forty-foot fall is expended upon the muscles of my back; a subconscious action wholly, for I have consciously known little about it.

During that instantaneous drop I may be out fishing, or walking along Fifth Avenue in New York, or practicing my act down in the old building in Shreveport, Louisiana. I see friends I have not met for years, scenes that otherwise have been forgotten. I look down upon my father, standing in his practice clothes in the building at Shreveport, and shouting directions to me as I fail in another attempt to learn the triple somersault.

My brain has completely sideslipped into one of those phenomena best described as a momentary dream, of the same type experienced by persons who sleep through the ramifications of a long vision, only to find that they have little more than closed their eyes.

Then comes the impact of the net and the swing into the air as I go upward on the rebound. I awaken to the realization that I have failed, that the audience is applauding after the gasping wait during my plunge while it has feared for my safety. A queer rage comes over me. My face flushes; for an instant I stand there like a schoolboy, shaking my fists. Sometimes the anger is uncontrollable. I claw at the net, I strike at it with my clenched fists; I have even fallen to my knees, tearing at the roped knots with my teeth.

My brain clears. I bow. I laugh—and go to the rope ladder, to climb upward for another try at the triple somersault.

Condensed from "Split Seconds" by Alfredo Codona as told to Courtney Ryley Cooper, *The Saturday Evening Post*, December 6, 1930. Reprinted with permission of *The Saturday Evening Post*. © 1930 Curtis Publishing Co.

AH, SO!

Bill Gold

Almost anything that's done by the daring young man on the flying trapeze is enough to make this old circus buff's heart do flip-flops. The triple somersault is in a class by itself.

The Barnum & Bailey Circus that arrived in town the other day has in its aerial company a 20-year-old Mexican lad named Tito Gaona. He does the triple somersault.

He was asked: "What's the secret in getting around three times?"

"The secret," he explained, "is to keep turning and not pause in between somersaults."

Thanks a bunch, kid. I thought you were going to say that all a fellow has to do is learn to count to three accurately.

From *The Washington Post*, March 15, 1968. Used by permission.

THE CRISTIANIS

Lawrence Lader

Imagine that the girl swinging from the high trapeze beneath the Big Top is your sister. Suddenly she slips, and with no net below her, starts to hurtle to the ground. The band stops playing; the crowd screams. But a second later, her feet catch the rung of another trapeze far below, and she swings there safely, unconcerned at the climax of her suicidal act.

Imagine that at the same moment, in another circus hundreds of miles away, your brother is somersaulting wildly around the ring on the backs of fast-moving horses.

Imagine that in a nightclub in another part of the country, your cousins are spinning through the air in double somersaults through loops of fire.

Imagine that on movie screens from coast to coast, millions are watching the performances of your brothers, sisters, cousins, nephews, and nieces, and that across the Atlantic, another branch of your family is running the largest circus in Italy.

Imagine all this and you'll begin to have some idea of what it is like to be a member of the illustrious Cristiani family—wizards of bareback riding, tumbling, and the high trapeze. The Cristianis are not only the largest circus family, they are by far the oldest. Compared to five generations of them, the Ringlings are almost newcomers to the big top.

When the drums roll and Lucio Cristiani comes into the ring, even the rest of the family holds its breath. The big white circus horses are trotting in a fast circle. Lucio jumps to the back of one, then somersaults through the air,

turning head over heels and spinning sideways at the same time. He lands, not on the horse directly in front, but two horses away. Almost instantly he is off on another somersault, from the third to the fifth to the seventh horse, around and around the moving circle of animals in a series of wild, thrashing somersaults that no one else in the world has ever been able to duplicate.

When the Cristianis did their four-high act at the Music Hall, the usually sedate audience got up and cheered. At the Circus Medrano in Paris, the audience refused to leave at the end of the show, insisting that the troupe repeat the act.

There is good reason for such acclaim, for in their four-high act, three Cristianis get on each other's shoulders to form a human totem pole more than fifteen feet tall. Benny Cristiani stands at the lower end of a teeterboard; then Pilade Cristiani jumps on the raised end, catapulting Benny high in the air, to land on top of the human totem pole without even shaking it.

Louise and Daviso Cristiani are the greatest "perch" artists in the circus [1947]. He balances a long pole on his shoulder. She climbs to the top of the pole, and then, placing her palm on its tip, executes a perfect handstand. Even the rest of the Cristianis can't do it.

When Adolpho Cristiani does his Arab pirouette he leaps through the air, twists and turns four times, lands on his feet, and then he repeats the pirouette some twenty-five times around the ring. Every other member of the family has tried to imitate him, but failed.

High-speed cameramen who have tried to photograph Adolpho in the air have been unable to move their cameras fast enough to keep up with his mad gyrations. But the Cristianis are trying to keep Adolpho from repeating the act too often. On a wet ring there's always the danger that he will slip and break his neck.

Yet danger is obviously part of the Cristiani's business. Once when they were using borrowed circus horses, pretty, dark-haired Conchita made a routine leap from the ground to one of the animals, but the horse suddenly halted, Conchita fell, and a hoof broke her arm. In 1946 Lucio suffered a fall while performing at the Pan-Pacific Stadium in Hollywood.

The most terrifying act of all is Louise Cristiani on the high trapeze. She has hurtled through space dozens of times to clutch a lower trapeze, but the risk is always there. In 1942, when the Cristianis were with Ringling Brothers, she missed the lower trapeze at Madison Square Garden and fell twenty feet to the ring, breaking her spine and four ribs. She spent six months in a hospital, and more than a year in training before resuming the act. Many circuses have refused to let her make the fall without a net, but Louise won't perform any other way.

"With the net, where is the thrill?" she asks.

All these miracles of bareback riding, trapeze, and tumbling, began in Italy almost one hundred years ago, with great-grandpa Cristiani, who was a blacksmith for the king. After serving for sixteen years, he retired on a royal grant, but idleness irked him, so he opened a great smithy of his own, employing thirty-five workers, and took up tumbling as a hobby. One day when the circus came to town, the inevitable happened: great-grandpa's son fell in love with a rider, married her, and joined the troupe.

Once the circus got into the Cristiani blood, it not only stayed there, but spread. Grandpa's son, the present Papa Cristiani, was born in Modena, and traveled everywhere his father went. When he was a young man, the Cristiani troupe arrived in Turin, to find another circus competing for local patronage. The Cristianis won, but among the spectators was a pretty brunette tumbler from the other circus. Papa Cristiani fell in love with her, and they were married in 1904.

Now, Papa started his own show, and took it all over Europe. He put horses into the tumbling act for the first time, and also a dog. The crowds loved it. When Papa played the Circus Medrano in Paris, in 1910, Mrs. Medrano presented him with a medal. When they played there again in 1931, Papa's son Lucio won the same honor.

By 1932, Papa disagreed too much with Mussolini's policies to stay in Italy, so he and his brother Pietro left for good. The show played England, Scotland, and Belgium, and it was there that John Ringling saw them for the first time. He invited the Cristianis to come to America. In March, 1934, just before the gala circus opening at Madison Square Garden, they arrived in New York.

The Cristianis immediately became one of the top attractions, but they insisted on playing alone in the center ring, without other acts to distract them. Ringling refused, so they joined another circus. In 1942, John Ringling North, now head of Ringling Brothers [1947], asked the Cristianis to return on their own terms.

Today the Cristianis have become too large to play with any single circus. They usually split their acts between the King Brothers on the East Coast and the Cole Brothers in the West, and have enough performers left over for separate units in nightclubs, theaters, and the movies. Millions of people have flocked to see them, for which the circus, theaters and movies pay an average of $3,500 a week. Thus, the Cristianis have become more than a circus family; they are now big business.

Cristiani children start training young. Nadio, for instance, was riding bareback before his second birthday. But the Cristianis never force their children to join the act; they don't have to: the urge comes almost by instinct. They see their mothers riding or their fathers tumbling and immediately want to do it themselves.

In Papa's day, the children started intensive training at the age of five. Now the family realizes that ballet is an essential background for all acts, and the children are usually sent to ballet school first. Conchita, for instance, one of the prettiest of Papa's daughters, studied ballet for two years before working out with the horses.

When she was seven she learned to sit side-saddle; then she mastered the fundamentals of balancing on one knee or one foot while the horse was running. Next, she went through the long, grueling process of learning how to leap on a horse, how to do ballet steps and handstands and acrobatics while the animal was circling the ring. She entered the show for the first time at the age of fourteen.

The Cristiani horses must be trained as carefully as the members of the family. The big animals are either Percherons or Belgians, purchased when two years old, and usually are not ready to enter the ring until they are finished with three years of training. Polo, the most famous of the stable, lived to the ripe equine age of twenty-nine. He was the only horse in the troupe that could hold five Cristianis on his back at the same time.

In their hometown of Sarasota, Florida, the Cristianis own seven big houses, but every once in a while the whole family converges on the little house that Mama and Papa bought first, and where they still live, and when they all get together it's like a convention.

Papa Cristiani, a wiry man with smiling eyes, who didn't retire as a tumbler until '55, rushes around buttonholing all his sons, daughters, nephews, and nieces, to tell them plans for the coming season. One of the bareback riders is over in a corner, demonstrating a new ballet step. One of the tumblers has discovered a new twist to his somersault. Everyone is laughing and talking at once.

Lucio Cristiani is business manager of the family, but the Cristianis run their affairs on a democratic basis—whenever an argument starts, the whole family joins in. A decision is only reached as the Cristianis get tired arguing and drop out, one by one. By that time, Mama bustles into the room, shouting, "The spaghetti, she is ready!" and the Cristianis forget their argument in a rush for the table.

To keep their place as first family of the circus, the Cristianis are constantly adding new acts or improving old ones. Old-timers in the circus wonder what new marvels the Cristianis will develop next. But the family not only gets better all the time, it also gets bigger. With more always on the way, there's no doubt that the great Cristiani tradition will continue to flourish.

The only renegade is little Antoinette. She has become an outstanding pianist, and her father expects her to have a musical career. "I like to hear her play," he says, "but somehow it doesn't seem right. When I see her sitting there making beautiful music, I ask myself, 'How did a Cristiani ever get in front of a piano?'"

THE LIMIT OF HUMAN DARING

Octavie LaTour

Human daring has but one limit: human imagination. Human courage dares all, and there is no task, no feat, no exploit of bravado you can suggest to it that it will not venture. But there is a limit to the field imagination can invent for human daring.

In the years of old, everyday life presented dangerous situations for everyday people. There was war, and the jousts of chivalry, and crusades to the East. Then the New World opened its gates to adventurers, and men sailed west to brave the terrors of the unknown.

But nowadays such experiences—if you except automobiling and subwaying—are rare. [This was written in 1905.] Civilization has been so busy for hundreds of years eliminating danger from the common routine that the type of men that would have been heroes long ago find sports the only outlet for their venturesome spirits. They drive racing autos; they launch forth in airships and balloons; they turn explorers and penetrate remote corners of the earth: Tibet and the desert vasts of the Himalayas, the jungles; they force their way to the North Pole and the South, by ship, sledge, and balloon, to satisfy the cravings of courage to be up and doing.

And as the field grows each year narrower, as this mountaineer scales that peak, and this explorer maps out another island in the Arctic Zone, human invention sits down and ponders on something for human daring to do next.

Then there is the class of the professionally brave, so-called, to which I belong. Our function is to satisfy the public taste for a certain form of excitement that comes from witnessing dangerous feats; the sensation of beholding some human being grappling with death in a hair-raising spectacle relieves the humdrum of modern life.

Courage, not merely moral courage that copes with ethical problems and wins the battles of the soul, but physical courage, is a primitive instinct with us humans. Persons who are not called upon to be brave themselves satisfy their natural inclinations with the admiration of another's thrilling feat.

So we professional heroes and heroines fill a necessary bill in life's vaudeville. We foster the spirit of bravery and daring, and we risk our lives every day and think no more of it, probably less, than a lawyer does of his case at bar.

And there is nothing too daring to attempt. Demand what feat you will that requires physical skill and physical courage, and we in the circus will attempt it. Nay, we will perform it successfully.

At present, I am courting death each day in La Tourbillon De La Mort, the supposed limit of human daring. But this act of plunging down the steep incline in an automobile that turns a back somersault in mid-air and lands on a runway is not really the limit of human daring. It is only the most perilous act that human imagination has so far devised for human daring. But it is the limit for only a moment. Hundreds of inventors are hard at work trying to perfect a machine that will make a double turn.

The trouble is not in finding people with courage to perform the feats, but in working out a stunt more terrible than anything ventured before, that will menace life and all but take it. For hairbreadth as the escape must seem, the probability of accident must be really small.

No one wants to see people die. The game is one of mettle, not of death.

So get your minds fermenting; give your imagination free play; and invent the real limit of human daring. Show us how to fly to the moon; direct the way to Mars; point the signboards down the roads of human daring. And I for one will go.

From *New York World*, April 8, 1905.

A HIGH DIVE
L. P. Hartley

The circus-manager was worried. Attendances had been falling off and such people as did come—children they were, mostly—sat about listlessly, munching sweets or sucking ices, sometimes talking to each other without so much as glancing at the show. . . . What did people want? Something that was, in his opinion, sillier and more pointless than the old jokes; not a bull's-eye on the target of humor, but an outer or even a near-miss—something that brought in the element of futility and that could be laughed at as well as with; an unintentional joke against the joker.

The clowns were quick enough with their patter but it just didn't go down; there was too much sense in their nonsense for an up-to-date audience, too much articulateness. They would do better to talk gibberish perhaps. Now they must change their style, and find out what really did make people laugh, if people could be made to; but he, the manager, was over fifty and never good himself at making jokes, even the old-fashioned kind. What was this word that everyone was using—"sophisticated"? The audiences were too sophisticated, even the children were: they seemed to have seen and heard all this before, even when they were too young to have seen and heard it.

"What shall we do?" he asked his wife. They were standing under the Big Top, which had just been put up, and wondering how many of the empty seats would still be empty when they gave their first performance.

"I don't see what we can do about the comic side," she said. "It may come right by itself.

Fashions change, all sorts of old things have returned to favor, like old-time dances. But there's something we could do."

"What's that?"

"Put on an act that's dangerous, really dangerous. Audiences are never bored by that. I know you don't like it, and no more do I, but when we had the Wall of Death—"

Her husband's big chest-muscles twitched under his thin shirt.

"You know what happened then."

"Yes, but it wasn't our fault; we were in the clear."

He shook his head.

"Those things upset everyone. I know the public came after it happened—they came in shoals, they came to see the place where someone had been killed. But our people got the needle and didn't give a good performance for I don't know how long. If you're proposing another Wall of Death I wouldn't stand for it—besides, where will you find a man to do it?—especially with a lion on his bike, which is the great attraction."

"But other turns are dangerous too, as well as dangerous-looking. It's being dangerous that is the draw."

"Then what do you suggest?"

Before she had time to answer a man came up to them.

"I hope I don't butt in," he said, "but there's a man outside who wants to speak to you."

"What about?"

"I think he's looking for a job."

"Bring him in," said the manager.

The man appeared, led by his escort, who then went away. He was a tall, sandy-haired fellow with tawny leonine eyes and a straggling moustache. It wasn't easy to tell his age—he might have been about thirty-five. He pulled off his old brown corduroy cap and waited.

"I hear you want to take a job with us," the manager said, while his wife tried to size up the newcomer. "We're pretty full up, you know. We don't take on strangers as a rule. Have you any references?"

"No, sir."

"Then I'm afraid we can't help you. But just for form's sake, what can you do?"

As if measuring its height the man cast up his eyes to the point where one of the two poles of the Big Top was embedded in the canvas.

"I can dive sixty feet into a tank eight feet long by four feet wide by four feet deep." The manager stared at him.

"Can you now?" he said. "If so, you're the very man we want. Are you prepared to let us see you do it?"

"Yes," the man said.

"And would you do it with petrol burning on the water?"

"Yes."

"But have we got a tank?" the manager's wife asked.

"There's the old Mermaid's tank. It's just the thing. Get somebody to fetch it."

While the tank was being brought the stranger looked about him.

"Thinking better of it?" said the manager.

"No, sir," the man replied. "I was thinking I should want some bathing trunks."

"We can soon fix you up with those," the manager said. "I'll show you where to change."

Leaving the stranger somewhere out of sight, he came back to his wife.

"Do you think we ought to let him do it?" she asked.

"Well, it's his funeral. You wanted us to have a dangerous act, and now we've got it."

"Yes, I know, but—" The rest was drowned by the rattle of the trolley bringing in the tank—a hollow, double cube like a sarcophagus. Mermaids in low relief sported on its leaden flanks. Grunting and muttering to each other the men slid it into position, a few feet from the pole. Then a length of hosepipe was fastened to a faucet and soon they heard the sound of water swishing and gurgling in the tank.

"He's a long time changing," said the manager's wife.

"Perhaps he's looking for a place to hide his money," laughed her husband, and added, "I think we'll give the petrol a miss."

At length the man emerged from behind a screen, and slowly walked toward them. How tall he was, lanky and muscular. The hair on his body stuck out as if it had been combed. Hands on hips he stood beside them, his skin pimpled by goose-flesh. A fit of yawning overtook him.

"How do I get up?" he asked.

The manager was surprised, and pointed to the ladder. "Unless you'd rather climb up, or be hauled up! You'll find a platform just below the top, to give you a foot-hold."

He had started to go up the chromium-plated ladder when the manager's wife called after him: "Are you still sure you want to do it?"

"Quite sure, madam."

He was too tall to stand upright on the platform; the awning brushed his head. Crouching and swaying forty feet above them he swung his arms as though to test the air's resistance. Then he pitched forward into space, unseen by the manager's wife who looked the other way until she heard a splash and saw a thin sheet of bright water shooting up.

The man was standing breast-high in the tank. He swung himself over the edge and crossed the ring toward them, his body dripping, his wet feet caked with sawdust, his tawny eyes a little bloodshot.

"Bravo!" said the manager, taking his shiny hand. "It's a first-rate act, that, and will put money in our pockets. What do you want for it, fifteen quid a week?"

The man shook his head. The water trickled on to his shoulders, oozed from his borrowed bathing-suit and made runnels down his sinewy thighs. A fine figure of man: the women would like him.

"Well, twenty then." Still the man shook his head.

"Let's make it twenty-five. That's the most we give anyone."

Except for the slow shaking of his head the man might not have heard. The circus-manager and his wife exchanged a rapid glance.

"Look here," he said. "Taking into account the draw your act is likely to be, we're going to make you a special offer—thirty pounds a week. All right?"

Had the man understood? He put his finger in his mouth and went on shaking his head slowly, more to himself than at them, and seemingly unconscious of the bargain that was being held out to him. When he still didn't answer, the knot of tension broke, and the manager said, in his ordinary, brisk voice, "Then I'm afraid we can't do business. But just a matter of interest, tell us why you turned down our excellent offer."

The man drew a long breath and breaking his long silence said, "It's the first time I done it and I didn't like it."

With that he turned on his heel and walked off unsteadily in the direction of the dressing-room.

The circus-manager and his wife stared at each other.

"It was the first time he'd done it," she muttered. "The first time." Not knowing what to say to him, whether to praise, blame, scold or sympathize, they waited for him to come back, but he didn't come.

"I'll go and see if he's all right," the circus-manager said. But in two minutes he was back again. "He's not there," he said. "He must have slipped out the other way, the crack-brained fellow!"

From the collection, *Two for the River*, Hamish Hamilton Ltd. © L. P. Hartley, 1961.

THE TUMBLERS

Thomas Mann

How forcibly I was struck by a troupe of tumblers and tightrope-walkers distinguished by their agreeable trick of consulting briefly before each of their hair-raising performances, as though they had to come to an agreement. Their star, who was obviously a favorite with everyone, was a boy of fifteen who bounded from a springboard, turned two and a half somersaults in the air, and then landed without so much as a wobble on the shoulders of the man behind him, apparently his elder brother. He was, to be sure, successful in doing this only on his third attempt. Twice he failed, missing his brother's shoulders and falling; his laughter and the way he shook his head at this failure were just as enchanting as the ironic gallantry of the gesture with which his senior summoned him back to the springboard. Possibly it was all intentional, for naturally enough the applause and *bravo's* of the multitude were all the more tumultuous when on the third attempt he not only completed his *salto mortale* and landed without a quiver, but managed to heighten the storm of applause by a gesture of his outspread hands which seemed to say *"Me voilà!"* It is certain, however, that his calculated or half-intended failures had taken him closer to a broken spine that his triumphant success.

What fabulous creatures these artists are! Are they really human at all?

PART FIVE

THE SIDE SHOW

WHAT MORE?

The big show had commenced, and the Curio Hall was deserted by all save the performers. The room took on the air of a private home when the guests have deserted and the household, a little tired but happy over the success of the function, are discussing the events and breathing normally once more.

Colonel George Augur, the giant who stands eight feet tall, was conversing with little Mr. Ernest Rownell, the midget.

"Wait a minute and I'll come down," he said, and it was an interesting sight to see him descend. One trembled for the ladder more than for the man. He inspires confidence.

"The ordinary giant would find that rather a difficult feat," he said, "but I've discovered that if a man wants to do anything he can do it. A chair, Ernest."

This to the midget, who complied with the request.

"I'm a Welshman—but you're probably not interested. To tell you the truth, I myself am not particularly in love with rehashing it. And yet, after all, it is not monotonous; we are proof against that affliction after a year or so on the platform. We learn another lesson—to keep our temper. It is my contention that the stronger a man is the gentler he should be."

"You talk well, Mr. Augur."

"I was educated at Eton—at least I was graduated there—but the crowd that presses against this platform is really giving me my education. We on exhibition here get a deep insight into human nature."

"Does there ever come to you a desire to reach down and hold some shivering pigmy up to the ridicule of the crowd?"

"No, I really like the crowd."

"When it tries to be funny at your expense?"

"Shall I tell you something? I have begun to believe that there is but one joke in existence."

"And that is?"

" 'How's the weather up there?' That joke is beginning to irritate me. It should be on exhibition here as the oldest joke in the world. Give me a cigarette, Ernest."

"Aren't you afraid cigarettes will undermine your health?"

"I don't believe I'm afraid of anything, and I'm not boasting when I say it. I suppose it's my superior height that gives me a sense of security, but in the old days in Cardiff, I was a professional wrestler."

"That arm is strong enough to draw a big salary." A harmless little jest, you will admit, but the big man did not smile.

"Yes," he said. "There are some of us in here that draw bigger salaries than the ring performers, and yet the ring performers do not hanker for our society. Among us in this room there is no jealousy, but with those in the rings, well, sometimes there is. We are considered freaks by them."

"You don't like the word 'freak'?"

"I do not. The word just does not apply to me or to anyone who is not malformed. I am a curiosity, perhaps. People look at me and I believe they envy me; why shouldn't they? I am strong, I am healthy, and I am young."

"What about your leisure hours?"

"Books. Ancient history in general, giant history in particular. Being a giant, I'm naturally interested in them. I've traced my genealogy back to the 12th Century. I've written a brochure on giants and some day I mean to write an exhaustive work on the subject."

And this is Colonel George Augur of Cardiff, Wales, on duty as the biggest man in the world. Directly across from him sits Marie, surnamed "The Beautiful." She is known as "The Fat Lady" but she is not losing any sleep over it or over anything else. Perhaps it is freedom from worry that has gifted her with so much solid flesh. An Englishwoman, she calls Hull, Yorkshire, her home.

"What do you think of the crowd?" I asked.

"Bless you, Hi love them all. Hit's my food and drink; hit's my life. Leave hit? For what?"

"For some man, perhaps?"

The platform shook with her laughter.

"Some man? Not on your bloomink life."

"Do you like being stared at?"

"Of course. That's what Hi'm paid for."

Then she grew intensely feminine. "Hi want you to look at my h'arm," she said.

"What's the matter with it?"

"Nothing," she said, "but hain't hit a beauty?"

It certainly was. Beautiful Marie probably sells more photographs than any one of the other curiosities. She is good to look at, unless you're a vegetarian.

"Pardon me, but don't you grow tired carrying yourself about?"

"Hi'm used to it. Hit's a great deal like the little boy who starts to carry the calf when it's a day old, and—"

"Tell me, do you feel pity for any of the curiosities?"

"Not a bit. We're all friends, and we're better h'off than some Hi know."

Ernest Rownell is the spokesman for the midgets. "Why should I not love it?" he said. "People are kind to me. Of course it is because

I'm small. I know that, but we are human."

"Does it strike you as being odd that your best friend should be the giant?"

"That is nearly always the case. Perhaps because there is no room for jealousy."

"But I understood there was no jealousy."

The little fellow smiled, twirled his cane, and said, "You have the wrong idea. You think we are different in every way from other folk. Why, the tattooed man is as proud of his pictured skin as a woman would be of her clear complexion. I'm glad to be small, and do you know, I believe it is the little fellows that get the best of it. We're looked after."

"And does a man of your age like that?"

"A man of any age likes it."

Frank Bentenia, of Sicily, the three-legged boy: "It is my business, this, and I keep my father, mother, two brothers, and two sisters by it. They live in Middletown, Connecticut. You ask how I would care to go to them. How would I live? How would they live? This is a matter of business with me. You pay your money and I eat my meals."

"Do you feel any embarrassment when you are on the street?"

"Why should I? This is my living, I tell you. And I am no more ashamed than a carpenter would be ashamed to be seen with his tools."

And this is the refrain of the room. At least to the casual observer, these folks are happy and content. They seem to believe themselves normal or, rather, better than normal.

In one corner of the room sits a brown, flat-nosed little woman, "Karo, the Missing Link," they call her. She comes from Burma, and if you forget the freak nature and think only of human nature, you will not smile at her strange looking face. Talk with her and you will forget her ugliness. Educated in England, she speaks many languages.

"Men I like at a distance—women not at all. Why? Perhaps it's because the only emotion I could possibly arouse would be pity."

"And you do not want to be pitied?"

"Why should I be? I have my books and my painting; what more do I need?"

From the *New York World*, March 25, 1905.

HAVE MIDGET, WILL TRAVEL

Carlton Brown

Charles Sherwood Stratton, whose fantastic life spanned the years from 1838 to 1883, was a midget whose height ranged between 2 feet, 1 inch from his infancy into his teens to 3 feet, 4 inches at his fullest growth. He was not the smallest human on record or even on view in his time and his claims to superlatives of other sorts were negligible. Neither his modest talents nor his cocky charm would have been likely to earn much cash or praise if he had been of normal size.

Yet, little Charles Stratton, after P. T. Barnum transformed him into General Tom Thumb, became the most celebrated entertainer of his century, winning world-wide and life-long acclaim and earning millions for himself and his discoverer.

He toured the U.S. and Europe repeatedly without ever wearing out his welcome. With Mrs. Tom Thumb and another midget pair, he travelled to the Orient and North Africa and wound up with a fourth triumphant tour of Europe. About mid-way in Barnum's long career, the showman estimated that a total of 82,464,000 people had paid to see his various attractions and that 20,400,000, or nearly a quarter of them, had come to see Tom Thumb. And the little make-believe general then had many more lucrative years ahead of him on his own and under Barnum's banner.

The tot who was to build Barnum's first fortune was born on January 4, 1838, to Sherwood Stratton, a carpenter, and his wife, Cynthia. He was a husky baby weighing 9 pounds, 2 ounces, at birth. Then, at the age of five months, measuring 2 feet, 1 inch, and weighing 15 pounds, 2 ounces, Charlie stopped growing.

Chance brought Charlie Stratton and Barnum together one day in November, 1842, in Bridgeport, Connecticut, the midget's birthplace, some twenty miles distant from Barnum's home-town of Bethel. Barnum gravely shook hands and sized him up in a glance as a likely attraction. He proposed that the Strattons let him exhibit their "wonderful little man" for four weeks at a fee of three dollars a week and the expenses of travel and board for the boy and his mother.

When Mrs. Stratton arrived in New York with Charlie, on December 8, she was at first shocked by the "Barnumizing" already being applied to Charlie. Banners, posters, and hand-bills proclaimed the first appearance a week later of "General Tom Thumb, a dwarf, eleven years of age, just arrived from England."

Mrs. Stratton's chief anxiety, that the public might expect more of an eleven-year-old Britisher than her little one could deliver, was soon allayed. The lad's speech was remarkably free of the lisping accents of infancy and he was, Barnum noted, "an apt pupil with a great deal of native talent and a keen sense of the ludicrous." In the scant week between Charlie's arrival and his debut, Barnum taught him the military bearing and manners that went with the uniform of a continental officer which had been tailored in advance to his measure. He drilled him in some simple songs, dances, and recitations and introduced him to his role in the sort of stunts which made Barnum the first great master of the art of press-agentry.

P. T. had the midget tricked out in an elegant gentleman's outfit which was an exact duplicate in miniature of his own. Thus attired, the brawny, six-foot-two Connecticut Yankee, then thirty-two, and his knee-high counterpart, not quite five, set off in a rented coach on a round of Sunday visits.

At the home of Colonel James Watson Webb, editor of the *Courier and Enquirer*, Barnum brushed aside the butler's objections that the family and several guests were at their midday dinner and led his tiny protégé to the dining room. Before the colonel would give voice to his anger at the showman's brash intrusion, the children at the table caught sight of the incredible mannikin and set up a delighted hubbub.

Barnum boldly hoisted the midget onto the table, standing him next to a roast turkey that might well have outweighed him. At his sponsor's cue, the animated centerpiece bowed formally and said, "Good evening, ladies and gentlemen. I'm General Tom Thumb." Then stepping nimbly amid the dinnerware he made the circuit of the table top, bowing politely to each diner. A chair was drawn up at once for Barnum and another heaped with cushions for his little marvel, and the two interlopers were made the most adulated of guests.

"Of a verity, General Tom Thumb is the greatest curiosity we have ever seen," Colonel Webb wrote in a long and glowing account of the visit in his paper. "And we are quite sure that all who omit to pay their respects to him at the Museum will forever regret it."

Visits to James Gordon Bennet of the *Herald*, Horace Greeley of the *Tribune*, and other editors resulted in similar free eulogies. At the same time Barnum bought columns of advertising in the newspapers and filled the streets with "bulletin wagons" papered with flamboyant posters heralding the forthcoming appearance of his latest discovery. The ballyhoo brought record crowds to the Museum on the evening of General Tom Thumb's first appearance.

"Good evening, ladies and gentlemen," the General began, when the din had subsided. "I'm only a *Thumb*, but a good *Hand* in a *General* way at amusing you. . . ." He went on to recite the rest of the pun-filled piece Barnum had written for him. He sang Yankee Doodle. He strutted up and down, flourishing his tiny sword. He told a joke or two and backed into the wings, bowing and waving his cockaded hat. The audience gave him as resounding an ovation as had ever greeted any famous actor of the day.

Barnum voluntarily raised the boy's wage to $25 a week and then to $50 [and eventually they become equal partners]. Meanwhile, he had drilled his protégé in some additions to his repertoire. The General now posed in a series of "living statues" representing Hercules, Ajax, Samson, the Dying Gladiator, and other heroes. Wearing flesh-color tights and gauzy wings, he impersonated Cupid, shooting tiny arrows over the footlights, from a miniature bow. Women scrambled to retrieve the arrows as wildly as any latter-day teenagers have fought for souvenirs of their idols.

The mayor of New York took his daughter to see General Tom Thumb and wrote appreciatively of him in his diary, and journalists —possibly influenced by Barnum's lavish distribution of "seegars"—went on filling columns with praise of "that Wonderful Little Man," long after his debut had ceased to be news.

When P. T. took Tom Thumb to England, he became the darling of London's nobility and gentry. The General appeared at Buckingham Palace by command of Her Majesty. The young queen and her court were charmed by the toy General's impersonation of Napoleon, his other little acts and songs, and his saucy deportment. He was rewarded with a gold-filled purse, Barnum with the exceptional privilege of dictating his own glowing account of Tom

Thumb's audience for the court circular, which was printed verbatim in all the newspapers the next day.

"This notice of my visit to the queen wonderfully increased the attraction of my exhibition," P. T. wrote. Queen Victoria sent for them twice more to entertain the King and Queen of the Belgians, the infant Prince of Wales (later King Edward VII), and sundry others of the royalty and nobility. Dukes and Duchesses showered him with jewels, swords, pistols, canes, snuff boxes, and other costly gewgaws.

Once Barnum had touched off what an English lord called "midget fever," it hopped boundaries and oceans and raged like an epidemic. In France, an invitation came from the king the day before the troupe's well-publicized arrival and the royal family strove to outdo the British in their lavish presents to "le General Tom Pouce." The French press reported the audience in enraptured detail, and at a mere request from Barnum, the mite's gorgeous little carriage was granted a place in a mid-Lent parade next to those of the king, the court, and the diplomatic corps. Crowds cheered Tom Pouce and mobbed the theater where he soon opened with tickets reserved for two months in advance.

"The French are very impressible," noted Barnum. "What in England is only excitement in Paris becomes furor."

In two carriages, a van to carry their baggage, and the General's coach and four they travelled through southern France into Spain where fifteen-year-old Queen Isabella II was added to the list of the fifteen-pound tyke's royal patrons. Then north to Belgium in a performance for King Leopold, Queen Louise, and the royal children. The spectacular retinue itself was enough to advertise the appearance of General Tom Pouce along the way and to bring commoners flocking to the village halls for his performances. His tutor taught him songs and recitations in the language of each country as they went along.

Recrossing the channel, the General shook another steady shower of shillings out of England,

Scotland, and Ireland. Sailing home three years after their arrival, the prospectors totted up total receipts of an astounding three-quarters of a million dollars.

Heralded by hyperbolic accounts of his triumphs abroad, Tom Thumb drew greater crowds than ever before to his "grand debut" at the American Museum. His talents now included the ability to saw out some squeaky tunes on a wee violin, dance the horn pipe and the Highland Fling, and to sing and speak some French and Spanish lines.

Charlie's personal thoughts and feelings were completely concealed behind the public figure of General Tom Thumb, which had been fashioned in all its essentials in the first four years of association with Barnum.

Thus, on the one hand there was a genuine spontaneous romance in a privately agreed-upon marriage between Charles Sherwood Stratton (age 24, height 35 inches, 47 pounds) and Mercy Lavinia Warren Bump (age 21, 32 inches, 29 pounds), who had taught school back home in Massachusetts. No doubt, that union was motivated in part by the same urgings of the flesh that are felt by full size men and women, and consummated to scale in the usual fashion.

But all that posterity has been given is Barnum's lacy press-agenting of the courtship and wedding of the General Tom Thumb and Lavinia. The wedding while as "genteel and graceful" as Barnum pledged Lavinia's mother it would be, was well staged and ballyhooed, a social event of the first order. There was a discreet though furious scrambling for invitations among New York's elite. It was Barnum, of course, who made out the list. The ceremony took place in Grace Church, one of the oldest houses of worship in Manhattan and the most socially prominent. Artfully, Barnum kept the wedding party diminutive; the best man was the rejected suitor, "Commodore Nutt" [29 inches, 24 pounds], the maid-of-honor, tiny Minnie, Lavinia's sister. Readers of the New York Times, the staid grey old lady of the nation's newspapers, will be amazed to learn that almost ten percent of the February 11, 1863, paper was devoted to a description of the wedding. . . .

After the simple Protestant ceremony, the couple left the quiet and dignity of the church and were immediately surrounded by throngs of well-wishers and the merely curious who crowded the streets.

Among the lavish gifts showered on the elfin couple were jewelry, silverware, and porcelain from such notables as the Belmonts, Astors, Vanderbilts, and Roosevelts, and a set of Chinese fire screens inlaid with gold, silver, and mother-of-pearl from Mrs. Abraham Lincoln. The President and his wife invited the bride and groom to the White House on their honeymoon and Lincoln remarked that he had been thrown completely in the shade by General Tom Thumb, who had become the national center of attraction.

Everyone was happy—the public, Tom Thumb, Lavinia. Everyone, that is, except P. T. Barnum. He was pacing the floor, wracking his brains for a new angle, a new peg on which to hang front page stories in the press. Then it hit him. What was the natural follow-up for a wedding? A baby, of course. He even let Lavinia in on the scheme after he'd made all the plans. But a quick check with the doctor showed that parenthood was impossible—by the usual means. Undaunted, Barnum released the story in due time anyway, documented it with photographs. They enjoyed a brisk and profitable sale of the General and Mrs. Thumb holding a beaming infant. Barnum had borrowed it for the occasion. America took the new addition to its heart.

Realizing that the fiction would be difficult to maintain, Barnum milked all the publicity he could for the nonexistent baby and then, alas,

let the tot die, thus tinging the charmed lives of his little ones with the humanizing touch of tragedy which gave millions of their feminine fans the therapeutic benefit of a good cry.

The wee general was always and genuinely devoted to Barnum and several times volunteered to help fill the coffers of his mentor. Long after he had proved himself equally adept at drawing crowds on his own, when Barnum was dragged into bankruptcy in 1856 by the failure of a large clock company for which he had endorsed notes for huge loans, Charlie immediately wrote that he would cancel the tour he had started and put himself, carriage, ponies, and assistance at P.T.'s service. Barnum took him on their second tour of Europe which lasted two years and was so lucrative that the showman's half share of the profits paid off most of his debts, amounting to more than a half million dollars.

Finally when Barnum joined with Bailey to open the three-ring circus in Madison Square Garden, in March of 1881, Tom and Lavinia came out of semi-retirement to add their still great drawing power to the Greatest Show on Earth, joining in a torch-light procession witnessed by half the population of Manhattan and helping mightily to attract turnaway crowds to the opening performance.

When Charlie died of apoplexy two years later at the age of 45, he was buried in Bridgeport beneath a life-size granite statue of himself which the vain little man had commissioned when he was nineteen. He was buried with the honors of a Thirty-Second Degree Mason and a Knight Templar, and ten thousand people, as great a crowd as he had ever drawn, attended the service.

Condensed from *Cavalier,* September 1958. Used by permission.

THE SIAMESE TWINS

J. P. McEvoy

Chang and Eng, later known as Chang-Eng Bunker, were born in 1811 in a tiny fishing village on the Meklong River not far from Bangkok, Siam. But their father was full Chinese and their mother half Chinese, which made them only one-quarter Siamese—or perhaps if you wanted to be quizzical, the world-famous Siamese Twins were only one-eighth Siamese apiece.

Lucky for them, they made their appearance in a deeply religious Buddhist community where even the humblest villagers revered the old law "shed not the blood for the blood is the life." Otherwise some helpful neighbor might have started cutting them apart, which would have finished the twins right then and there.

So they grew to their full height of five feet one inch for Chang and five feet two inches for Eng (Chang wore special lifts in his shoes so his twin couldn't top him), and they made themselves useful around the house raising ducks and peddling eggs—and everyone remarked how lively and smart they were at driving bargains, for it seems in those days they both talked together, each finishing the other's sentence, and the ordinary haggler was no match for them.

One day, when the twins were 18 years old, a Yankee skipper dropped anchor in the harbor not far from where they were living and accidentally met the twins while trying to peddle some guns to the King of Siam. Immediately he forgot all about gun running and shanghaied the twins.

By the time the good ship *Sachem* arrived in Boston, after a five months' voyage, the skipper was able to announce piously that the Siamese twins were "under his protection." They created a sensation, not only around Boston but in Europe where their protector journeyed with them. We are told he toured 2,500 miles in the British Isles alone, exhibiting the twins to 300,000 Britishers for once startled out of their proverbial complacency. Even the august Royal College of Surgeons deigned to invite the twins to tea and after discreetly examining them broke down and pronounced them "an extraordinary *Lusus Naturae*."

They were all of that. Joined as they were, "they could run and swim, take walks of eight and ten miles, play battledore and shuttlecock, and on many occasions went hunting." They could walk only side by side. They slept face to face, changing positions by the simple expedient of rolling over and over, which they learned to do automatically without awakening each other.

They were normal in every way except for a small band only three and a half inches long and some eight inches in circumference connecting them from the extremity of the breast bone of each and extending downwards to the abdomen. It was quite flexible. The upper part was strong and firm—the under part soft, fleshy, and apparently containing a connecting cavity.

There was a great difference of opinion among the medical experts of the time concerning what went on inside this cavity and they never did find out until the post mortem, which was a world event, but all agreed that surgical divorce would have proved fatal. Meanwhile, it was an intriguing fact that a pin prick in the exact center of the "band" was felt by both twins but a puncture to the right or left was only felt by the twin nearest the injury. As children they contracted measles and smallpox at the same time and recovered simultaneously, but as adults one twin was a periodic souse while the other was a complete teetotaler—and the alcoholic ecstasy of the one brother was in no way communicated to nor did it affect the pious sobriety of the other.

They came back to America from their first trip, richer only in experience, the skipper having skipped (with the booty) out of their lives. But the twins, who were of age now, had other connections, including the immortal Barnum—with whom they sojourned in New York City at the corner of Anne Street and Broadway (The American Museum) and finally accumulated an estate of $60,000.

The twins provided plenty of legal puzzles for our own American lawyers, who used to sit around the cracker barrels of those far-off days, arguing about how the twins, whom the medicos had said were individuals, could own property as individuals. Weren't they inevitably partners in ownership as they were in life? It was finally legally decided that they could hold property and sign contracts either as individuals or as joint partners, one signing for the other, but they must marry as individuals and their children would inherit separately.

But if one committed a crime, which should be guilty? Could the other be held as an accessory? And if one was innocent how would you punish or imprison the other without making the innocent party suffer? No one could argue lack of knowledge on the part of the other— for the twins fell asleep at the same time, woke up at the same time, were hungry simultaneously, ate the same food in similar quantities, and

smoked and chewed tobacco when the other did, and though many people tried, it had been proved impossible to engage the two of them in separate conversations or on different subjects. While they disagreed violently about many things, they could only talk on the same subject at the same time—each finishing the other's sentence as in childhood.

Curiously enough, they seldom spoke to each other. They explained this once, saying they both saw the same things at the same time and felt the same way about them so there was nothing to discuss. For the same reason they disliked playing games in which they were pitted against each other, such as chess at which they were quite good—explaining they took no more pleasure playing competitively "than you would by playing your right hand against your left." Politics was something else again. During a local Congressional election in 1847 they differed so violently they insisted upon voting for different candidates.

For by now these three-fourths Chinese were American citizens. A special act by the legislature of North Carolina had done it. They had learned to speak English pretty well, to read and write. They had adopted American style of dress except that each wore his hair in a queue (old Chinese style) three-and-a-half feet long, wrapped tightly around his head. They were prosperous farmers, too.

Somewhere in their travels two sisters fell in love with them. Contemporary meanies were ungallant enough to say the $60,000 estate had something to do with it. Perhaps. Anyway, on April first, 1843, in Wilkes County, North Carolina, Chang married Adelaide Yeats and Eng married her sister, Sarah Ann—and we would like to add that they lived together happily ever after, but they didn't. For the sisters didn't get along and the brothers weren't too congenial about their sisters-in-law. A working solution was finally arrived at—they built separate houses for their wives three miles apart near Mount Airy, North Carolina, and lived three days at a time in each house—a design for living that intrigued the countryside.

The twins were married for more than 30 years and between them had a total of 22 children, all of them exceptionally bright. Eng was the champ, with seven boys and five girls—all normal. Chang had seven girls and three boys—and they, too, were normal except that one boy and one girl were deaf-mutes.

The Civil War came along and the twins, sympathetic to the Confederacy, shared its defeat. Impoverished, they came to New York to recoup their finances and exhibited at Wood's Museum, but the public had lost interest. Despondent, neglected, they faded out of the public view and spent their last days on their farms—faithfully going back and forth to each other's house every three days regardless of the weather.

Some of the old chronicles say this was the death of them—that Chang caught a severe cold riding in the rain. Other accounts have it that Chang went on one alcoholic spree too many. In any case, on Friday evening, January 23, 1874, in the sixty-third year of their amazing lives, they retired to a small room by themselves and went to bed. But Chang was restless. Sometime between midnight and daybreak they got up and sat by the fire in a special chair which had been made for them. Eng was sleepy and wanted to go to bed. Chang complained that it hurt his chest to lie down. They argued about it while Eng smoked his pipe. Finally Eng knocked out his pipe and they went to bed, and Eng fell into a deep sleep.

And now the curtain. Surely Edgar Allen Poe never conceived of anything more macabre: "Eng waked up and asked his son, 'How is your Uncle Chang?' The boy said, 'Uncle Chang is cold. Uncle Chang is dead.' Then great excitement took place. Eng commenced crying, saying to his wife whom they called in, 'My last hour has come.' As he turned in alarm to the lifeless form by his side he was seized with violent nervous paroxysms. In two hours he was dead, although he had been in perfect health when they went to bed."

The autopsy, held at a special meeting at the College of Physicians in Philadelphia, settled a number of questions for the medical world with words like teratology, omphalopagus Xiphodidymus, and duplex bilaterality. It also showed that any attempt to separate the twins in life would have been fatal. It showed that Chang died of a cerebral clot. But no cause could be found for the death of Eng. It was generally believed he died of fright.

Condensed from *Kiwanis Magazine,* September 1943. Used by permission.

A DIME, TEN CENTS ONLY

Carl Sandburg

When the circus came to town we managed to shake out of sleep at four o'clock in the morning, grab a slice of bread and butter, and make a fast walk to the Q. [railroad] yards to watch the unloading in early daylight. A grand clear voice the man had who rode his horse a half-block ahead of the elephants in the parade and cried out as though there might be hell to pay, "The elephants are coming, watch your horses!" First to one side of the street and then the other he cried it and those who had skittish horses watched them.

After the unloading we went home for a quick breakfast and a run to the circus grounds, a big pasture at Main and Farnham near the city limits. If we were lucky we got jobs at carrying water for the elephants or lugging to the big tent the boards for the audience to sit on. After three or four hours of this useful and necessary work we were presented with slips of paper that let us in to see the big show in the afternoon. If we hadn't been lucky and if we didn't have the fifty cents for a ticket we tried to slide under the canvas and crawl to where we could peek through boards and between legs to see the grand march, the acrobats, the trapezists, the clowns, the hippodrome chariot race given before our eyes as it was in the time of Nero in Rome. Once as I was nearly through the canvas a pair of strong hands caught me by the ankles, yanked me out and threw me for a fall, and a voice told me I could get the hell out of there.

I walked around to the Side Show. There out front as a free show I saw the man with the elastic skin. He would pull it out from his face and neck and it would snap back into place. There I saw the tattooed man with fish, birds, brunette girls, ships, and many other shapes inked deep into his skin—and there too the Oriental Dancing Girl wearing few clothes and smiling about it to some giggling farm hands. The spieler, a man with a thick upcurled mustache, leaned toward the farm hands and said in a voice as if for them only to hear, "Go inside, boys. You can't lose. She takes off everything, every last stitch, and her muscles shake like a bowl of jelly. She makes a sick man feel like a wild monkey. What did you come here for, boys? She's got it. You can't lose."

Then the spieler dropped his confidential way and turned to the main crowd and let go in a smooth, loud voice. You could tell he was used to what he was saying and had spoken the same words in the same way a thousand times. "La·deez and gen·tul·men, beneath yon canvas we have the curi·aw·si·ties and mon·straw·si·ties—the Wild Man of Borneo, the smallest dwarf ever seen of mankind and the tallest giant that ever came into existence, the most marvelous snake ever brought to your fair city, a man-eating python captured in the darkest jungles of Africa ever penetrated by man. And I would call your particular attention to Jo Jo the dog-faced boy, born forty miles from land and forty miles from sea." At this last you couldn't be sure he was taking a laugh inside of himself, for his eyes twinkled. Us kids did imitations of him and when trying to rattle a pitcher or a batter, we would bawl, "Beneath yon canvas we have the curi-aw-si-ties and the mon-straw-si-ties," or "Look who's to bat. It's Jo Jo the dog-faced boy, born forty miles from land and forty miles from sea." And we learned too from the spieler, the barker, about the dime. "The price of admission, la-deez and gen-tul-men, is a dime, ten cents only, the tenth part of a dollar. Buy your tickets now before the big rush comes."

I had a dime and a nickel in my pocket. With the dime, the tenth part of a dollar, I bought a ticket. I went in and heard the ventriloquist and his dummy: "Will you spell a word for me, Danny?" "I'll try, what's the word?" "Constantinople." "Why do you tell me you can't stand on an apple?" I saw the Wild Man of Borneo and I could see he was a sad little shrimp and his whiskers messy. The Fat Woman, the Dwarf, the Giant, they seemed to me to be mistakes God had made, that God was absent-minded when he shaped them. I hung around the midget and his wife, watched them sign their names to photographs they sold at ten cents—and they were that pleasant and witty that I saw I had guessed wrong about them and they were having more fun out of life than some of the men in the Q. shops.

I stood a long while watching the Giant and noticed that he was quiet and satisfied about things and he didn't care one way or another whether people looked at him. He was so easy and calm about the way things were going that he reminded me of a big horse that didn't have to work and eats regular and never buys patent medicines. If a smarty asked, "How's the weather up there?" he might lift one eyebrow and let it pass, for he had heard it often enough. Nor did I feel sorry for the python. He may have been a man-eater but he was sleeping as if he had forgotten whoever it was he had swallowed and digested. After a third or fourth time around, the only one I felt sorry for was the Wild Man of Borneo. He could have been the only lonely creature among all the freaks. The Oriental Dancing Girl certainly was no freak, an average good-looking showgirl, somewhat dark of skin and probably a gypsy. She twirled, she high-kicked, did a few mild wiggles, and when it was over I heard a farm hand saying, "It's a sell. I thought from the way he talked outside that we was going to see a belly dance." "Yeah," said another, "and she didn't take off a stitch. It's a sell."

Years later it came over me that at first sight of the freaks I was sad because I was bashful. Except at home and among playmates, it didn't come easy for me to be looked at. I didn't like the feel of eyes being laid on me. I would pass people on the street and when they had gone by, I would wonder if they had turned their heads for another look at me. Walking down a church aisle between hundreds of people, I had a feeling of eyes on me. If three or four men stood in front of a store when I came along and one of them made some remark like, "Better hurry, kid, you're late," or "Does your mother know you're out, son?" I didn't have the answers and walked on with a feel that their eyes were on me. This was silly, but when you're bashful you have that feeling of eyes following you and boring through you. And there at the side show were these people, the freaks—and the business, the work, of each one of them was to be looked at. Every week, day by day they sat or stood up to be looked at by thousands of people and they were paid to be looked at. If some one of them was more looked at than any others there was danger of jealousy on the part of those who didn't get looked at as much as they wished. Only the Wild Man of Borneo and the python seemed to be careless about whether anyone looked at them or not.

I walked out of the side show with my nickel still in my pocket. I passed the cane stand where a man held out rings and spoke like his tongue was oiled. "Only ten cents for a ring and the cane you ring is the cane you get." I watched fellows throw one ring and quit. One stubborn farm hand spent thirty cents for rings and didn't get a cane and laughed he didn't want a cane anyhow. I walked on and later came back and the man with the oily tongue was still calling out, "Only ten cents for a ring and the cane you ring is the cane you get." Now I saw a man ring a cane and look at it from end to end and laugh, "I s'pose maybe it's worth ten cents."

I stopped where a man was cheerfully calling with no letup, "Lem-o-nade, ice-cold lem-o-nade, a nice cool refreshing drink for a nickel, five cents, the twentieth part of a dollar." Then in a lower tone as if talking to himself, "Lem-o-nade, made in the shade and stirred with a rusty spade." I passed by him to hear a laughing voice, "Here's where you get your hot roasted peanuts, those big double-jointed humpbacked peanuts, five a sack." I passed him by and still had my nickel.

Then I came to a man sitting on the ground, a deep-chested man with a face that had quiet on it and wouldn't bawl at you. I noticed he was barefoot. I looked up from his bare feet to see his arms gone, only stumps of arms at his shoulders. Between the first two toes of his right foot he held a card and lifted it toward me and said, "Take it and read it." I read a perfect handwriting, every letter shaped smooth and nice. It said, "I can write your name for you on a card for you to keep. The charge is only ten cents." I looked into his face. I said, "I would if I had the ten cents. All I've got is a nickel." I took out the nickel and turned my pockets inside out and showed him that besides the nickel there was only a knife, a piece of string, and a buckeye. He took the nickel in his left foot. He put a pen between the first two toes of his right foot and on the card wrote "Charles A. Sandburg," lifted the foot up toward me, and I took the card. I looked at it. It was the prettiest my name had ever been written. His face didn't change. All the time it kept that quiet look that didn't strictly belong with a circus. I was near crying. I said some kind of thanks and picked up my feet and ran.

The great P. T. Barnum himself never met my eyes but I did see Mr. Bailey of the firm of Barnum & Bailey on a bright summer morning in a black swallowtail coat giving orders and running the circus in the big green pasture that soon was subdivided into city lots. I told the kids who hadn't seen Bailey that I had seen him real as life. And with the kids who had seen him I joined in saying, "Wasn't he something to look at? And think of it, he's nearly as great a man as Barnum himself."

PART SIX

BEHIND THE SCENES

TAKING THE CIRCUS SERIOUSLY

Ralph Bergengren

"Professor" Manuel Herzog, irreproachably garbed as beseems a representative of that most carefully and expensively costumed enterprise, a modern circus [1909], had just come out of the ring in which he had been putting six magnificent black stallions through a series of graceful and complicated evolutions. His horses had been led away to their temporary stable, and the trainer paused a moment at the curtained entrance of the arena, watching with an idle eye the fruitless efforts of the Auguste clown to make himself useful in helping the ring attendants to arrange the paraphernalia of a troupe of Japanese acrobats. It is the business of an Auguste clown to make himself fruitlessly useful. Joining Mr. Herzog, I remarked that the antics of Auguste made a striking contrast to the grace and beauty of his own performing stallions.

The trainers eye kindled. "Ah, that is it," he replied gravely; "the grace and beauty! It is for that that the artist must work."

For it seems in very truth that the circus has its claim to be regarded as an expression of art.

As there are two ways of reading a novel, one for the conclusion of the story, the other for the more attentive pleasure of traveling the path by which the author gets to the end, so there are two ways of taking our satisfaction at the circus. The first is, and must always be, the more widely popular. But as the second may lead to many re-readings of the same story, each time with some new sense of pleasant discovery, so it may lead many times to the circus, with a fresh enjoyment in each repetition of performances that are, in their general intent, necessarily and eternally identical. That this enjoyment, if we care to analyze it, will be found akin to the aesthetic pleasure that we recognize so tangibly in painting and sculpture, and more intangibly in literature, music, and the drama, is the circus performers' claim to be considered an artist. . . .

Like art, the circus is cosmopolitan, speaks a universal language, and cares not a whit for national politics. Its names are foreign, not for pictorial effect, but because its men and women are of all countries. The American circus performer preceded the American actor before European audiences. If his feats cannot be intrinsically new, there is a further analogy in that they vary in the style in which they are executed. There may be dash, daring, and vigor in the riding of an American bareback equestrian, and yet a lack of the distinctive elegance that marks the exponent of European training in arenic equestrianism. And this on examination may be traced to differences in tradition. Almost from the beginning the American rider has practiced on horseback, but the European rider must first of all have acquired the art of ballet dancing. The difference is characteristic. The eye of a performer—not all performers, but of the minority that here as elsewhere represents the higher altitudes of the profession—sees these distinctions and looks for style much more keenly than for the successful achievement of some startling dénouement.

They are by no means easy to know, these circus people, living as they do in a world of their own, into which the outsider is not too carelessly invited to penetrate. As M. Hugues Le Roux says of them: "The Mountebank is too jealous of his freedom to talk openly to everyone who approaches him. The same patience which travelers use in their relations with savages must be employed before one can hope for any intimacy with this people, who are still as much scattered, as varied, as strangely mixed, as vagabond as their ancestors, the gypsies, who, guitar on back, hoop in hand, their black hair encircled with a copper diadem, traversed the Middle Ages, protected from the hatred of the lower classes and the cruelty of the great by the talisman of superstitious terror." Here, in a few words, is the genealogy of the circus; but the word "vagabond" as applied to modern conditions, hardly connotes the fact that many a circus performer, when not actually on the road, maintains a home for his family in some quiet community, where life of the circus is temporarily forgotten in the luxury of being commonplace and domestic. Taken as a whole, however, so unrestricted and wandering are their lives, in which the one thing stable the whole world over is the size of the ring in which they make their appearances, that what is said of any one country applies, broadly speaking, to any other. But without personal acquaintance it is impossible for us on this side of the water to understand what the performer means when he refers to himself as an artist, or to realize how fully there exists under the dome of the "big tent" a point of view by no means dissimilar to that of the other arts.

In using the term "other arts," and thus frankly admitting the circus performer to the great (and little) company of artists, I am by no means seeking the cheap triumph of establishing a paradox. If such inclusion be a paradox, it is already established by the position which the circus performer has attained in the larger European cities. There, in the winter circus that competes with the theater, he is admittedly an artist, without quotation marks. At the Circus Schuman, Berlin, audiences have recalled the Banvards, an American troupe of aerialists, with an enthusiasm quite equal to that with which American audiences have recalled the famous singers in German opera. Nor is this inclusion altogether surprising, for art in its broadest sense, is a far-reaching democracy.

Combine the definitions and we shall see that it demands of its citizens only that they seek to express something of beauty, and seek to express it in all sincerity—on the other side of their natures let them be moral or immoral, humble or conceited, austere or extravagant, refined or uncultivated. . . . So long as they produce beauty in some one of its infinite manifestations, that is all that the term "artist" demands of them—no slight demand, mark you, for it means the sincere expression of what is best in the individual. And if some betray us with false coin, it is the inevitable result of conditions that make art, not only a form of religion, but the means of earning a livelihood.

It is in the visible expression of strength, grace, and vitality, that the artist of the circus holds himself at one with the painter and sculptor; but this art, like that of the actor, is necessarily alive and impermanent. Let the painter set on canvas his fixed presentiment of lion, tiger, or leopard. The trainer, by his dangerous medium of whip and training stick, will make the living animals exhibit endless graces of subtle line and lovely color. When he puts his head in the lion's mouth, he considers it nothing better than a concession to the groundlings—a mere vulgar, necessary pot-boiler. When he compels the great tawny thing to repeat the grace of a natural movement (the training of wild animals being always along the line of what they do naturally), and leap in a long, gracious curve across the arena to an unstable landing on a rolling sphere, he feels that he is doing something worthy of himself and his animals.

Or, again, let the sculptor depict a flying Mercury; Mercury must at least have a point of arrival or departure. But for one brief moment the young woman of the circus, swinging through space from one trapeze to another, *is* the grace of the flying Mercury. To attain this movement of self-expression she has given as long and arduous an apprenticeship as the artist who works in clay, bronze, or marble. And her tradition, like his, is to do this thing naturally, easily, without apparent effort— in other words, to acquire that highest attribute of the mechanical side of art, the ability to conceal itself. Similar analogy the thoughtful artist of the circus can carry into practically every act on the programme. And others will argue that their own art is superior to the stage, in that the actor is not an independent artist but must depend on the playwright.

It is hardly surprising that this comparison, the art of the circus with the art of the stage, should have an objective interest to many circus performers, although it has no interest whatever to the professional actor. It merely amuses the more intelligent people of the circus— those, in fact, who see clearly that there is no real basis for such comparison. Analogy can here go no further than the fact that stage and arena are both directly visible to an audience; the performer appears personally before it, and hears personally whatever applause may reward his efforts. Beyond this point the man or woman of the circus is doing one thing, and the man or woman of the stage something altogether different. The circus artist cannot be an interpreter; he creates no human character, tragic, comic or melodramatic; and such creation is no more to be expected of him than that Forbes Robertson should illuminate the madness of Hamlet by turning somersaults. Nor do we expect in this performance of Hamlet the rhythmic—almost melodic—charm of motion that gives its own excuse of beauty to circus equestrianism.

The appeal to the mind, which is so large a factor in the highest expression of the artist in human emotion, is the least important factor in the work of the artist in human grace, strength, agility, or domination over brute force. The appeal to the emotions—our admiration of courage, our enjoyment of suspense, our interest in any struggle between opposing forces—that makes another vital element of the stage, is to be found in the circus, but it is so modified and reduced to first principles that it affords no real ground for comparison. Truth to tell we are deceived by the skill of a great actor into the belief that his fictitious danger is real, and by the skill of a great circus performer into the belief that his real danger is fictitious. It is the test of art in both cases.

But the existence of the play, the presence of a specific tale to be told, completely separates the art of the stage from that of the arena, and so places our friend of the circus much more substantially in the company of those other artists whose professional pride is that they tell no stories. What he does must reach his audience through the sense of vision; let it delight the majority as a stunt, the few as yet another of the many varied expressions of beauty, and the initiated as an example of masterful technique. And so the art of the circus, even more perishable than that of the stage because it has no historians, actually invades for a fleeting moment the province of those arts which are considered most perishable.

But an audience, taken as a whole, cares little enough for art, and makes no bones of preferring that which is boldly startling to that which is subtly difficult. It wants the end of the story. It so little appreciates the strain and nervous tension felt by even a long experienced performer during the deeply concentrated effort of mind and body necessary to his act in the ring, that it fondly imagines the act not so very difficult after all, if one has the knack of it. The typical murmur of the artist that his best work is unrecognized and his worst applauded is therefore no more characteristic of the studio than of the circus. I have known an elephant trainer whose soul mourned daily over the satisfaction of audiences in seeing an elephant made ridiculous.

So, too, the individual point of view of the performer toward his work is full of surprises. Rarely, if ever, is he worried over the things that the audience imagines makes him uneasy— and never about his own equipment of nerve, muscle, and judgment. The bareback rider worries about his horse, for the slightest deviation from the animal's customary course and gait ruins a harmony between horse and rider upon which depends the success, and even the life, of the performer. The man on the trapeze is not at all disturbed at being so high up in the air; the higher up he is the more security he feels that in case of accident he will have time enough instinctively to twist his body into the right position for falling into the net. What worries him most is the fear of some unsuspected weakness in his apparatus.

The animal trainer is more afraid of an accidental scratch from a good-natured but blood-poisoning claw than of any actual conflict with an angry animal; more than that, he has real affection for his animals and dislikes the stern necessity of punishing them. The very clown is not so much pleased by the laughter of his audience as disturbed by the thought that it quite fails to appreciate the time and care he has expended in working out the details of his humorous contribution.

That the typical circus performer should be illiterate is a natural conclusion for those who believe that the beginning of all circus experience is a running away from school. But such would be few in number in the roll-call of an average circus. The circus, in fact, is too much a domestic institution to need this assault on other domestic circles. When a boy runs after it, it is not because the circus wants the boy but because the boy wants the circus. The institution recruits itself largely from its own family circles, and the very tendency of these families to have homes of their own during at least some part of the winter, supplies a legitimate connecting link between the ring and the world.

The true type of performer, the real artist of the arena, is born into the life, and honestly proud of his ancestry. By its very isolation from the rest of humanity, the circus has become domestic; its own convention is stoutly anchored to the institution of matrimony, and disinclined, with an almost aristocratic disinclination, to marry outside its traditional circle. The circus family may often trace its lineage through several generations of performers; and you will to-day find members of the same family in the rings of two continents.

Among these people it is a commonplace to have an aunt who rides bareback, but it is equally possible, and extremely likely, that she also knows how to make her own dresses. The remarkable thing would be to have a relative who isn't somehow or other connected with the show business. Like any other successful worker—doctor, lawyer, college professor, financier, artist, editor, or what not—the circus performer is knit by habit and association into the fabric of his occupation; criticise it he may on occasion, with all the harshness of an old acquaintance; respect it he must at bottom, and be by no means sorry when his children elect to continue the tradition that he may have inherited from his father's father.

As for the child, it sometimes happens that he reverses the usual order of things and runs away from the circus. His young life, at all events, must be passed away from it (which, in this country of public schools, casts an interesting sidelight on the supposed illiteracy of circus performers), for a circus on the road burdens itself with no such superfluities as useless children. Man and wife must each have something to do, in the ring or in some other capacity about the show, or they must separate during the season. If they do an act together, so much the better; and better yet if it is one in which they can include the children as they grow old enough. Thus the nucleus of the poster family is likely to consist of parents and children, and such is the tonic wholesomeness of this careful living, fresh air and vigorous exercise, that they are, to all intents and purposes, all young together.

The circus child, moreover, is born with a

livelihood, and learns almost by instinct the fundamental feats of flexibility, strength, and agility that are the A B C of every arenic performance. The lowest type of performer teaches his children these rudiments as a matter of business; he means the children to become so many financial assets, and their education is likely to be confined as closely as possible to the arena. But, even so, the wandering life of the profession is itself a university; he whom we regard from the audience as probably illiterate may have a conversational knowledge of several languages.

To the higher type of performer, he who regards his work most seriously, and realizes also that it outlaws him from the life of that great majority of "other people," the instructions of his children is a matter of precaution, taking the hour when it is ripe to provide a sound foundation for future bodily agility. The parent in this case recognizes his other responsibilities; the boy or girl is sent away to be educated, and there is no compulsion, save the call of the blood, to force a return to the circus. Yet the chances are that the child will follow in the paternal and maternal footsteps.

About this nomadic existence there is unquestionably a potent fascination. The performer, we say, lives by applause and cannot get on without it. But we forget that, in the three-ring circus, no one performer can be certain that the applause is his own instead of his neighbor's, in which case his satisfaction must obviously supply a new quality to be reckoned with by students of human nature. The canvas man, equally wedded to the circus, gets no applause whatever.

Applause is only a partial explanation; a fuller one is that the circus artist lives in a state of freedom to which his own nature, however varied may be its other manifestations, is peculiarly suited. "It is a free life"— such is the current phrase in which many a performer, and many a canvas man, expresses the call of the circus.

And yet, from the point of view of the man in the office-chair, they deceive themselves heartily, for this "free life" consists of most unremitting discipline, both of the individual over himself and the circus over the individual. Seen from the outside, it is the freedom of leisure and the emancipation of morals—a brief period of work each day and a long period of irresponsible idleness. But the boy who longs to become a part of this nomad life sees more clearly than his elders. What attracts him is the ability of these wonderful people to perform feats; he envies the strong man his muscles, the animal-trainer his courage, the rider his horsemanship, the acrobat his agility, the clown his humor. And these things—even in the case of the clown, who is also an acrobat— do not comport with riotous living. The circus, to be sure, has its "booze-fighters"; incredible things have been done on the flying trapeze by men who were actually intoxicated when they climbed the swaying rope-ladder—but such are the exceptions to a rule of rigid training and in a way, almost monastic living.

The exigencies of the life forbid dissipation, as a mere matter of self-preservation, and in the circus artist who has attained distinction, the temperate life has usually acquired the tenacity of a confirmed habit. As the trainer of wild animals is usually a kindhearted individual with a philosophical toleration for the inherent strain of treachery in the beast-nature, so the typical first-class performer is usually a decent enough fellow himself, with a philosophical toleration of vice in others.

Hence it follows that no young woman is more carefully chaperoned than the girl of the circus. A circus mother is often honestly scandalized at the latitude which mothers outside the circus allow their daughters. And this chaperonage is by no means confined to these circus families whose instinctive morality is fully as high as the instinctive morality that creates social respectability the world over, in or out of circuses. The purely mercenary desire to keep together the several performers in a family act tends to extreme watchfulness over the members lest sex-attraction should draw them into other affiliations. The management itself is zealously watchful, divides its employees into married and unmarried, and keeps the sexes carefully separated except where matrimony has joined them together and man or management may not put asunder.

If this matrimony is fictitious, it must at least last out the season; and that this sometimes happens may be fairly conceded, to appease the popular notion that all circus people are disreputable. But genealogies, although even the best of them have their black sheep, cannot be founded on fictitious marriages, and the aristocracy of the circus is singularly free from either the convenience of divorce, or the irresponsibility of race-suicide. Said a young trapeze performer in a confidential moment, "Real circus families are like that Four Hundred you read about, only it ain't so easy to break into one of 'em."

Condensed from *The Atlantic Monthly,* May 1909.

RENDEZVOUS OF LOVE

Ben Hecht

One sunny July morning many years ago, Mr. Gilruth, the city editor of the Chicago *Daily News*, called me to his desk. "This ought to be a good story for you," he said, and handed me a sheaf of morning newspaper clippings. Disaster had come to the Hagenbeck-Wallace Circus, traveling in Wisconsin. The circus train had caught fire in the night and scores of performers had been killed and injured.

"Go to Beloit where the circus is reopening today," said Mr. Gilruth. "It ought to make a good feature story."

I arrived in Beloit in time for the parade. It was a brave and heart-touching affair—this parade of a battered, grief-stricken circus.

There were empty seats in the red-and-gold wagons. There were riderless horses, and clowns were missing from the comic contraptions. But there was no hint of mourning; all was as gaudy and blaring as a circus parade should be in a small town on a summer day long ago. Listening to the band and watching the razzle-dazzle of the march, the young and old citizens along the Beloit curbings forgot that almost half the show lay dead and dying in hospitals.

I hunted up Mr. Thompson, the circus press agent. His hands shook and his eyes were red with grief and sleeplessness. Suddenly, as we watched the parade, his mouth opened and he seemed to be looking at a ghost. "That's Gus," he said. "I can't believe it."

He was looking at a man in an ill-fitting red jacket, green silk trousers, and patent-leather boots who sat in the front seat of the lead lion wagon, clutching a whip. He held his head stiffly, eyes front, as the gilded cage rolled past. I got the impression he was asleep, with his eyes open.

"I can't imagine what he's doing there," said Mr. Thompson. "He doesn't belong in the parade. The poor fellow must have gone mad last night."

Mr. Thompson told me the story as we drove out to the circus grounds. Gus was the young Swiss husband of Mademoiselle Lola, the lion tamer, whom he looked on as the greatest woman in the world. He stood outside the big cage during every performance and handed her the whip, the kitchen chair, and other accessories she used for her animal act. At his belt he carried a loaded gun.

"You will use it in case anything happens in the cage," she had said to him. "But be sure it's *necessary*."

Lola and Gus were in one of the sleeping cars when the fire swept the circus train. Gus was knocked unconscious. When he came to, he was lying on the ground beside the burning cars.

Gus got to his feet and pushed his way through the firelit rescue workers. He saw Lola lying on her back. An iron bar had caught her as she was crawling half-burned from under the car, had gone through her body like a harpoon and pinned her to the ground. A large timber had fallen across her chest. But she was still alive. Wild screams came from her as the men toiled in vain to lift the broken section of the car. There was no chance of saving her.

Suddenly the screams stopped. Lola had seen Gus. He was bending over her, sweating and groaning and trying fiercely to help raise the wreckage.

"Gus," Lola whispered, "it's *necessary*."

Gus looked at the agonized face. A doctor spoke.

"There's no chance," the doctor said. "She'll be dead before the wrecking crew can free her."

"It's *necessary*," the whisper came again from Lola. "Please, Gus!"

Gus drew the gun he had never used. He stood listening for a moment to the drawn-out moan from his fearless Lola. Then he fired. Lola became silent.

This was the story Mr. Thompson told me as we drove to the circus.

I looked Gus up in the dressing tent. Two men were arguing with him. "You can't take Lola's place in the cage," one was saying. "You've never worked with the cats, Gus. They'll tear you to ribbons."

"I must do her act," Gus said. He still looked like a man asleep, with his eyes open.

"What good will it do, Gus," the other man argued, "for you to go in there and get hurt?"

"I must do her act," Gus repeated. "It was promised me."

In any other business Gus would have been led away and put into custody for his own good. But the circus is a special world and the things behind the staring white face of Gus in his red jacket were powerful and legitimate arguments.

At the afternoon performance I sat near the animal cage and watched the lions and tigers glide in from the tunnel. The band was playing gaily and the spectators were waiting eagerly. There was a fanfare and the ringmaster stepped into a spotlight. His voice rose in the traditional singsong of the arena,

announcing that Lola, the world-renowned trainer of lions and tigers, had died in the disaster but that her place would be taken by her husband, who was determined to carry on her breathtaking and unrivaled performance as queen of the jungle beasts.

Gus in his red jacket and patent-leather boots, whip in hand, stepped to the door of the cage. The spectators, thrilled at this bit of "the-show-must-go-on" drama, applauded wildly. But no applause came from the watching circus people. They knew that Gus was walking into death.

I saw his face as he stood for a moment outside the little door. It was lighted and eager. Gus was keeping some sort of rendezvous with the wife into whose head he had sent his mercy bullet. I could almost see Lola in the cage, a shadow among the roaring and snarling beasts. And for a moment I knew, as if Gus had told me, that he hoped to find her and become one with her and the wild animals she had loved.

The small door opened and Gus stepped inside the cage. Hardly breathing, I watched. Gus cracked Lola's whip and called the lions and tigers by their names as she had done. The beasts snarled at this impostor, and backed away, roaring.

For several minutes it seemed as if Lola's famous act would go on as it always had. The lions circled angrily toward their tubs. The tigers slid along the sides of the cage toward their pedestals.

Then suddenly Lola's act disintegrated. One of the lions leaped. Two tigers leaped. Gus lay on the ground, claws tearing him and teeth rending him. Men with iron bars rushed into the cage. Guns barked.

Gus was rushed to the hospital. I learned from the doctors that he would survive; but they said he would come out less an arm and a leg.

I sent the story in, and next morning was back at the *News* office.

"That wasn't a bad yarn," Mr. Gilruth greeted me. "But what made the fellow do that? He must have been crazy."

Mr. Gilruth was more in the dark than the reader of this story today. For in the story the *Daily News* had printed there was no mention of what Gus had done under the burning car the night before. I had omitted the detail of Gus's shooting his doomed and screaming wife—because the police are not so sentimental about such things as newspapermen.

"Yes," the sharp Mr. Gilruth continued, "it was a good yarn, but a little confusing. You missed out somewhere on the facts. I felt that as I read it."

Well, here they are, Mr. Gilruth—29 years later—all the facts of the greatest love story I ever saw.

CIRCUS FOLKS ARE FOLKS

Sarah Comstock

During the long years that I have known the circus—have enjoyed a confidential chat with the Strong Lady, have discussed cross-stitch with the supreme Equestrienne, or have dished up gossip with flying families—I have often wondered vaguely just what the lure might be. For me it isn't the lure of spangles and tinsels and gaudy electric glares, or of Breathlessly Hair-Raising, Spectacularly Sensational, and Unparalled Feats of Daring Never Before Attempted. Spangles and Spectacular Sensations alike tarnish with the years and the glitter is no more.

No, it isn't any of these obvious enthrall-ments. I am not agreeably stunned or paralyzed or petrified by the performance. Rather, it is the performers themselves who hold me chained by an affection that age cannot wither. It is the circus people as they are, beyond the spotlight, minus the rouge and tinsel—homely sometimes, and often middle-aged and out of curl, and not especially heroic—it is they themselves that call forth the *neighbor* in me. Few things more warmly call forth that hidden neighbor in me than to enter the great dressing-tent of the circus women, to see a hand waving from one corner, to hear a "hello" ring from another, to have a contortionist's baby goo-goo at me, to meet a smile here, a bit of bursting news there as I pass along the aisle of trunks.

"Look at my sofa pillow! The Sword Swallowing Girl showed me that stitch, and I'm going to embroider this for home next winter," announces an aerialist.

"Oh, I've got a new recipe for spiced peach marmalade, and if we get back before the peaches are all gone, I'm going to put up three dozen jars," declares a bareback rider.

I love these people, not because they raise my hair but because they warm my heart. I love them not because they are performers of intrepid feats, but because they are human beings who like home, husband, wife, children, family cat, baked beans, darning bag, "The Suwanee River," and homemade piccalilli. They are not theatrical, they are not *poseurs*; they leave florid adjectives to the press agent and speak commonplace Americanese; they don't for a moment think of themselves as Unrivalled Marvels of Dauntless Heroism, but as Jennie's husband or Bill's wife or the father or mother of freckle-nosed Dicky.

They don't, during the half-year off the road [1924] live in an atmosphere of glittering splendor, but of simple home comfort—the sort of comfort where a husband gets into his shirt sleeves and takes the clock to pieces because he knows how and that confounded clock tinker down the street doesn't understand his business; where a wife dons her checked apron and makes the waffles herself because Jim always did like her waffles better than any others. Is there any reason why a clown should not take the family clock to pieces or why an acrobat should not perform somersaults with the waffle iron? For the simple but seldom realized truth is that circus folks are folks.

It's a curious little world, entirely sufficient unto itself, this world of the circus actors. It is walled about and seldom approached by outsiders. From generation to generation passes the art of bareback riding or animal training or trapeze flying; "Gran'ma's a grand aerialist, her ring work is only beat by two others, and she's fifty-eight last March." Intermarriage is as much the rule as with royalty . . . rider marries contortionist, juggler marries acrobat, bear trainer marries high-wire dancer. So closely bound, unknown to the outside world and indifferent to it, these people go their own way; and it's a happy, wholesome, sane, homey, folksy way. The other day I asked a trapeze performer if she wanted her seven-year-old son to follow in her own and her husband's footlights.

She shook herself out of the green-and-gold trunks and ostrich feathers of Mlle. Adele, stepped into a cotton kimono, and became Mrs. Muldoon.

"Well, he'd have a grander time outside the circus," she reflected. "S'ciety, and a chance to go to shows and dine at restaurants. He could lay around."

Maternity brooded in Dellie Muldoon's eyes as she kicked off the slop-shoes. "Of course, I'd like him to have the grandest time he can," she went on thoughtfully, "but I'll feel safer about him if I know he's growing up with the show. One boy left us, got into one of those swell sets—my, it was terrible—nearly broke his mother's heart. He went to the dogs till she lost her nerve and fell one day when there wasn't any net. Yes, for health and morals, the one sure place is the circus every time."

Mrs. Muldoon had summed up the attitude of these few hundred people toward the rest of the world. We are the idlers of the earth. We stroll through a life of pleasure . . . seeking leisure, we "lay around" while they toil by the sweat of their brows and at the risk of their necks for our capricious pleasure. We are a good enough sort, but we don't grasp the fact that life is real, life is earnest—a trapeze is not our goal. Many of us may be virtuous, but in our midst vice exists, and to permit a young person

to mingle with the world of outsiders is to run a risk. Acquaintance with that world beyond the wall is discouraged; boys are kept busy at their training, girls are held under a duenna system.

The six acrobatic Hoppe maidens turned to Prunellas at my query:

"What happens when unknown young men write you notes and send you candy?"

They pursed twelve rosy young lips and folded twelve hands primly in the laps of their sky-blue tights.

"We always give them to Momma right away," replied the spokesman of the six. "Three of us are too young to have anything to do with gentlemen. And we three older ones only know those that are properly introduced. Momma reads the letters first, and if they are very respectful, just that they admire our work, then she lets us write and thank them for their kind appreciation. But if they are one speck sentimental—"

"There!" broke in Momma dramatically, and pointed with a direly significant finger to the wastebasket.

The Hoppes are as perfect an example of the old-time circus family as remains with us today. Both grandparents on both sides were acrobats, even as the third generation is now. Poppa Hoppe has trained his flock from the cradle up; their first word is said to have been "flip-flap" and their first step to have been taken on their hands. Momma Hoppe, meanwhile, has clucked like a tiny solicitous hen from the arrival of the first chick, twenty-four years ago, until now that she is followed by six strapping daughters and one son of ten—"all born in Michigan except Arabella, and she was born on the train. I says 'Poppa' says I, 'I think I'd better stay in the Pullman and you go and see if somebody won't come from one of those houses over there.'"

The circus woman's manner of meeting this problem is disheartening to those earnest reformers who strive to convince us that legal measures must be taken to give every woman leisure during her period of contributing to the census. The tent performer simply laughs to scorn the idea that it is any problem at all. She "takes a little time off" and promptly "feels fine again." This wiry Mrs. Hoppe, whose daughters stand inches above her and outweigh her by many pounds—powerful as boy athletes, blooming as a dairymaids' chorus —observes, "I never stop up to two or three weeks before—that's always been aplenty for me. Those that lay around have time to feel bad. I feel better when I go right back to my flipflaps."

It is with the same simple courage that the circus woman meets sickness, pain, or grief wherever she happens to find it. No elaborate systems of mental science, autosuggestion, or Coueism help her to it; she merely takes the knocks as they come, in the arena or out, as all in the day's work. She is totally devoid of the vanity in ill health that leads so many of her sex to select embroidered negligees for future headaches and to date all history from "my operation". She will show all the sympathy in the world to others in trouble, but she has none for herself. I remember coming upon a little aerialist lying curled like a sick kitten on her trunk. A rider, pink tighted and crystal decked, was laying compresses on her head.

"I've got to go now, Honey—that's my call," the rider said, clapping a golden wig over shorn gray hair. "The other girls'll help you in the trapeze. Think you can stick it out?"

"I'll try to," came faint but firm from the heap on the trunk.

Twenty minutes later the sick kitten pulled herself together and went on. I saw the performance.

"Heavens! You've beaten your own record!" I cried as she staggered back to the dressing-tent. "You must have made at least five extra twirls!"

"I'll show myself I don't lay around if I am sick!" she declared stubbornly, and unpretentiously fainted into a Wild West rider's arms. The show, departing that night, left her in a hospital with pneumonia.

And, of course, letters and gifts showered on her up to the day when she swam airily back up into her familiar heights of the Big Top. For these people are knit together in a freemasonry which neither years nor miles can break. Once with the show means forever with it in heart. The other day as the tents were going up in New Jersey, a throng was collected in the midst of swaying elephant trunks, arriving performers, bustling managers, woofing tigers, incoming baggage, peevish midgets carrying their own suitcases, and thumping red vans. I found that the center of the throng was a little old lady, spectacled, snowy, tremulous with delight—her hand being shaken almost to politician's cramp while she beamed up at everybody from ringmaster to cook.

"It's Mrs. Black!" everybody was crying, and more came running to welcome her. They pelted her with news.

"Remember the Lion-Faced Boy? He's back this year. You used to make him lemonade in hot weather; he complained so of being shaggy in the heat."

"The Noonans? Yes, they're with us again. Mrs. Noonan tried settling down but she says people are so cranky outside the show. She kept lion cubs in the apartment and the landlord objected, though she always shut them into the bathroom when he called."

"This is my baby—you wouldn't believe it, would you?" triumphed a pretty gymnast, swinging to her shoulder a lusty cherub of three as you or I might handle a bean-bag.

And all this outpour of welcoming news was by way of proving to a little old lady that because she had been thirty-five years with the circus she would always belong to its innermost circle, even though the infirmities of age have brought her to a life of church sewing societies and pie-making in Newark, New Jersey. "In 1872 Mr. Barnum made me wardrobe mistress," she preens herself, and the very tone in which she utters it carves the name's niche in the Hall of Fame.

The wardrobe mistress is far more than a mere needle and thread. She is guide, philosopher, and friend-in-general of the women's tent. She clk-clks to their babies while they are performing, bathes their sprains when they come off damaged, comforts them when home letters do not arrive, chaperones them through their love affairs, and stands patroness to their social gatherings.

These are many and exclusive. Every season is gayly littered with them, but rarely does anyone outside this happy family enter in. The woman's dressing-tent hums with the buzz of teas and cards; sometimes the girls give a vaudeville and invite the men; and the coffee clubs, bridge clubs, sewing clubs, and reading clubs would warrant a Federation of their own.

The prime social event is a wedding, but this seldom occurs on the road, although romance flourishes like a green bay tree. A gymnast may fall in love with the poodle trainer, carry chocolates to her Pullman section, and take her riding on Sundays, but the wedding is usually put off until the season is over, "so's not to interrupt."

"A fine crop we had last spring," the wardrobe mistress tells me. "Six weddings before we started on the road. And every one inside the show, as it ought to be. Twelve of our finest. A great crop."

The winged god now and then gets ahead of practical considerations. One young aerialist lost his heart to the pretty Cinderella who rode beside him in "The Spec," and slipped off and married her on the sly because she was so vigilantly chaperoned that it was his only chance. The elopement turned out the event of the season. Parents forgave, clowns had a special performance in its honor, the band gave a private concert, teas and card parties and dinners overwhelmed the couple. . . .

Domesticity being the keynote of the circus performers' life, they enjoy a portable domesticity even on the road. No sooner are the car sections and staterooms assigned for the season than up go the curtains which each woman has made for herself. Magazines, photographs, cushions, flowers turn every Pullman section into a miniature home. Mrs. Barna, the rider, confesses in a whisper that "it isn't allowed, but I have to carry a little stove in our stateroom so that I can do a chicken with mushrooms now and then for my husband: he gets so homesick if I don't."

The two fundamental arts of womankind are at the finger tips of every one. Not one but is adept with the needle and the kitchen spoon. Their free hours are divided between the Pullmans in which they sleep, the dining tent served like an army mess, and the dressing-tent; in the latter, eighty-eight women have summered together without one quarrel, which is their boast. . . . There they gather to sew for their babies; to discuss "how hard bears and tigers are on your clothes"; and to repair the arena's daily wreckage of torn ruffles and spilled spangles.

Sunday finds some of them attending church; they usually belong to the Y.W.C.A. and I know some acrobats who always doff lavender tights to teach Sunday School when they reach their home town. But one Darby and Joan couple may be caught of a Sabbath morning slipping off from the Pullman like children at hooky to seek the nearest stream; in their dingy old fishing garb you would never guess them to be the Beau Brummel master of the ring and his devoted spouse, the glittering queen of equestriennes.

A quiet home in the country is the circus performers' dream. Some of them are kept busy through the winter in vaudeville; even so, there's a farm or a small-town house somewhere awaiting them. Their art must be sandwiched in between such domestic acts as shaking down the furnace or seasoning the pot roast; it won't do to get out of practice, therefore the rider lays out a ring in his backyard and the acrobatic parents build a concrete gymnasium under the house and drill the children there after school. "I don't believe in being hard on 'em," Poppa declares. "I don't punish 'em when they don't make thirty flipflaps. I says 'Dicky, what do you want most? I'll give it to you when you get those backward revolutions down fine.' He's only ten, but he says 'A typewriter.' And now he's got it, and he's written a letter on it to a senator, and he's got an answer, too."

Parenthood is proud among these people, but it is wholesomely rigorous as well. A substantial respect for the Three R's prevails; some children are left with relatives to attend school, others travel with the show, but even here their mental sprouting is not neglected. Although you may never have heard the Ringling brothers named with Doctors Eliot, Finley, or Butler among the nation's educators, it is nevertheless true that they have maintained a traveling school.

Manners and morals, too, are given strict attention. A little acrobat came from school in her home town crying bitterly:

"The gym teacher don't like me anymore."

"Now what did you do?" began the maternal investigation.

"I didn't do noth-anything, I did everything she told me in class, even if it was baby work, but while we were waiting I thought I'd put in a little practice, and one of the girls had to yell, 'Look at Ada: she's walking on her hands!' Then another one said, 'Teacher, can you walk on your hands? Course you can, being a gym teacher.' And the teacher got just as red, she was so mad, and she said, 'Well anyhow, I can stand on my head!' and she hasn't spoken to me since."

"Serves you right," came the prompt reproof. "How many times have I told you girls never to show you were superior?"

. . . But in spite of occasional human yearnings, the "circus kid" will cling to his own from birth to death. He will grow up, love and marry, and some day die within it.

There is a story of a bareback rider who was thrown one day by a humping horse. She lay still where she fell.

Her husband, a clown, ran and picked her up, flung her over his shoulder, like a sack of meal, and made a grimace to the audience as he ran off with her. Pausing once, with a comical gesture, he seized her hand and waved it. The audience roared applause for what they took to be a rehearsed finale.

Out back he collapsed. But, "She was always bent on making an artistic exit. Leave the arena artistic, that was her hobby an' I was bound she should do it even then. It's the way she'd want it."

He said it over and over all that day, and all the next day—"It was the way she'd want it"—even when, in a Middle West drizzle the line of black hacks drove to the cemetery. Other clowns and a great rider and even one of the circus owners were the pallbearers. Thus do these people live with, work with, play with, and bury their own.

A CIRCUS BRIDE

Lucia Zora

An investigative child, and by my predilection to stray from home, more than the usual source of annoyance to watchful parents, I wandered, one day when I was about five down the shady street upon which stood our home in the sleepy little upstate town of Cazenovia, New York. The sound of brass-throated music came from a distant street and I hurried there to stand with other children, watching the meager parade of a small wagon show. The clown fascinated me, the horses were beautiful, the performers held for me the same magic lure that they would possess for any child, but the one thing that stood out above all others was the elephant. It became the personification of dreams which are natural to childhood: far-away places, strange, mysterious happenings, adventures, and fields of golden fulfillment, just beyond the horizon. . . .

My parents occupied a position in the world then known as "comfortably fixed." Their ambitions for me took the usual line. I would be given the best education which they could afford, my natural talents would be heightened, and I would be made ready to become the educated and accomplished wife of some good man, according to the dictates of the average conservative American home. Against this cut-and-dried existence I instinctively rebelled even before I had reached my teens. At nineteen my opportunity came. I ran away to the circus. . . .

Years that were comparatively uneventful followed, unless one considers the danger of the hippodrome races, the adventures of the circus in wind and storm and rain, the injuries attendant upon a crash in the chariot races when, four speed-maddened horses plunging before me, I was catapulted into the seats by the breaking of a wheel; unless one counts as events such things as train wrecks, the frenzied cry of "fire" in the darkness of night, the slash of shattering canvas and the dancing of wind-jerked quarter poles in the grip of a hurricane, those years were unpunctuated by anything save the commonplace, as I dragged along, one of many performers in the big top, my ambitions toward the training of animals still far from realized. In fact, it was not until a circus romance entered my life that I found myself truly on the road to the fulfillment of a childhood ambition.

I had been on the Sells-Floto Circus with him for more than a year. He knew that I was Lucia Zora, a "generally useful" actress, and I knew that he was Fred Alispaw, one of the men "working on elephants." That was all. The season came and went—and a new one arrived. With it arrived the information that I was to take a position I had occupied before on other shows, that of riding the leader of the elephant herd during parade. It was good news to me—eager as I was to be near animals, particularly elephants. How good it was even I did not know, for seated on the head of the old elephant as we made our first parade was the newly promoted menagerie superintendent, Fred Alispaw.

We became acquainted, and with our first conversation, I made known my love of animals. It led to other meetings, gradually resolving itself into a sort of professor and pupil arrangement, by which I went into the menagerie every afternoon to learn from the superintendent the things I craved to know: little stories about the natures of caged animals, their habits, peculiarities, and methods by which they were trained. A natural sequence followed: friendship, love, and finally the reception of a marriage proposal while seated on a bale of hay behind a lion cage.

However, it really was more romantic than it sounds. For more than a week, Fred Alispaw and I had been endeavoring to save the life of a malformed lion cub suffering from rickets. Each day, during my lesson hour, it was a part of our duties to minister to the stricken baby, until it became to us almost like a human child, and we watched over it with the care a physician would bestow upon a dying infant.

One afternoon the end came. I had the cub in my arms, and Fred and I were seated on a bale of hay behind a den of roaring lions. He had been massaging the beast's muscles, and suddenly ceased.

"Seems to me he's mighty quiet," he said.

I looked down. The eyes were glazed, the skin drawn from the tiny teeth.

"Why, Fred!" I exclaimed. "He's dead!"

Then the tears came. A second later, I felt an arm go about my shoulder.

"Don't do that, Zora, please don't," came in pleading tones. "I—I just can't bear to see you cry."

Then with a dead lion in my arms, I heard a man tell me that he loved me, and rather dazedly, I admit, heard myself answer that his love was reciprocated. Six weeks later, we attempted to elope—for weddings in the circus are riotous affairs. We managed the ceremony very well, but in some manner the information became known. That night, as we made ready to take our positions on Old Mom, the leader

of the herd, for our entrance in tournament, pretext after pretext was made to delay us, until finally we rushed for our places at the last possible moment, to be boosted to the back of Old Mom so hastily that we failed to notice much of anything save the fact that the procession was starting.

We entered the tent, to find the audience suddenly boisterous. Fingers pointed. Children yelped with merriment. I looked somewhat vacuously toward my husband, bobbing before me on the elephant's head, and he, in turn, stared as blankly at me. Then I happened to glance toward the rear.

Tied to Old Mom's tail, and dragging in the wood chips of the hippodrome track, was the greatest collection of old shoes that I ever had seen, while behind us marched a clown collection of a minister, a groom, a clown-faced bride, carrying a beautiful bouquet of cabbages, and flanked by her bridesmaids and flower girls, daintily distributing "flowers" of carrots, onions, potatoes, and spinach in the path of the happy "bridal couple," while accompanying clowns pointed up at us, and with their mimicry sympathized in turn with both Fred and me. About this time I became aware of the fact that Old Mom was carrying a banner, and leaning over the side of the howdah, I saw:

LOOK US OVER!   JUST MARRIED!
BRIDE AND GROOM!

Then the Wedding March by the band— and deluges of rice. Scattered every ten feet around the entire hippodrome track were canvasmen, each with a big bag of it, intent upon showering us. The audience, of course, roared with merriment, and I learned what it really meant to be a circus bride.

But at that, I had little time for details. As soon as the tournament was over, the boisterous circus crew promptly kidnapped my husband, hid him somewhere around the show train and held him prisoner for three days.

From *Sawdust and Solitude* by Lucia Zora, edited by Courtney Ryley Cooper. Little, Brown & Co., Boston, 1928.

THE RING OF TIME

E. B. White

After the lions had returned to their cages, creeping angrily through the chutes, a little bunch of us drifted away and into an open doorway nearby, where we stood for a while in semidarkness, watching a big brown circus horse go harumphing around the practice ring. His trainer was a woman of about forty, and the two of them, horse and woman, seemed caught up in one of those desultory treadmills of afternoon from which there is no apparent escape. The day was hot, and we kibitzers were grateful to be briefly out of the sun's glare. The long rein, or tape, by which the woman guided her charge counterclockwise in his dull career formed the radius of their private circle, of which she was the revolving center; and she, too, stepped a tiny circumference of her own, in order to accommodate the horse and allow him his maximum scope. She had on a short-skirted costume and a conical straw hat. Her legs were bare and she wore high heels, which probed deep into the loose tanbark and kept her ankles in a state of constant turmoil. The great size and meekness of the horse, the repetitious exercise, the heat of the afternoon, all exerted a hypnotic charm that invited boredom; we spectators were experiencing a languor—we neither expected relief nor felt entitled to any. We had paid a dollar to get into the grounds, to be sure, but we had got our dollar's worth a few minutes before, when the lion trainer's whiplash had got caught around a toe of one of the lions. What more did we want for a dollar?

Behind me I heard someone say, "Excuse me, please," in a low voice. She was halfway into the building when I turned and saw her—a girl of sixteen or seventeen, politely threading her way through onlookers who blocked the entrance. As she emerged in front of us, I saw that she was barefoot, her dirty little feet fighting the uneven ground. In most respects she was like any of two or three dozen showgirls you encounter if you wander about the winter quarters of Mr. John Ringling North's circus, in Sarasota—cleverly proportioned, deeply browned by the sun, dusty, eager, and almost naked. But her grave face and the naturalness of her manner gave her a sort of quick distinction and brought a new note into the gloomy octagonal building where we had all cast our lot for a few moments. As soon as she had squeezed through the crowd, she spoke a word or two to the older woman, whom I took to be her mother, stepped to the ring, and waited while the horse coasted to a stop in front of her. She gave the animal a couple of affectionate swipes on his enormous neck and then swung herself aboard. The horse immediately resumed his rocking canter, the woman goading him on, chanting something that sounded like "Hop! Hop!"

In attempting to recapture this mild spectacle, I am merely acting as recording secretary for one of the oldest of societies—the society of those who, at one time or another, have surrendered, without even a show of resistance, to the bedazzlement of a circus rider. As a writing man, or secretary, I have always felt

From pp. 51-55 "The Ring of Time" —Fiddler Bayou, March 22, 1956—in *The Points of My Compass* by E. B. White. Copyright © 1956 by E. B. White. Originally appeared in *The New Yorker*, and reprinted by permission of Harper & Row, Publishers, Inc.

charged with the safekeeping of all unexpected items of worldly or unworldly enchantment, as though I might be held personally responsible if even a small one were to be lost. But it is not easy to communicate anything of this nature. The circus comes as close to being the world in microcosm as anything I know; in a way, it puts all the rest of show business in the shade. Its magic is universal and complex. Out of its wild disorder comes order; from its rank smell rises the good aroma of courage and daring; out of its preliminary shabbiness comes the final splendor. And buried in the familiar boasts of its advance agents lies the modesty of most of its people. For me the circus is at its best before it has been put together. It is at its best at certain moments when it comes to a point, as through a burning glass, in the activity and destiny of a single performer out of so many. One ring is always bigger than three. One rider, one aerialist, is always greater than six. In short, a man has to catch the circus unawares to experience its full impact and share its gaudy dream.

The ten-minute ride the girl took achieved—as far as I was concerned, who wasn't looking for it, and quite unbeknownst to her, who wasn't even striving for it—the thing that is sought by performers everywhere, on whatever stage, whether struggling in the tidal currents of Shakespeare or bucking the difficult motion of a horse. I somehow got the idea she was just cadging a ride, improving a shining ten minutes in the diligent way all serious artists seize free moments to hone the blade of their talent and keep themselves in trim. Her brief tour included only elementary postures and tricks, perhaps because they were all she was capable of, perhaps because her warmup at this hour was unscheduled and the ring was not rigged for a real practice session. She swung herself off and on the horse several times, gripping his mane. She did a few knee-stands—or whatever they are called—dropping to her knees and quickly bouncing back up on her feet again. Most of the time she simply rode in a standing position, well aft on the beast, her hands hanging easily at her sides, her head erect, her straw-colored ponytail lightly brushing her shoulders, the blood of exertion showing faintly through the tan of her skin. Twice she managed a one-foot stance—a sort of ballet pose, with arms outstretched. At one point the neck strap of her bathing suit broke and she went twice around the ring in the classic attitude of a woman making minor repairs to a garment. The fact that she was standing on the back of a moving horse while doing this invested the matter with a clownish significance that perfectly fitted the spirit of the circus—jocund, yet charming. She just rolled the strap into a neat ball and stowed it inside her bodice while the horse rocked and rolled beneath her in dutiful innocence. The bathing suit proved as self-reliant as its owner and stood up well enough without benefit of strap.

The richness of the scene was in its plainness, its natural condition—of horse, of ring, of girl, even to the girl's bare feet that gripped the bare back of her proud and ridiculous mount. The enchantment grew not out of anything that happened or was performed but out of something that seemed to go round and around and around with the girl, attending her, a steady gleam in the shape of a circle—a ring of ambition, of happiness, of youth. (And the positive pleasures of equilibrium under difficulties.) In a week or two, all would be changed, all (or almost all) lost: the girl would wear makeup, the horse would wear gold, the ring would be painted, the bark would be clean for the feet of the horse, the girl's feet would be clean for the slippers that she'd wear. All, all would be lost.

As I watched with the others, our jaws adroop, our eyes alight, I became painfully conscious of the element of time. Everything in the hideous old building seemed to take the shape of a circle, conforming to the course of the horse. The rider's gaze, as she peered straight ahead, seemed to be circular, as though bent by force of circumstance; then time itself began running in circles, and so the beginning was where the end was, and the two were the same, and one thing ran into the next and time went round and around and got nowhere. The girl wasn't so young that she did not know the delicious satisfaction of having a perfectly behaved body and the fun of using it to do a trick most people can't do, but she was too young to know that time does not really move in a circle at all. I thought: "She will never be as beautiful as this again"—a thought that made me acutely unhappy—and in a flash my mind (which is too much of a busybody to suit me) had projected her twenty-five years ahead, and she was now in the center of the ring, on foot, wearing a conical hat and high-heeled shoes, the image of the older woman, holding the long rein, caught in the treadmill of an afternoon long in the future. "She is at the enviable moment in life [I thought] when she believes she can go once around the ring, make one complete circuit, and at the end be exactly the same age as at the start." Everything in her movements, her expression, told you that for her the ring of time was perfectly formed, changeless, predictable, without beginning or end, like the ring in which she was travelling at this moment with the horse that wallowed under her. And then I slipped back into my trance, and time was circular again—time, pausing quietly with the rest of us, so as not to disturb the balance of a performer.

Her ride ended as casually as it had begun. The older woman stopped the horse, and the girl slid to the ground. As she walked toward us to leave, there was a quick, small burst of applause. She smiled broadly, in surprise and pleasure; then her face suddenly regained its gravity and she disappeared through the door.

It has been ambitious and plucky of me to attempt to describe what is indescribable, and I have failed, as I knew I would. But I have discharged my duty to my society; and besides, a writer, like an acrobat, must occasionally try a stunt that is too much for him. At any rate, it is worth reporting that long before the circus comes to town, its most notable performances have already been given. Under the bright lights of the finished show, a performer need only reflect the electric candle power that is directed upon him; but in the dark and dirty old training rings and in the makeshift cages, whatever light is generated, whatever excitement, whatever beauty, must come from original sources—from internal fires of professional hunger and delight, from the exuberance and gravity of youth. It is the difference between planetary light and the combustion of stars.

Three rings: Ringling Bros.-Barnum & Bailey

The Flying Gaonas from Mexico

The three Mecners

Prince Paul, midget clown

Friends: clowns, an elephant, and a boy

Otto Griebling

— La Toria (Victoria Unus), whose act is similar to that of the immortal Leitzel —

Ingeborg Rhodin

Charly Baumann and his tigers

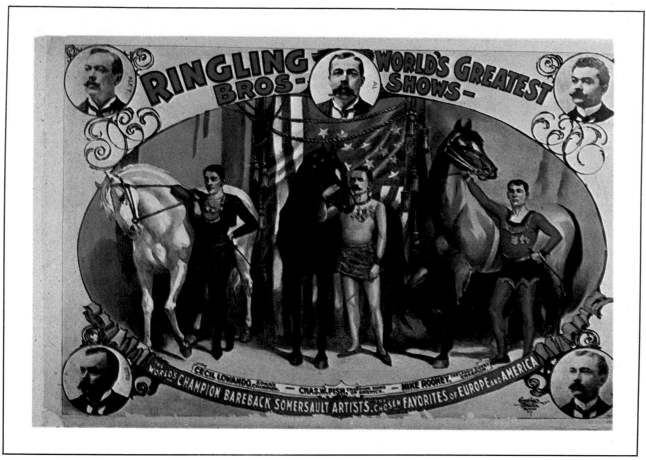

1895

1891

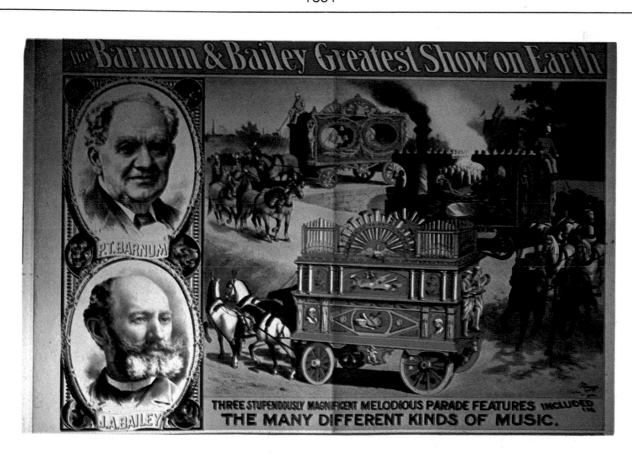

1897

1899

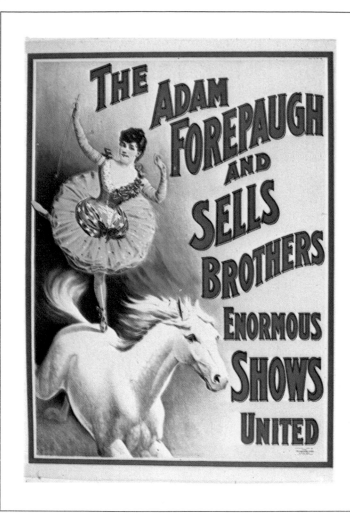

1900

1892

1904

1900

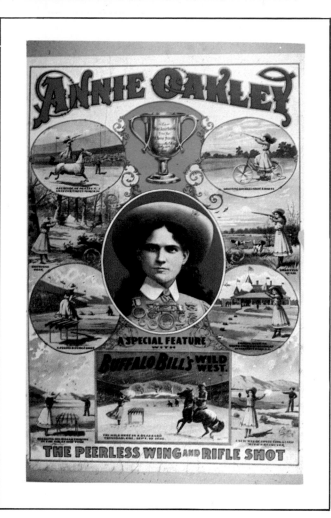

1898

1908

Circus Room, Tom M. Scaperlanda Collection, San Antonio, Texas

The Circus, A. Logan, Collection of Edgar William and Bernice Chrysler Chrysler Garbisch

Bareback Riders, W. H. Brown, National Gallery of Art, Washington, D.C., Gift of Edgar William and Bernice Chrysler Garbisch

Clowns by Charles Hammond, 1969

Family of Saltimbanques, Pablo Picasso, National Gallery of Art, Washington, D.C., Chester Dale Collection

UNDER THE BIG TOP IN INDIA

Zarine Merchant

A visit to the circus is an enchanting experi-ence for children of all ages. Be they six or sixty-six, they sit rapt and wide-eyed as all the wonders of fairyland parade before them. But if one looks behind the scenes, if one sees through the gilt and the grease-paint to the tragic actuality of circus life, fairyland more often than not dissolves into a heart-breaking world more akin to that of Cinderella, a cruel world of drudgery and back-breaking work that kills all but the most hardy.

At show time all is aglitter. The Big Top reverberates to the fullthroated applause of thousands of voices, young and old. But the morning after, silence reigns and all is still.

The animals laze in quiet contentment. There are more than 200 of them, but each one is an individual whose likes and dislikes are known and catered to. There is Fantoosh the elephant, a huge tusker, the only male amongst 19 females, who likes to live alone with his mate Anarkali. Despite his two and a half tons, Fantoosh is so sensitive that he once ran amuck in the streets of Bombay after a small tiff with Anarkali. At the other end of the scale is Giddoo, the dog who acts as guardian angel to the horses (he once got lost and walked more than 50 miles to find his way back to the horse enclosure, where he collapsed), and Ramu, the pelican who prefers the company of the elephants to that of his own kind.

In sharp contrast, the circus humans are the picture of industry and perseverance. For many of the feats that one sees performed so casually—with seemingly effortless coordina-tion and balance—have taken years to perfect.

Shobha, a cute, grinning, eight-year-old, practices balancing and somersaulting till her bones ache. But that is no signal for rest. The grin disappears but she continues dog-gedly on in sheer determination till the act becomes second nature with her. That is the only way to learn, the trainers emphasize. There can be no shortcut to perfection and anything short of perfection can endanger a life.

The acrobats must have bones of rubber and muscles of steel. That is why all circus folk are either born to the life or join it at a very early age. Young bones set early, if broken, and young hearts know no fear.

Just as the animals, when they come to the circus, give up most of the habits of the jungle, the children, on joining, renounce most of the pleasures of ordinary youngsters. They can have no family ties except with the circus family, an education that is sketchy at best, or altogether non-existent, no life other than the circus life of thrills and chills, of accidents and constant travelling, of hard work and only a few rewards. These consist of a rare visit home or an occasional trip to the cinema to relieve the routine. Three shows a day plus constant practice and exercise hardly leave time for anything else.

For most of them the circus is not only their family, it is their only world. They never know any other and they are content to live and die within its all-embracing folds.

Take lithe, swarthy Konnan for instance. At 60 he is today the oldest performing circus artiste in India, still does his daily stint on the flying trapeze and hopes to keep at it till he dies, or at least "till I am 80." He is a remarkable man who looks about half his age because he is always brimming with youthful ideas. "I am atomic," he says proudly in his limited English, and a horde of children and grandchildren bear him out. Konnan, like almost all circus people, comes from the home of the circus—Tellicherry, in north Kerala.

For circus folk there is neither the glamour of the cinema nor the fame and the monetary rewards of the sports world. Yet the lure of the Big Top is so strong that few ever leave the circus once the sawdust and the sequins, the applause and the excitement get into their blood.

The light that comes into a little child's eyes or the occasional smile that flits across the face of a bored adult is their only compensation.

The circus fraternity is the most democratic in the world, and all performers, from the star of the show to the smallest "extra," live and work in complete harmony and cooperation. They must, for their lives depend on team-work. In spite of their hard and dangerous lives circus people are the most hospitable and friendly of all.

Condensed from *The Illustrated Weekly of India,* February 11, 1968. Used by permission.

THE IMPROBABLE CIRCUS

"Mr. Harper"

On the evening before the circus opened in New York in April, I went to a dress rehearsal. Well, not exactly a dress rehearsal, for although the trapeze clowns did not deign to dress, and at the moment when my wife and I—a little late—entered the vast arena of Madison Square Garden, the great Emmett Kelly was standing at the edge of a group of them under a strong spotlight in mid-arena, wearing nothing more comical than a gray suit with a gray fedora and a light overcoat over his arm. As representatives of the press we had the run of the whole place, so that we could alternate between sitting with a few hundred other people to watch the dancing horses and the swooping aerialists go through their magical acts, and strolling through the backstage passageways where the performers were awaiting their cues. It was our exploration of those concrete corridors that made the greatest impression on me, I confess; for it is one thing to look at the improbable when it is on public exhibition under the glare of the lights, and another thing to come upon it casually, off guard. The net effect, I found, was curiously destructive of one's sense of what is normal and expectable.

Out in those backstage corridors there were a great many people coming and going, or gathered in little groups. Some of them were presumably visitors like ourselves, though a few may have been clowns in street dress; but one was eight feet tall or thereabouts, and several were only waist-high. One was walking on his hands; another, in tights, had a little girl with him, also in tights, and every now and then, with a fine economy of effort, he would hoist her about his head and hold her there at arm's length. We came upon two little rooms opening off the corridor; in one of them was a woman in a dashing evening dress spectacularly ornamented with plumes. The bear's attendant, perhaps? The costume didn't seem quite right for that, but by this time one answer seemed just about as logical as another.

We arrived at the wide ramp which leads up to the corner of the arena and had to draw back to let a herd of elephants go by. Suddenly there was a cry of, "Watch it!" just behind my ear and I jumped nimbly forward out of the way of a pair of horses dragging a neat Victorian carriage. A little further along a group of acrobats were chatting together in a language unintelligible to me, and for that matter unidentifiable; and a little later—just after we had passed the man walking on his hands and a tall man practicing cuffing a dwarf—we confronted a pretty girl in a black leotard, standing behind a large object on the floor which appeared to be a rather elaborate chandelier. She informed us in a distinctly Vassar accent that five acts later she would be going on with the chandelier balanced on her head. This now seemed such an altogether reasonable thing to do with a chandelier that we didn't think to ask her what, if anything, it was supposed to symbolize.

Presently we turned and walked down the wide, curving ramp—watch out here for elephant dung—to the basement, where they have the power plant, and the stable, and the lions, and things like that. And as we passed the sideshow platform on our way out to the world of the probable, we saw on it just one person—a woman in perfectly ordinary clothes, engaged in a matter-of-fact way in packing a trunk. But there was something a little queer even about this operation, for the blankets she was packing seemed to be heaving of their own accord, and I caught a glimpse of something long and slinky that she was poking into place.

She was packing her python. Of course.

CIRCUS KIDS

Bill Ballantine

The circus—super colossal, splendiferous, spangled spectacle—is just a homey, pleasant place to children who travel with it. A shabby stray dog sniffing around the circus backyard (behind the big top) is much more fun for a circus kid than the same old elephants, giraffes, and lions-'n-tigers which, seen week in and week out, become commonplace.

Actually, the most fascinating attraction to the canvas-covered kids of the Ringling Bros.–Barnum & Bailey circus [1952] is a runty green parrot owned by the manager's wife.

Even clowns can't get much of a tumble. Their wild-eyed shenanigans are taken for granted in a community alive with snake charmers, aerialists, midgets, sword swallowers, fire eaters, giants, and people who can balance on many parts of their anatomies, including the forefinger.

Circus kids like clowns well enough (most of the littler boys want to be one) and they're often fond of the real men behind the false noses, but their interest in buffoonery tends to be coldly professional.

Take for instance, David and Alan, Welsh tykes with the Alzana troupe of highwire walkers (Hairbreadth Harold! He walks and *leaps!* Where *Ayn-n-gels* fear to tread!). Twice daily for one entire season, rain or shine, they watched Lou Jacobs, famous clown in the center ring with his Lilliputian comedy auto. If Lou left out one tiny bit of familiar funny business, they'd be around to his dressing room after the act and solemnly tick him off about it.

Little Jimmy, the midget stooge in the number, finally asked Alan why all this gigantic interest, and was told that when they got bigger, the kids planned to "take over the act." They were only four years old then or Lou might have worried.

In one respect circus youngsters are like most other kids: they all think Mama and Papa are the greatest people on earth! At performance entrances to the big top during the show usually there will be a circus kid watching a circus parent.

Maybe it's one-year-old Mousie in open-mouthed awe of her bespangled daddy making fools of his wild performing bears. Mousie always stands quite alone at the edge of the Hippodrome track, but at least one pair of discreet but alert eyes is looking out for her— the ring master's perhaps, or a roughneck prop hand's or an usher's.

Tony Albertino (Zoppe) will likely be in the center back-track entrance during the riding act perched on the shoulders of the Hungarian acrobat who is a genuine gypsy, watching his father ride the big bouncy rosinbacks.

And Gilbert, aged four, stands way-off down by the bandstand straining through the maze of lights, aerial rigging, and quarter poles, to see his Mama swinging on her trapeze high above the center ring. "Oo la la! Mama!" says Gilbert as his Mama (billed as

La Norma, Denmark's Bird of Paradise) hangs by her teeth and whirls so fast her shock of wavy golden hair looks like spun maple sugar.

During the summer usually more than a dozen children travel with the Ringling Bros. Circus, a few less in the fall when schoolagers return to Sarasota (the winter-quarters-town in Florida) to add book learning to sawdust learning.

Circus families are never too busy to celebrate their children's birthdays. Tino Zoppe's party was especially festive. Colored balloons and serpentine tape were strung from the dressing-room wagon to the big top's sidewall; there was a large cake drooling with globs of pink roses. Refreshments were jelly beans, chocolate buds, peanuts, and soda pop—laid out on the flat round side of one of the big reels that carry light cables into the main tent. All the kids were there, along with several performers and a couple of wistful-looking ushers whose kids were back home, faraway.

Albertino didn't rate the full circus band (as grown-up circus birthday celebrators do), so little Jimmy, the midget, played *Happy Birthday* on his trumpet. He also brought each of the kids a present (trinkets from the local Five-and-Dime). Antoinette, Tino's big sister, wouldn't let Jimmy kiss her because her mother told her never to let little boys get fresh. Jimmy is twenty-eight. The baby gorillas couldn't come at the last minute as Mlle. Toto had a slight sniffle, and the keeper was afraid the kids might catch it.

There were plenty of up-ended buckets for the kids to sit on. The Zoppe wagon was occupied by eight people: Cucciola, the bareback-riding midget; Tino's parents Alberto and Jenny; his two sisters; Alberto's sister, Tosca; and the family's *Grandmacita* (her job is making the frilly pink paper hoops that Alberto leaps through in his act).

The kids had a big time. Young Alfie wore the cowboy outfit that one of the clowns had given him. (He wore it to bed the first night, just like any American kid.) Gilbert with his toes stuck in Dixie cups gave a credible imitation of Miss Lola dancing on her tight wire. Cucciola exhibited his baby alligator "(He don't bite; sticka-you finger in and you see").

Albertino's papa showed home movies on the wagon's open silver door: Albertino one day old, Albertino fourteen days old holding on to papa's finger, Albertino seven months old doing somersaults on a bed, and Albertino at one year poised on one foot on papa's hand held high overhead. Rose Hanlon, the lady clown, soulfully accompanied the cinema production on her trombone.

Circus children all get along together famously. For them, there is no racial intolerance and no wrong side of the tracks. They *all* live down by the railroad, right *on* the tracks.

Circus mamas are likely to be robustly healthy; they take childbirth casually.

Miss Lola rode a unicycle on her tightwire until she was seven months along with her little Emil. Lola kept her pregnancy secret until six months, her ballet tutu being a great maternity garment. At seven months she casually visited an obstetrician in Providence, Rhode Island. He didn't know her profession. "Is it all right if I keep on walking?" she asked.

"Depends on what kind of walking."

She flipped open a magazine which had a picture of her on the wire. The doctor blanched, then made her promise to get down off the wire right away. Well, maybe tomorrow, because he had tickets for the circus that night and he wanted to see with his own eyes a seven-months pregnancy riding a unicycle across a tightwire.

Circus kids all love circus life and hate to leave the sawdust world for school in the fall. I was sitting with Minnie Alzana, Fearless Harold's wife, in their wagon just after Alan had left for Sarasota.

" 'E didn't cry or make a fuss," Minnie said, "but 'e came right out and said 'ed rather stay on the circus. The day before 'e left for school 'is father took 'im on the wire. At first 'e didn't want to go, but I said, 'C'mon, ducks, I'll go too.' And when 'e went.' Arald wanted to see 'ow 'e'd react if e'd' get scared or not; 'e 'adn't been up for a long while. 'E liked being pulled up on a rope around 'im. 'Arald took 'im across on 'is shoulders. . . .

Minnie marked her place in a paperback she was reading (*Chad Hanna*) and continued. "We used to take 'im on 'Arald's shoulders before 'e was three. Arald would tie 'is foot in so 'e couldn't fall, but people made complaints and the police came and we 'ad to stop."

You know, if I was a circus kid I too would 'ate to leave such a wonderful place.

PART SEVEN

ON THE ROAD

TOURING EASTERN
U.S. AND CANADA

John Durang

About this time [1787] a Monsieur Placide, a celebrated tight rope dancer, and his wife, with a Frenchman called the Little Devil, famous on the slack rope and tumbling, all ar-rived. . . . Mr. Placide was the best tight rope dancer that ever was in America. I did the clown to the rope which got me a good benefit; at least I cleared three hundred dollars, which was a great sum at that time.

About this time [1793] the renowned equestrian, Mr. Ricketts, arrived in Philad'a from Scotland. He served his time to Mr. Hughes the equestrian near Black Friar Bridge, London. He visited our theatre on a night's performance. Next day he sent me a polite note to wait on him. I was punctuel to the appoint-ment. He told me he was much gratifyed in seeing me dance on the tightrope, slack rope, wire, a hornpipe and Harlequin; that I would be of infinite service in a circus—and thereupon offered me an engagement. . . .

[The troupe—John Ricketts with less than half a dozen other performers—toured Canada in 1797.]

We put up at a Captain Pomroy, a private French house, the stable bad, but the best hay I ever smelt, and good oats. In the course of a conversation with the Captain I drop'd a hint about supper, for we had not eat anything the whole day. They placet on the table a large earthen dish of milk and two spoons. Mr. Ricketts wished to eat his milk in a seperate dish. They brought him a large wash bason out of which he eat his milk and bread. The whole family sat round the table looking at us.

The Captain showed Mr. Ricketts and me into his bedroom to a bed prepared on the floor for us in the opposide corner to his own. The family still looking at us, we did not like to undress, so we pull'd off only our coats, west, and boots, and lay in bed. The groom and our boys slept in the hay loft. As for our parts, we did not sleep the whole night. . . .

[In Montreal] I laid out the circus in a drawing for the carpenters and mark'd out the skeleton of the circus. It was built without a top for day performance. In two weeks it was compleated with ring, state, dressing room, and stables. The house was devided, a row of boxes elivated, and the pit underneth.

The Canadian inhabitants thought our horses were supernatural, that it was impossible horses could dance and keep time to music, that the man dancing a hornpipe on the saddle while the horse was in full speed; Mr. Ricketts was very great in that. We were the first equestrans that ever was in Canada, therefore the Canadian inhabitants were ignorant of the science and thought the whole a conjuration. However, so far they were right that a horse can not keep time to music—we allways adapted our music to keep time with the horses. They soon were convincet that we are like other people, and much pleased with us.

From *The Memoirs of John Durang, American Actor 1785-1816*. Published from the original manuscript for the Historical Society of York County and for the American Society for Theatre Research by the University of Pittsburgh Press. Alan Downer, editor.

154

"HEY, RUBE!"

Dan Rice

The circus fight is not [at the turn of the century] what it used to be. Canvasmen have forgotten the traditions of their younger days, and it is no uncommon thing for the whole circus to go into a town, show two or three times, and then go on to the next town without having once heard the cry of "Hey, Rube!" and without having seen or heard of a single fight.

"Hey, Rube!" is the battle cry of the showmen. No one ever raises it unless he is in dire straits, and every man who hears it is bound by the law of self-preservation to go to an instant relief. The cry was raised in Montpelier some twenty-five years ago, and the fight that followed was so severe that the legislature for many years refused to grant circuses a license in Vermont.

Older men of today will remember some of the fights back in the days before the [Civil] war, when it really looked as if the spirit of the country had developed to such a point that a little blood-letting was necessary. But one does not need to go back to antebellum eras. Circus fights continued clear down to the end of the last decade.

Scranton, Pa., and, indeed, every coal-mining or iron-working district, was expected to furnish a fight every time the canvas was raised in it. And educational centres had a much worse name for this species of lawlessness than did the rude districts of the unlettered plains. It took unnumbered thumpings for the men at Yale to learn they could not successfully lam the whole travelling outfit, but they seemed to have imbibed wisdom at last. Ann Arbor, the seat of the Michigan University, was one of the last to learn the salutary lesson.

Down at Jacksonville, Tex., in 1873, Robinson's show undertook to exhibit and they got into one of the hardest fights on record. The battle lasted from three in the afternoon till midnight, and twenty-three men were killed and more than fifty wounded. At Somerset, Ky., in 1856, Barnum's show ran across a very bad gang of railroad men, and in the fight which followed, twenty persons were killed.

Showmen who tell about these things always lay the blame on the bad men of the town or neighborhood where the trouble occurs, or on too officious peace officers who try to exercise all their authority in a minute. But it often happens that the showmen are themselves to blame. Sharpers and gamblers of various descriptions travelled with the circus and kept in the favor of the fighters with the show by giving them a share of the money they would take from the countrymen. When the fleeced native would insist on the return of his money, he would be met with the whole fighting force of the company.

Of late years the big shows that chiefly go to large cities have had more peaceful experiences, and the fight that turns out a riot is fast becoming one of the obsolete things.

Quoted by Maria Ward Brown in *The Life of Dan Rice*. J. J. Little & Co., New York, 1901.

EXPERIENCES OF A PIONEER SHOWMAN

W. C. Coup

No other human being can realize like the showman the volume of dread hardship and disaster held by those two small words, "bad roads." At the time of my breaking-in [1860], we were passing through a section of the country in the Southwest, over such wretchedly constructed highways that the slightest fall of rain was sufficient to convert them into rivers of mud. The heavy wagons would sink to their hubs in the mire and the whole train would be stopped.

Then followed a scene too picturesque to escape the attention of even the poor fellows who were half dead from lack of sleep. By the light of flaring torches a dozen big draft horses would be hitched to the refractory wagon. Inspired by the shouts, curses, and sometimes the blows of the teamsters, the animals would join in a concerted pull that made their muscles stand out like knotted ropes. But often a battalion of six teams would fail to start a wagon.

Then the shout would go down the line for Romeo. In a few minutes the wise old elephant would come splashing through the mud with an air that seemed to say, "I thought you'd have to call on me!" He knew his place and would instantly take his stand behind the mired wagon. After he had carefully adjusted his huge frontal against the rear end of the vehicle the driver would give the command, "Mile up!" Gently, but with a tremendous power, Romeo would push forward, the wagon would

start, and lo! the pasty mud would close in behind the wheels like the Red Sea.

Perhaps the most disheartening of all bad-road experiences is that of losing the way—a thing which happened with perverse frequency. Just imagine yourself a member of such a caravan. You have slept four hours out of sixteen and are crawling along in the face of a drenching, blinding rainstorm—soaked, hungry and dazed. The caravan has halted a dozen times in the forepart of the night to pull out wagons and repair breakdowns. But it halts again, and the word "lost" is passed back along the line of wagons. This means retracing the route back to the forks of the road miles in the rear. Many an old circus man has wished himself dead on hearing the word "lost" under these conditions.

Some runs, however, were especially pleasant. For example, I recall one Sunday run, in the 1870's, of three hundred miles across an Indian reservation between a town in Kansas and another in southern Texas. The day was beautiful. . . . Towards noon we halted and erected cooking tents and stables. The horses and animals were looked after and a dinner was cooked by the attachés. After dinner they formed congenial knots and strolled around while the "hash slingers" washed the dishes and the men once more loaded up. We carried at that time an excellent troupe of Jubilee singers, and they burst into song, alternating their quaint camp-meeting songs with others in which the majority of the attachés could join. The band, too, caught the infection and produced their instruments and we enjoyed a vocal and instrumental feast. Just at dusk, when the stars were beginning to appear, before starting for the night's run, the Jubes sang "Nearer, My God, to Thee" to the full accompaniment of the band and with a refrain swelled by everyone able to sing. The rolling prairie, the beautiful trees, the perfect weather, the joyous spirits of every one present, the melodious voices of the Jubilee singers, and the grand strains produced by thirty skilled musicians, combined to produce music such as man seldom hears.

"All aboard!" is shouted, and every one climbs into the car. The whistle sounds and off you go, past miles of beautiful scenery and occasional Indian villages. Everything is quiet and everyone seems to be drinking in the beauty of the scene or sits lost in thought. With quiet "goodnights" one after another slipped off to bed to awake to another day's hurry and bustle.

One morning we started north from a small Missouri town, with our caravan—a mile in length—stretching out like a long serpent. The elaborate and gilded chariots, the piebald Arabian horses, the drove of shambling camels, and the huge swaying elephants gave a touch of genuine Oriental picturesqueness to the scene, strangely out of keeping with the wild Western landscape and surroundings.

On every hand the prairies were carpeted with wild flowers in the greatest variety and profusion. Their fragrance even reached me as I stretched out at full length on the top of a lumbering chariot.

Later the lurch of the wagon aroused me, and I started up with a sense of unaccountable alarm. The first object which met my eyes was a jackrabbit, sitting on his haunches not more than two rods from the trail we were following. Knowing the habitual timidity of these creatures, the boldness of this one

surprised me greatly. He sat there with his ears cocked straight up, his nose working nervously, and his heart pounding so heavily that its pulsations shook his gray sides. Not until the wagon had passed did the rabbit stir. Then he dropped upon all fours and vanished in a gray streak traveling in a line parallel with the course of the caravan and keeping only a few rods from our trail. While I was still pondering over the strange conduct of the animal I saw a rattler emerge from the grass into the beaten trail only a few feet in front of the "off leader" of our four-horse team. Naturally I expected to see the snake coil and strike the horse, but he did nothing of the kind—simply avoided the horse's hoofs and then slipped away into the grass beyond. What was the meaning of the strange spell which seemed suddenly to have taken possession of the wild animals and reptiles of the plain through which we were traveling?

Before I had arrived at any conclusions, the captive animals in the darkened cages began to show signs of unusual restlessness. The lions and tigers began a strange moaning unlike their ordinary roars and growls. From the monkey cages came plaintive, half-human cries. These sounds were taken up by all the animals big and little. The elephants trumpeted, the camels screamed, and every animal took part in the weird chorus. Then the air seemed to take on a hazy appearance, particularly in the direction from which we had come.

Finally the truth dawned upon me—the prairie was on fire! By turning backward and straining my eyes I fancied I could make out a cloud of smoke far in the rear of the caravan. Then I caught sight of a man on horseback on the crest of the rise in the prairie. He was riding towards us as fast as his horse could carry him. Passing us like a whirlwind, he shouted: "Whip up, man! the prairie's on fire! Move for the river straight ahead!" In a second he was gone, shouting the same word to every startled driver as he passed. His approach had been noted by the boss, who was at the head of the entire procession. That grand marshal of the day came riding back to meet the courier. Instantly, on learning the tidings, he wheeled about and rode like the wind for the chariot in the lead, drawn by six splendid horses white as milk.

Sharp orders emphasized by a liberal sprinkling of profanity were sufficient to impress the driver of the magnificent leaders with the awful gravity of the situation and with the fact that he must set the pace for the remainder of the caravan. It might be thought that the greatest drag on the speed of the terrified procession would have been the camels and elephants, but the way in which they swung themselves over the ground was a revelation.

"Where is the river? Are we nearing the stream? Can we make the water?" These were the questions in the mind of every person in that long wagon train. Sometimes they were yelled from one driver to another, but the only answer was to lay in the lash harder on the backs of the poor horses pulling the heavy wagons and chariots—leaping and straining like so many modern fire department animals responding to an alarm. It was a genuine chariot race—in which the stake was life and the fine, death by flames.

Suddenly I saw the boss put his horse into its highest speed, leaping on ahead of the six whites. Then he leaped from the saddle, struck a match to the grass, remounted, and rode back a short distance. As each team approached he ordered: "Wait till the flames spread a little and then break through the line of the back fire I've started and form a circle."

The grass which he had fired was considerably shorter than the general growth of the prairies; then, the fire it made had not acquired the volume, intensity and sweep of that hurricane of flame from which we were fleeing. One after another of the teams reared, pitched, and plunged, only to find that the back fire had gone under their feet leaving them inside a charred, blackened circle fringed with flame.

No sound I have ever heard approached in abject terror the awful symphony of roars, growls, screams, wails and screeches that went up from the maddened beasts in that caravan as the great sky-reaching cylinder of flame and smoke rolled down upon us and was met barely forty rods away by the rapidly spreading line of our own back fire.

Just as we were wondering if our next breath would be flame or air, the leaders of the white chariot horses leaped into the air like rockets. Instantly the whole six stallions became absolutely crazed with fear and made a plunge directly for the oncoming storm of fire and smoke. On toward the furnace of fire they ran, the driver tugging with might and main on the reins.

"Jump!" yelled the boss. And jump the driver did. He was not a second too soon, for an instant later the white charioteers had disappeared under the great red and black barrel that was rolling upon us. Then came a moment which was a dizzy blank to most of us, I guess. The fearful strain of the long race, the moments of awful suspense after the charred ground had been reached—it was enough to have dethroned the reason of every man and woman in the charmed circle! Small wonder that a few fainted dead away.

We had scarcely recovered the use of our faculties when the wag of the circus broke the long strain by the remark: "I reckon there's been more genuine praying done in circus circles in the last hour than since Noah let the elephants out of the Ark!"

One of the first things we did, when the burning ground became cool enough, after the tornado of fire had swept around our little oasis of burned ground and passed on towards the river, was to go out and look for the remains of the chariot and the six white stallions. We had not far to go before we came to a heap of wheel tires and other ironwork from the big vehicle. A little beyond it were the blackened remains of the splendid horses which had dashed into an unnecessary death.

From *Sawdust and Spangles: Stories and Secrets of the Circus*, Herbert S. Stone & Co., 1901.

ANNIE OAKLEY
Will Rogers

Annie Oakley is a greater character than she was a rifle shot.
Circuses have produced the cleanest living class of people
in America today, and Annie Oakley's name, her lovable traits,
her thoughtful consideration of others, will live as a mark for
any woman to shoot at.

Will Rogers, about 1926.

CIRCUS LOGISTICS

The only permanence of the circus is its impermanence. Leaving New York after a long April stand in Madison Square Garden, Ringling Brothers–Barnum & Bailey Combined Shows, Inc., annually hauls its Greatest Show on Earth on a tour of some 18,000 miles that ends in Sarasota, Florida, late in November. [This was written in 1947.] During this perambulation the Ringling show may play in as many as 150 communities, which is merely another way of saying that the Big Show habitually solves a problem in logistics that is complicated enough to muddle the most competent colonel of roving Marines.

Each time the circus leaves a city it tears itself down and packs itself on four railroad trains. On arrival at the new town in the early dawn of the next day, it reverses the process so neatly that when the new-town customer arrives on the new lot a few hours later, he feels at home. To him the circus looks exactly as it looked last year. The hardened Ringling employee has the same feeling. . . .

To demonstrate the constant movement of the circus, and to explain its illusion of stability in the midst of that constant movement, it is only necessary to detail a typical cycle such as the one that might begin tonight in the town of Imaginary, Wisconsin.

At 8:00 P.M. of this pleasant summer day in Imaginary, Wisconsin, the circus is poised to produce its evening version. The lot, conveniently close to town, is a tight-packed acreage, offering ticket buyers excitingly non-Wisconsin sights, sounds, and smells. Dominating is the gray canvas dome of the largest single tent in the world, the Big Top. When the show begins in a few minutes, on its oval track around three rings and two stages, there will be a "straw house"—a sellout.

Late arrivals, jostling in at the main entrance gate, find themselves on the midway. On the left side of this short, broad avenue are the ticket wagons, selling reserved seats for $3 and general admissions for from 80 cents to $1.50. On the left too are brightly lighted booths where hard-faced men with rasping voices peddle almost anything that is both edible and indigestible. They also sell a line of cheap, but not cheaply-priced, souvenirs. On the right is the side-show tent. . . .

Late-comers probably pass up the side show, display their tickets to takers at the front gate or marquee, and push on into the menagerie tent. Here they meet the satisfactory, muffled roar of a lion, the pungent, not-unpleasant wild-animal smell, the sight of monkeys and elephants; of Boston, the baby giraffe; of Gargantua, most publicized of all giant gorillas. They might linger a while trying to get a decent glimpse of Gargantua in his badly-lighted, glass-enclosed cage, but the blare of the Merle Evans twenty-eight circus band, as it begins its two-and-a-half-hour marathon of brass, hurries them to their seats under the bright lights and dark shadows of the Big Top.

To most, the circus means no more than the places just enumerated—the midway, the side-show tent, the front gate, the menagerie, and the Big Top. To many others there is much interest to be seen on the rest of the lot. Some of the non-spenders lack the price of a ticket; some maintain that the finest spectacle offered by the circus is outside the big top and free of charge. As these specialists, known as "lot lice," wander along the sides of the main tent or stand gawking in the growing dusk on the fringes of the back yard, they are looking at a circus that, while already vanishing, is well set up.

Much earlier today, Lloyd Morgan, circus man in charge of layout, arrived in Imaginary to find a rarely satisfactory piece of ground. The property, a comfortable mile from the railroad siding, was an eighteen-acre rectangle with one of the short sides on a main highway. The turf was almost level, requiring no grading. The soil was damp but firm; there would be neither dust nor mud. Vital water mains were handy.

After a brief look, Morgan knew he could use a straight away, or—as he would have called it—a "Yankee Robinson" circus layout. He placed the main entrance gate in the middle of the narrow side of the lot facing on the highway. This, to many circus performers, at once became the "Eighth Avenue" side. Circus actors, wherever they may be, are apt to orient themselves by thinking of the Big Top as New York's Madison Square Garden. Thus, when standing on Eighth Avenue and facing the front door of the main tent, the Forty-ninth Street side is to the left, the Fiftieth Street side to the right, the Ninth Avenue side at the far end. Many of the circus workers who travel with the show under canvas, on the other hand, have never laid eyes on Madison Square Garden. These refer to the area about the entrance as the "front yard" and call the opposite end of the lot the "back yard." To them, for technical reasons, the Forty-ninth Street side is called the "short side," the Fiftieth Street side is named the "long side." By the use of either set of these terms, a man or an object can readily be pinpointed, no matter where the show is playing. These

terms, also, give circus employees a comfortable sense of permanence in the midst of motion. Morgan spotted the Big Top so that its long sides paralleled the long sides of the lot. All in all, he spotted some forty-three tents, including the numerous canvas-walled chemical toilets known as "donnickers."

Even on such a big lot as this one in Imaginary, the operating circus is crowded. In addition to the tents, there are the 191 big, bright-red circus wagons that carry the show. There are the eighteen trucks and fourteen tractors that move the wagons. Tonight—it is exactly 8:17 P.M. when the show begins—there are also on the lot 900 animals, about 1,400 circus employees, approximately 10,000 customers. The size and the busyness of the place at this moment give it an air of permanence. Actually—even though it is barely dark and the show will run for two and a half hours—the Ringling Circus, for some time, has been quietly melting away.

The big cookhouse, the first tent to be set up early this morning, has long since vanished with its crew of 130 and its fourteen red wagons. Already waiting to be reloaded on the trains, also, are the specialty or service departments, which during the day functioned as blacksmith, cobbler, commissary, and harness maker. There is activity everywhere. Men are setting out and lighting ball-shaped kerosene flares. From a distance there comes a roar of tractor motors starting. As elaborate floats come out of the main tent at the conclusion of the "Spectacle," each is pounced on by a crew of three and swiftly laced into a canvas cover. Almost immediately the "Spec" wagons will be on their way to the trains. In the back yard, an elephant effortlessly pushes one of the heavy wagons with his head.

But the wise lot louse, who wants to get the most for his nothing, knows that the best free show of the moment is at the Eighth Avenue, or "front-yard" end of the Big Top, where a swarm of men is at work tearing the menagerie tent to pieces. He steps along the side of the Big Top under a web of guy ropes, passing "Clown Alley"—a narrow canvas lean-to where the clowns keep their props during the show—and the performers' side entrance, the "Forty-ninth Street Connection." When he gets to the menagerie tent the side walls have already been stripped away and the goings on inside are his for the looking.

The most impressive thing about any part of the circus teardown is the imparted sense of an urgent necessity for speed, and the sight of many men simultaneously doing many things without many orders. In the menagerie tent at this moment, men are taking away the overhead lights. Others are swathing seventeen wild-animal cages in canvas. The observer steps back to avoid being trodden on by a llama, which in company with a donkey is being walked away. The tent is shrill to the sound of whistles, as "cat handlers" direct the snarling small yellow tractors. Three quick whistle blasts cause a "cat man" swiftly to back his tractor up to a wagon. One blast stops him. Two doubles and he is away, pulling the $25,000 air-conditioned cage of Gargantua and his mate. A work elephant, with two men manipulating his dragging chain, begins to pull down the side poles that support the perimeter of the roof. The tent is emptied when forty-odd performing elephants, solemnly absurd in clown costumes, march away into the big tent. (When they emerge again, at the other end, thirty-two of them will keep right on walking the long mile to the train.) The last light goes out, and in a few moments the overhead canvas comes billowing down. The menagerie tent is no more.

Emotionally satisfied but physically hungry, the spectator takes himself over to the midway for a hot dog. He is just in time, for the "grab joints" and the "juice joints" concluding that they have squeezed the last dime from the last customer, are ready to leave. Across the way, the side show, too, is collapsing into its five wagons. In a matter of minutes the entire front section of the circus will be rolling down the road.

The show ends at precisely ten forty-five, but for twenty minutes there has been a pool of interest between the Big Top back door and the door of the main dressing tent. This deeply shadowed area, edged by silent spectators, has become more and more crowded. Clowns and midgets streaming from the arena at the end of a "clown break" cause an eddy in the double line of well-mounted, brightly costumed girl riders who are waiting to enter. An elephant, hitched to a prop wagon, edges forward to place his head against the canvas of the back door. Behind him follow the nineteen other wagons that will take away the contents of the Big Top.

A few minutes later, a burst of applause marks the end of the concluding high-trapeze act. Over the loudspeaker the master of ceremonies says, "Good-night, and thank you." The sudden silence of the band is almost as painful as its previous long-term noise. Two elephants move stolidly through the back entrance of the Big Top, pulling wagons. There begins a metallic clashing that will continue deafeningly until 6,000 chairs have been folded. The Big Top is on its way down.

Urgency is again the keynote, but now the urgency seems more intense. The big audience may think it files out of the tent in its own time; actually it is shoved. Ushers nag the slow-of-foot. The two lead elephants progress massively down either side of the track, only a half step behind the last of the crowd. At the end of seven minutes the 10,000th ticket holder steps out into the Wisconsin dusk, and in those seven minutes, work has been done.

Six hundred men toss themselves at the job of tearing out the insides of the Big Top. In addition to the standard gang of laborers, electricians, prop and rigging men, the teardown crew sucks in ushers, drink and peanut butchers, ticket takers, midway concession men, clowns, midgets—almost every male on the payroll who is not busy elsewhere. . . .

The biggest job in stripping the tent is to

remove the chairs and the framework they stand on. The framework consists first of plank platforms that hinge in the middle. (Since they fold with a slap, they are called "bibles.") The bibles rest on forty-foot alloy I beams called "stringers," and the stringers rest on jacks. The metal chairs are all folded in a space of seven minutes, and the end of their clamorous closing is a relief.

Ring makers and side-wall men are breaking away the heavy ring curbs into sections. Propmen tear at the performers' stages. A youth nimbly runs up a twenty-foot ladder leaning against one of the tent poles. He unties a big electric-light so that it swings free, comes rapidly down, runs with his ladder to the next pole, sweatingly repeats the job. Flying rigging is lowered and is tucked into canvas bags. The side walls of the big tent are disappearing. Electricians begin to uproot and reel in the four miles of cable that have supplied lights to a darkening arena. . . .

At eleven fifty-five the main tent is stripped. It stands vastly and dimly empty, with a lone workman beside each of the six towering main poles. Since more than half of the smaller poles have been removed, the canvas sags. A single, last light is blotted out, and from the canvas boss—invisible at the edge of the tent—comes the softly spoken order, "Let her go." The last half hitch is loosened in the main falls holding the canvas to the peaks. At the same time, the bases of the sixty-one standing poles are jerked free. The Madison Square Garden of the sticks begins its impressive collapse.

It takes forty-five seconds for the deflation of the Big Top balloon, which gives the six pole rigger men time to get out from under (These men seldom fall, but if one does he carries a sharp knife to slash himself free.) On the outside, teams of canvasmen are waiting. Even before the tent is flat on the ground they throw themselves at the heaving fabric, slipping, grabbing for hand holds, as they try to hasten the descent. When they finally

reach the bases of the center poles they begin to work rapidly outward, unlacing one piece of the great cloth pie from the next. Working again from the inside out, they compete in folding and rolling the segments into bundles for loading. The winners take pleasure in jeering the defeated. Tonight, the job of separating the eighteen canvas pieces of the Big Top takes exactly ten minutes.

Still standing are the six towering main poles of the Big Top, and the meticulous job of lowering them one by one begins at once. At the same time, the 486 stakes that anchor the guy-line ropes of the big tent are being pulled. These four-foot wooden spikes, about two feet of which show above-ground, are yanked in pairs by a tractor dangling two chains from a boom. Workmen loop the chains around the stakes. The tractor heaves; the stakes resist—finally dangle free. They lie where they fall until a workman called "Whitey" (he has palsy) collects them in his little wagon hauled by Sheby, the donkey.

The last free show of the night on the circus lot is the leveling of the last Big Top main pole, called "No. 1." Because none of the other poles are standing, its entire weight is held by a rope and cable angling from the peak to the ground. On the ground end the rope weaves through a maze of stakes that act as tether, hovered, over by George Smith, the circus general manager, and the canvas boss, Leonard Aylesworth (wearing dirty cotton gloves). As the rope is slowly let out, the strain on it is so great that it smokes, and must be doused with water. But in four minutes the No. 1 pole is safely horizontal. It is exactly 12:24 A.M., which means that one hour and thirty-nine minutes after the evening show ended, the Ringling Brothers Circus is about ready to say goodby to Imaginary.

Tonight the Big Show will travel slightly more than 100 miles from Imaginary to a one-day stand in Shortstop, Wisconsin, on four railroad trains made up of forty-eight double-length flat cars carrying red wagons, eleven stock cars for animals, and twenty-six coaches for employees. The first of these trains is called the "Flying Squadron." The other three are labeled the "second section," the "third section," and the "fourth section."

The principle guiding the make-up of the trains is that the Squadron must carry the equipment and personnel required to lay out the lot, as well as to make the lot livable for those who follow. On it, therefore, will be the cookhouse and staff, Lloyd Morgan with his layout equipment and crew of thirty, and the various specialty shops and personnel. To provide its own motive power it will take trucks, tractors, work horses, a car of elephants, the menagerie, and the front door. The basic ingredients of the second section are the side show and the canvas and poles of the Big Top. Section three lugs the contents of the Big Top. All other loadings are matters of the convenience of the moment; generally speaking, anything can be placed on any train. (Since performers and top executives are last to be needed on a new lot, their sleeping coaches comprise the fourth section.)

The trains leave and arrive in one, two, three, four order, but the loading sequence is one, three, two, four. The reason is that the Big Top contents are ready for the train before the Big Top itself, but cannot be used the next day until the main tent has again been set. The contents, therefore, are loaded first on section three. When the Big Tent arrives at the siding it is loaded on section two and departs in advance.

Ray Milton, the train boss, has the tricky task of loading the flatcars with circus wagons and other rolling stock. The trickiness of the job lies in the fact that it is never done by rote; i.e., wagons are not spotted at the same place on the same car night after night. While loading by the numbers would make Milton's life less worrisome, he cannot take advantage of it. For any one of many reasons

a wagon might be—often is—late in reaching the siding; this would immediately stall such a loading program. Milton is forced to fill his flatcars, not by prearranged plan but by juggling wagons according to their length.

The largest circus flatcars measure seventy and seventy-two feet and have two feet less of loading surface. If Milton is not to leave a wagon or two behind when the trains pull out, he must use almost every available foot of space on every car. To aid him in solving this puzzle, each wagon is plainly marked on all four sides with its number and loading length. Milton stands in the light of a flare at the end of the train and calls the numbers of the wagons he wants loaded. When two seventeen- and two eighteen-foot wagons have been hauled up the chute and spotted by the little "cats" that ride the ties alongside the train, Milton has a tidy carload. He will get the same result with three seventeens and a nineteen. A special problem is presented by the sixty-foot Big Top mainpole wagon. But the hood of a jeep will fit under its rear overhang, and the jeep body fills the remaining ten feet of space. There are many such loadings.

In Imaginary tonight, the loadings go smoothly, so that the Squadron puffs out of the siding at ten thirty. It is followed by the second section at one thirty, the third at two thirty, and the fourth at about three thirty. In some twenty hours since it arrived early this morning the Ringling Circus has set itself up, torn itself down, reloaded and departed— all for five hours of show time. Tomorrow morning the only physical remnant of the circus in Imaginary will be the so-called "twenty-four-hour-man." He will see to it that the lot is cleaned up to the satisfaction of the city fathers, and will take care of all bills and complaints before he leapfrogs ahead of the circus to another town. . . .

BUFFALO BILL HOLDS FOUR KINGS

Louisa F. Cody

Then arrived the beginning of Will's trip of triumph [1887]. We both had talked about it often, and made our arrangements. I was to stay at home and look after the business of the ranch while Will was away. And he—he was going to a new adventure, Europe!

It was through Will's letters that I followed him on that trip, through the chartering of the steamer *Nebraska* to carry his aggregation [his Wild West Show, which had opened on May 17, 1883, at the Omaha fair grounds] to England, his arrival there, his opening performance and then, the visits of Gladstone, of the Prince and Princess of Wales, and even of Queen Victoria herself. And judging from those letters, there was enjoyment in every bit of it all.

"What do you think, Mamma," he wrote me once. "I've just held four kings! And I was the joker! It wasn't a card game either. You remember the old stage coach [Deadwood Stage Coach, closing number of the show]? Well, I got a request from the Prince of Wales to let him ride on the seat with me, while inside would be the kings of Denmark, Saxony, Greece, and Austria. Well, I didn't know just what to say for a moment. I was a little worried and yet I couldn't tell the Prince of Wales that I was afraid to haul around four kings, with Indians shooting blanks around. So I just said I was as honored as all getout, and we made the arrangements.

"And, Mamma, I just had to have my joke, so I went around and told the Indians to whoop it up as they never did before. We loaded all the kings in there and the Prince got up on the seat with me, and then I just cut 'er loose. We sure did rock around that arena, with the Indians yelling and shooting behind us, fit to kill. And Mamma—I wouldn't say it out loud—but I'm pretty sure that before the ride was over, most of the kings were under the seat. It sure was fun.

From *Memories of Buffalo Bill* by Louisa F. Cody and Courtney Ryley Cooper. © 1919 by Appleton and Co.

"When the ride stopped, the Prince of Wales said to me that he bet this was the first time that I'd ever held four kings. I told him that I'd held four kings before, but this was the first time that I'd ever acted as the royal joker. Well, he laughed and laughed. Then he had to explain it to all those kings, each in his own language—and I felt kind of sorry for him.

"The Prince gave me a souvenir, a sort of crest, with diamonds all around it. It sure is pretty and I'm real proud of it."

Thus went Will's trip to England, and he came home a greater idol to the American small boy than ever. For three years his show did not move from Staten Island, and then it was only to return to Europe again, that he might repeat in France, Spain, Italy, and other countries, what he had done in England, there to meet the rulers and potentates and receive from them gifts and souvenirs of their appreciation. Nor did the Pope refuse his presence when Will Cody went to pay his respects.

By this time, Will had become a true showman. Everything he saw, everywhere he went, he found something to intertwine with the thing that had become the realization of a great dream for him—his Wild West Show.

ON TOUR IN AUSTRALIA, 1885

George Wirth

We [the Wirth Circus] found that there was one thing we could
not conquer, and that was the elements. The rain beat down
on us mercilessly, town after town and day after day. Our tents
were all soggy with water and beds were soaking wet.
At last, foot-weary, horses poor and knocked-up, broken in spirit
and nearly broken in pocket, we reached Murray Bridge
and decided to put all the tents, boxes, poles and paraphernalia on
the train—which had not long been opened across the 90 mile
desert. After sending off the material, we rested the
horses for a day or two, and then had them pull the empty wagons
across the dreary, monotonous desert.

Talk about the perversity of Fate. As we were waiting in
Murray Bridge to spell the horses, and at the very moment
our goods left per train, the rain ceased, and the following nights
were beautiful. We had lovely weather all the way across the
desert, which was one blessing, for, oh, the desert! One
can't imagine what it is to ride in an empty wagon over Mallee
roots, which have three or five short legs or prongs. When
one of the wagon wheels lodged on a root, the root seemed to rise
up on one of its short hind legs and hurl the wagon on to
another root yards away. This root would do the same thing, and
so it would continue all day. One would never know which
way the root was going to throw the wagon. Sometimes it would
even throw you backwards. At the end of the first day none of
us could stand, for we were so beaten and bruised and sore
from the throwing about on the wagons.

After four or five days we reached Bordertown, and intended to
play there three nights so as to give the horses another spell.
We pitched our tent on the town common, but no sooner was
it erected than the rain poured down, and the whole country was
very soon again under water. It was so bad that after an hour

or two we could not reach the tent from the railway. We pulled the empty wagons on to the hard road some distance away, and whilst the horses were resting we were pulling down the wet, soggy tent, dragging it over to the road, and loading it on to the wagons.

We were days doing this, because all our workmen left. They had had enough, so they quit and got jobs somewhere else, so we four brothers, with our agent and four old German musicians, pulled down and packed up the tents, seats, poles, etc., on to the wagons and made for the next town. My mother and sisters had to drive a wagon apiece as we were so short-handed.

Luck and rain were dead against us again as we went from town to town. Day after day it rained, and yet we struggled on. When we put up the tents, several hundred venturesome persons turned up to the show, but we were hard put to it to give a show at all, as we had no men to wait on the ring or harness up the horses for the ring, but we managed it, wet and miserable as we were. We stuck to the business as a loving parent would to a dying child.

After a few more weeks, we got a fine day at Donald. It was show time, and that meant the town full of people. We forgot all about our last few weeks' nightmare in getting the wet and mildewed tent up and erecting the seats in anticipation of a bumper house that night, and we were not disappointed. No one to have seen that performance that night would have thought we had gone through such heart-rending times for the last six weeks. This was in the winter of 1885.

Soon it was spring, glorious spring, and all our hopes and confidence returned as if by magic.

From *Round the World with a Circus* by George Wirth (one of Philip Wirth's sons), Troedel & Cooper Pty Ltd., Port Melbourne, Victoria, Australia 1925. Used by permission.

THE BIG TOP IN SOUTH AMERICA

Jay Zarado

With the big top in South America, life was in many ways different from circus life in the United States. Most of our journeys were by sea; on land we traveled always in a special train, but our trips were not long. At home we played in all weathers; but on our South American journey, if the weather was bad, we did not show. We gave but two matinees a week, the principal one on Sunday. Our tent was smaller and had but one ring. Adventures of all kinds befell us and many times we were in actual danger. We were nearly four years making the tour, and played throughout most of South America.

On the way to San José, Costa Rica, we were delayed by a landslide. We waited three days for a temporary track to be laid and then walked forward as far as we could and watched the operation. As fast as the track could be set another landslide wrecked it. We waited three days more and decided to take a chance the next time the slide came to a temporary halt. We had the railroad crew lay the track and then had an engine push us over with another engine on the other side to pick us up. It was a hurry-up job and the crew did not want to attempt it, but we won our way.

Our most exciting experience on a railroad occurred in the southern part of Brazil. We were on our way to Santa Maria. At noon, with about five hours of our journey left, a strike went into effect. We did not know what all the agitation was about when the train stopped and the crew refused to take us any

further. After an argument they consented to go on, and we arrived in the town where we were to play about dusk. At the station we were met by a howling mob, armed with guns, knives, and clubs. The strikers took the attitude that if we were friendly to them we should have stayed out in the jungle until the strike was decided. A meeting, to be attended by everyone interested, was to take place in the plaza in the heart of the town.

The meeting started late in the afternoon and was still in progress when we made ready for the show at night. There we were in the tents ready to give the show, and two blocks away in the plaza an embittered mob that might suddenly be filled with an appetite for destruction! We heard the sound of their excited voices as the meeting broke up.

They started as one man for the circus tents!

With our band playing, we stood waiting behind our canvas walls. There was a rush of many feet, and the mob had surrounded us. In our dressing-room tent, we tried to guess what the shouting might mean. We could not make out a single word. Then the leaders of the strike appeared at the door with a score or more friends and raised the shout: "¡Viva el circo!"

Our hearts went back to their proper places and we showed to an enthusiastic audience in a packed tent. One of the railroad officials had turned the tide for us by a most eloquent and earnest plea for mercy. Faced with the possible injury and destruction of the property of so many innocent Americans, he put aside all thoughts of the company's part in the dispute, and pleaded solely for us.

Only one month in the year is it possible to show in a tent in Bolivia, on account of the extreme cold and snow. When we arrived in our first town in that country, Oruro, we were greeted by the cheerful news that people died there suddenly from the effects of the rarefied air. An opera troupe just closing its engagement had buried some of its number. A business man arrived from the United States the night before we came and was found dead in bed the next morning. And we were supposed to do acrobatic and gymnastic stunts!

The snow came down on the big top so heavily that it broke one of the center poles. But none of us noticed any difficulty in working, except a back-bending contortionist who contorted and could not straighten again. We took him out of the ring into the dressing room and unkinked him, and he did not try to twist himself so severely for a while.

If our acrobats did not find the atmosphere of Bolivia unpropitious, it seemed as though other members of the circus did. A beautiful white horse that belonged to the bareback riders died in La Paz of indigestion. One of our clowns lost his mind. He did not become violent, but suffered from delusions.

All the way down the west coast we were disturbed by earthquakes. We grew so accustomed to them that we could distinguish their characteristics; we could almost tell how severe they were likely to prove by the particular kind of shaking they gave us. The common variety seems to shake with a side-wise motion; but those that cavort up and down are the kind that demolish cities. A matinee in Lima, Peru, was almost disorganized by an earthquake accompanied by subterranean rumbling.

In the United States, danger was an ever-constant presence; but in South America we seemed to skate continually on the thin edge of destruction. By the time we had reached São Paulo, Brazil, two of our number had died— one in Ecuador of yellow fever and one in Southern Brazil of heart disease.

We had been playing in São Paulo some six weeks when influenza broke out. The natives in the congested part of the town died like flies. All day long processions carrying the dead to the cemeteries filled the streets. The very poor died so rapidly and in such numbers that it was not possible to bury them that way. Yet in the heat of the tropics the dead must be cared for at once, especially during an epidemic. They went to the incinerator.

The foreign women established relief stations throughout the poor districts and did what they could to relieve the sufferers. The North American women established a soup kitchen and distributed soup, milk, and groceries among them. The government closed every place where the public could gather, and we lost forty-two possible show days. I worked in the soup kitchen, and many of us helped the doctors, too.

Gradually the epidemic diminished and we took the train for Rio de Janeiro. We thought that we had encountered every perilous experience that the southern continent had to offer. But we found that we were mistaken. The crowning episode completed the tour.

Of course we knew why, from the Isthmus to the Cape and back again, the store fronts are protected by steel curtains, well oiled. They shed bullets. In the province of Pernambuco we ran right into a revolution in full swing. Not a little spluttering revolution but a very active and genuine one.

We had played in a theatre for two days to a very good business in a sleepy town on the seacoast. It was a hot day and a number of us were watching the band as they climbed into the red and gold band wagon for the late afternoon parade. The driver started the team, the band struck up a lively march, and the parade swung off. As the wagon reached the first intersection, we heard a sound of running feet and a scattered volley of shots. We saw the driver bend low and whip up the team and the band boys get under their seats. All but the drummer, who climbed inside the bass drum. Around the corner they raced and back to the stable beside the theatre.

Then we could see nothing more, and the deserted street was still. People who a few moments before had been going in and out of the stores had vanished completely. The steel curtains of the store fronts came down with a bang like the report of a cannon and presented a solid front of metal. Silence everywhere. In the foyer of the theatre was a cigar store. A steel curtain was drawn also over the theatre entrance, and here too admission was only by a small door in the sheet of metal. Quite a few people had gathered at the ticket booth inside the cigar store. A few cars drew up to the curb and a crowd began to enter through the small door. Without any warning, a party of the revolutionists swept around the corner on foot. They opened fire on the crowd in front of the theatre. There was a rush for the small door, some of that crowd never reached it, but lay still on the walk.

I lived a block from the theatre and I wanted to go to the hotel, as it was decided that we should not attempt to give a performance. Many of our number, who had put up at a distance, decided not to risk attempting to reach their hotels. They made temporary beds in the dressing rooms and prepared to spend the night there. I started out with several others for the hotel on the next corner. The old stage doorman assured us that we should not be harmed because we were foreigners, but he cautioned us not to run. He said that if we ran we might be fired on, for then the revolutionists could not see that we were not natives.

With this advice ringing in our ears, we set out. The street was lined with trees and not well lighted. We had gone about half the distance when a man behind one of the trees fired as we passed it at someone in the shadows across the way. I forgot all about not running, and made the rest of the distance in zero flat. I did not stop until I was safely inside the hotel.

All entrances were being barricaded, and the proprietor told us that most of the garrison had joined the revolutionists. The revolt was against the governor, who took his loyal troops to the palace; the barracks and the town were in the hands of the rebels.

The whole northern part of Brazil seemed in imminent danger of rising in revolt, and we thought that the time had come to return to the United States.

It was one thing to reach a decision, but quite another to be on our way. However our route was mapped out, its path lay through cities and towns that had joined the revolt. We appealed to the government. The officials were only too glad to get us out of the country and made all haste to ask an oceanliner to put into a port town for us. We faced an all-day journey to reach the appointed port. In automobiles we were carried to the railroad station—past the death cart and its gruesome burden again, past bodies lying in the gutters, past soldiers standing guard. Our driver tried to set a record for speed. We protested. He told us that we were fortunate to find a driver at all. We were, yet it was hard to determine the greater danger—the stray bullets or the lurching car. Even the station had a room full of dead waiting the trip to the incinerator.

Toward the end of our journey, in the cool of the early evening, we sighted the little port town. How welcome was our first glimpse of the liner lying at her dock with the British flag at her masthead! On the high seas we relaxed.

Condensed from *The Atlantic Monthly*, April 1931.

PART EIGHT

CHILDREN OF ALL AGES LOVE THE CIRCUS

A CIRCUS GARLAND
Rachel Field

This is the day the circus comes
With blare of brass, with beating drums,
And clashing cymbals, and with roar
Of wild beasts never heard before
Within town limits. Spick and span
Will shine each gilded cage and van;
Cockades at every horse's head
Will nod, and riders dressed in red
Or blue trot by. There will be floats
In shapes like dragons, thrones and boats,
And clowns on stilts; freaks big and small,
Till leisurely and last of all
Camels and elephants will pass
Beneath our elms, along our grass.

THE PERFORMING SEAL

Who is so proud
As not to feel
A secret awe
Before a seal
That keeps such sleek
And wet repose
While twirling candles
On his nose?

ACROBAT

Surely that is not a man
    Balanced on a thread in air
But a brightly colored fan
    Folding and unfolding there?

GUNGA

With wrinkled hide and great frayed ears,
Gunga the elephant appears.
Colored like city smoke he goes
As gingerly on blunted toes
As if he held the earth in trust
And feared to hurt the very dust.

EQUESTRIENNE

See, they are clearing the sawdust course
For the girl in pink on the milk-white horse,
Her spangles twinkle; his pale flanks shine,
Every hair of his tail is fine
And bright as a comet's; his mane blows free,
And she points a toe and bends a knee,
The while his hoofbeats fall like rain
Over and over and over again.
And nothing that moves on land or sea
Will seem so beautiful to me
As the girl in pink on the milk-white horse
Cantering over the sawdust course.

EPILOGUE

Nothing now to mark the spot
But a littered vacant lot;
Sawdust in a heap, and there
Where the ring was, grass worn bare
In a circle, scuffed and brown,
And a paper hoop the clown
Made his little dog jump through,
And a pygmy pony-shoe.

Reprinted by permission of Coward-McCann, Inc., from *The Three Owls, Third Book* by Anne Carroll Moore. © 1931 by Coward-McCann, Inc., renewed 1959 by Anne Carroll Moore.

174

THE CIRCUS-DAY PARADE

James Whitcomb Riley

Oh, the Circus-Day Parade!
　How the bugles played and played!
And how the glossy horses tossed
　their flossy manes and neighed,
As the rattle and the rhyme
　of the tenor-drummer's time
Filled all the hungry hearts
　of us with melody sublime!

How the grand band-wagon shone
　with a splendor all its own,
And glittered with a glory
　that our dreams had never known!
And how the boys behind,
　high and low of every kind,
Marched in unconscious capture,
　with a rapture undefined!

How the horsemen, two and two,
　with their plumes of white and blue,
And crimson, gold and purple,
　nodding by at me and you,
Waved the banners that they bore,
　as the Knights in days of yore,
Till our glad eyes gleamed
　and glistened like the spangles
　　that they wore!

How the graceless-graceful stride
　of the elephant was eyed,
And the capers of the little horse
　that cantered at his side!
How the shambling camels, tame
　to the plaudits of their fame,
With listless eyes came silent,
　masticating as they came.

How the cages jolted past,
　with each wagon battened fast,
And the mystery within it
　only hinted of at last
From the little grated square
　in the rear, and nosing there
The snout of some strange animal
　that sniffed the outer air!

And, last of all, The Clown,
　making mirth for all the town,
With his lips curved ever upward
　And his eyebrows ever down,
And his chief attention paid to
　the little mule that played
A tattoo on the dashboard
　with his heels, in the Parade.

Oh! the Circus-Day Parade!
　How the bugles played and played!
And how the glossy horses tossed
　their flossy manes and neighed,
As the rattle and the rhyme of
　the tenor-drummer's time
Filled all the hungry hearts of us
　with melody sublime!

THE CIRCUS
Tom Prideaux

THE PARADE

Here it comes with all its clamor,
All its grand and gaudy glamour,
    Tell me when such spangled wonder
was displayed?
All of Solomon's possessions
And the emperor's processions
    Never rivaled half the pomp of this parade.

See the harem maids Circassian
Garbed in Oriental fashion
    From the earrings to the henna on their feet,
In the gilded howdahs swaying
And majestically surveying
    All the awed and gaping people in the street.

See the herds of jeweled dragons
Coiling over crimson wagons,
    Watch the unicorns a-whirling on the wheels!
And the fat and portly cherubs
Sailing under scarlet scarabs,
    Who are fleeing for their lives from copper eels.

THE SIDE-SHOW

Tremendous! Stupendous!
    Zaboo, the giant!
    Joz, the magician!
    Lynn, death-defiant!
    Ten cents admission!

THE MENAGERIE

Wistful lions' eyes behind bright cages
Lit with tolerance like matyred sages.
    Hippopotamuses dream of sprawling
Where a river thick with ooze is crawling.
    Slim giraffes display their mottled graces,
Longing for a desert's cool oasis.
Monkeys screech in panic as if mocking
    Chewing-gum posterity for gawking.

THE BIG SHOW

Troupes of boisterous strutting clowns
    With yellow cheeks and painted grins,
A far cry from the love-sick frowns
    Of sad pierrots and harlequins.

Careening through the polished paraphernalia
    Like birds among the jungles of a dream,
The acrobats in glittering regalia
    Dazzle life with their own sequin's gleam.

Then bowing when their lauded act is ended,
    And tossing kisses, jaunty and so glib,
I wonder if they really comprehended
    They've tickled Death along his bony rib?

From *Creative Youth* (Lincoln School Verse, 1923-25, Lincoln School of Teachers College, New York City), edited by Hughes Mearns, Doubleday, Page & Company, 1925, Garden City, New York. Used by permission of Tom Prideaux, who wrote the poem when he was a tenth-grader.

THE BIG TENT UNDER THE ROOF

Ogden Nash

Noises new to sea and land
Issue from the circus band.
Each musician looks like mumps
From blowing umpah umpah umps.

Lovely girls in spangled pants
Ride on gilded elephants.
Elephants are useful friends,
They have handles on both ends;
They hold each other's hindmost handles
And flee from mice and Roman candles.
Their hearts are gold, their hides are emery,
And they have a most tenacious memory.

Notice also, girls and boys,
The circus horses' avoirdupois.
Far and wide the wily scouts
Seek these snow-white stylish stouts.
Calmer steeds were never found
Unattached to a merry-go-round.
Equestriennes prefer to jump
Onto horses pillow-plump.

Equestriennes will never ride
As other people do, astride.
They like to balance on one foot
And wherever they get, they won't stay put.
They utter frequent whoops and yips,
And have the most amazing hips.
Pink seems to be their favorite color
And very few things are very much duller.

Yet I for one am more than willing
That everything should be less thrilling.
My heart and lungs both bound and balk
When high-wire walkers start to walk.
They ought to perish, yet they don't;
Some fear they will, some fear they won't.

I lack the adjectives, verbs and nouns
To do full justice to the clowns.
Their hearts are constantly breaking,
        I hear,
And who am I to interfere?
I'd rather shake hands with Mr. Ringling
And tell him his circus is a beautiful
        thingling.

FATHER GOES ON AN ORGY
Irvin S. Cobb

Once a year, when the circus came to town, my father went on a real debauch, an orgy carried through to its triumphant conclusion without regard for cost.

He believed, with almost a passionate fervor, that every child should go to the circus. So he took his own children; and he took the children of neighbors who through religious scruples or for other reasons couldn't go themselves. He collected from all over our part of town children whose parents had not the means with which to buy tickets, and on the way to the show grounds usually managed to pick up a few more penniless urchins. For these two latter groups he would provide at his own expense. His appearance under the big top, shepherding along his flock of gaping, happy youngsters, was an anticipated event. Sometimes it was marked by a spatter of applause which made the show-folk wonder why there should be this small sudden outburst of hand-clapping when the performance hadn't even started yet.

We sat, all of us, on a racked-up rank of narrow blue planks. The flap-backed reserved seats were not for us. Anyhow he must husband his resources since red popcorn and parched goobers (roast peanuts to you) must be provided. Because what would the circus have been without goobers and popcorn? I figure that the total expenditure must have equaled a week's income for my father, but I'm sure he counted it as money wisely invested.

When the performance was over he would shuffle them out—his convoy of tired, gorged children—and distribute them at their several addresses. Then, he would repair to the Palmer House, two "squares" down Broadway from our house and pre-empt a private place at the far end of the bar and, drink by drink, get gently but firmly tight. He might not touch liquor after that for another year. . . .

Often I get to thinking about those long-gone circus days. I get to thinking that of all the wasteful and wanton excesses to which men are addicted, my father's was about as excusable a one as ever was. I used to hear of an aged Kentuckian named Hill, a man who as a boy knew Lincoln; and this old Mr. Hill had, in his later life, a belief that Paradise was a place where a man did forevermore what he had done best and most contentedly on this earth. . . . And—meaning no irreverence—if old man Hill had the rights of it, then I like to picture my sorrel-topped, spry-stepping little dad, rounding up the overlooked cherubim and the neglected seraphim and taking them with him to some Heavenly circus where the bareback riders are all lady angels and, in the grand entry, Gabriel as the drum major leads a saintly brass band playing an umph-pah tune twice around the hippodrome track; and the gentlemanly Apostles will pass among the blest, selling tickets for the grand concert and minstrel-carnival for after-show.

SPRING RITE

Bill Gold

A teacher at a private school in Virginia was puzzled when one of her pupils brought in a note from home asking that the child be excused from school for a religious holiday. The teacher authorized the absence, but phoned the child's mother to ask: "What religious holiday falls on the day Bobby will be absent from school?"

"Oh," the mother explained gaily, "that's the day we're going to take a holiday and see the circus. We go to the circus every year, religiously."

From *The Washington Post*, February 20, 1964. Used by permission.

CIRCUS DAY IN THE 1890's
Booth Tarkington

The bright sun of circus-day shone on Platt-ville. The length of Main Street and all the Square resounded with the rattle of vehicles of every kind. Since earliest dawn they had been pouring into the village, a long procession on every country road.

The air was full of exhilaration; everybody was laughing and shouting and calling greet-ings; for Carlow County was turning out, and from far and near the country people came; nay, from over the county line, clouds of dust rising from every thoroughfare and highway, and sweeping into town to herald their coming.

A thousand cries rent the air; the strolling mountebanks and gypsying booth-merchants; the peanut vendors; the boys with palm-leaf fans for sale; the candy sellers; the popcorn peddlers; the Italian with the toy balloons that float like a cluster of colored bubbles above the heads of the crowd, and the balloons that wail like a baby; the red-lemonade man, shouting in the shrill voice that reaches every-where and endures forever: "Lemo! Lemo! Ice-cole lemo! Five cents, a nickel, a half-a-dime, the twentiethpotofadollah!"

Timid youth, in shoes covered with dust through which the morning polish but dimly shone, and unalterably hooked by the arm to blushing maidens, bought recklessly of peanuts, of candy, of popcorn, of all known sweet-meats, perchance; and forced their way to the lemonade stands; and there, all shyly, silently sipped the crimson-stained ambrosia. Every-where the hawkers dinned, and everywhere

was heard the plaintive squawk of the toy balloon.

But over all rose the nasal cadence of the Cheap John, reeking oratory from his big wagon on the corner: "Walk up, walk up, walk up, ladies and gents! Here we are! Here we are! Make hay while we gather the moss. Walk up, one and all. Here I put this solid gold ring, sumptuous and golden eighteen carats, eighteen golden carats of the priceless mother of metals, toiled fer on the wild Pacific slope, eighteen garnteed, I put this golden ring, rich and golden, in the package with the hangkacheef, the elegant and blue-ruled note-paper, self-writing pens, pencil and penholder. *Who* takes the lot? Who takes it, ladies and gents?"

His tongue curled about his words; he seemed to love them. "Fer a quat-of-a-dollah! Don't turn away, young man—you feller in the green necktie, there. We all see the young lady on your arm is a-langrishing for the golden ring and the package. Faint heart never won fair wummin'. *There* you are, sir, and you'll never regret it. Go—and be happy!"

Down the middle of the street, kept open between the waiting crowd, ran barefoot boys, many of whom had not slept at home, but had kept vigil in the night mists for the com-ing of the show, and, having seen the muffled pageant arrive, swathed, and with no pomp and panoply, had returned to town, rioting through jewelled cobwebs in the morn-ing fields, happy in the pride of knowledge of what went on behind the scenes. To-night or tomorrow, the runaways would face a woodshed reckoning with outraged ancestry; but now they caracoled with no thought of the grim deeds to be done upon them.

In the court-house yard, and so sinning in the very eyes of the law, two swarthy, shifty-looking gentlemen were operating (with some greasy walnut shells and a pea) what the fanciful or unsophisticated might have been pleased to call a game of chance; and the most intent spectator of the group around them was the Town Marshal. He was simply and unofficially and earnestly interested. Thus the eye of Justice may not be said to have winked upon the nefariousness now under its vision; it gazed with strong curiosity, an itch to dabble, and (it must be admitted) a growing hope of profit. The game was so direct and the player so sure. Several countrymen had won small sums, and one, a charmingly rustic stranger, with a peculiar accent (he said that him and his goil should now have a smoot' old time off his winninks—though the lady was not manifested), had won twenty-five dollars with no trouble at all. The two operators seemed depressed, declaring the luck against them and the Plattville people too brilliant at the game.

It was wonderful how the young couples worked their way arm-in-arm through the thickest crowds, never separating. Even at the lemonade stands they drank holding the glasses in their outer hands—such are the sacrifices demanded by etiquette.

There was a fanfare of trumpets in the east. Lines of people rushed for the street, and as one looked down on the straw hats and sun-bonnets and many kinds of finer head apparel, tossing forward, they seemed like surf sweeping up the long beaches.

The parade was coming at last. The boys whooped in the middle of the street; some tossed their arms to heaven, others expressed their emotion by somersaults; those most deeply moved walked on their hands.

There was another flourish of music. Immediately all the band gave sound, and then, with blare of brass and the crash of drums, the glory of the parade burst upon Plattville. Glory in the utmost! The resistless impetus of the march-time music; the flare of royal banners, of pennons on the breeze; the smiling of beautiful Court Ladies and great, silken Nobles; the swaying of howdahs on camel and elephant, and the awesome shaking of the earth beneath the elephant's feet, and the gleam of his small but devastating eye; then the badinage of the clown, creaking along in his donkey cart; the terrific recklessness of the spangled hero who was drawn by in a cage with two striped tigers; the spirit of the prancing steeds that drew the rumbling chariots, and the grace of the helmeted charioteers; the splendor of the cars and the magnificence of the paintings with which they were adorned; the ecstasy of all this glittering, shining, gorgeous pageantry needed even more than walking on your hands to express. Last of all came the tooting calliope, followed by swarms of boys as it executed "Wait till the clouds roll by, Jennie" with infinite dash and gusto.

The band began to play, and the equestrians and equestriennes capered out from the dressing-tent for the "Grand Entrance" and the performance commenced. Through the long summer afternoon it went on: wonders of horsemanship and horsewomanship; hair-raising exploits on wires, tight and slack; giddy tricks on the high trapeze; feats of leaping and tumbling in the rings; while the tireless musicians blatted inspiringly through it all, only pausing long enough to allow that uproarious jester, the clown, to ask the ring-master what he would do if a young lady came up and kissed him on the street, and to exploit his hilarities during the short intervals of rest for the athletes.

From *The Gentleman from Indiana*, Grosset & Dunlap, New York, 1902.

THE CIRCUS
William Saroyan

Any time a circus came to town, that was all me and my old pal Joey Emerian needed to make us run hog-wild, as the saying is. All we needed to do was see the signs on the fences and in the empty store windows to start going to the dogs and neglecting our educations. All we needed to know was that a circus was on its way to town for me and Joey to start wanting to know what good a little education ever did anybody anyway.

After the circus *reached* town we were just no good at all. We spent all our time down at the trains, watching the gang unload the animals, walking out Ventura Avenue with the lions and tigers in their golden wagons, and hanging around the grounds, trying to win the favor of the animal men, the acrobats, and the clowns.

The circus was everything, everything else we knew wasn't. It was adventure, travel, danger, skill, grace, romance, comedy, peanuts, popcorn, chewing-gum and soda-water. We used to carry water to the elephants and stand around afterwards and try to seem associated with the whole magnificent affair, the putting up of the big tent, the getting of everything in order, and the worldly-wise waiting for the people to come and spend their money

One day Joey came tearing into the class-room of the fifth grade at Emerson School ten minutes late, and without so much as removing his cap shouted, Hey, Aram, what the hell are you doing here? The circus is in town.

And sure enough I'd forgotten. I jumped up and ran out of the room with poor old Miss Flibety screaming after me, Aram Garoghlanian, you stay in this room. Do you hear me?

I hear her all right and I knew what my not staying would mean. It would mean another powerful strapping from old man Dawson. But I couldn't help it. I was just crazy about a circus:

I been looking all over for you, Joey said in the street. What happened?

I forgot. I knew it was coming all right, but I forgot it was today. How far along are they?

I was at the trains at five. I been out at the grounds since seven. I had breakfast at the circus table, with the gang.

How are they?

Great, the same as ever. Couple more years, they told me, and I'll be ready to go away with them.

As what? Lion-tamer, or something like that?

I guess maybe not as a lion-tamer, Joey said. I figure more like a workman in the gang till I learn about being a clown or something I don't figure I could work with lions right away.

We were out on Ventura Avenue, headed for the circus grounds, out near the County Fairgrounds, just north of the County Hospital.

What a breakfast! Joey said. Hot-cakes, ham and eggs, sausages, coffee. Boy.

Why didn't you tell me?

I thought you knew. I thought you'd be

down at the trains same as last year. I would have told you if I knew you'd forgotten. What made you forget?

I don't know. Nothing, I guess.

I was wrong there, but I didn't know it at the time. I hadn't really forgotten. What I'd done was *remembered*. I'd gone to work and remembered the strapping Dawson gave me last year for staying out of school the day the circus was in town. That was the thing that had kind of kept me sleeping after four-thirty in the morning when by rights I should have been up and dressing and on my way to the trains. It was the memory of that strapping old man Dawson had given me, but I didn't know it at the time. We used to take the strappings kind of for granted, me and Joey, on account of we wanted to be fair and square with the Board of Education and if it was against the rules to stay out of school when you weren't sick, and if you were supposed to get strapped for doing it, well, there we were, we'd done it, so let the Board of Education balance things the best way they knew how. They did that with a strapping. They used to threaten to send me and Joey to Reform School but they never did it.

Circus? old man Dawson used to say. Well, bend down, boy.

So we'd bend down and old man Dawson would get some powerful shoulder exercise while we tried not to howl. We wouldn't howl for five or six licks, but after that we'd howl like Indians coming. They used to be able to hear us all over the school and old man Dawson, after our visits got to be kind of regular, urged us politely to try to make a little less noise, inasmuch as it was a school and people were trying to study.

It ain't fair to the others, he said. They're trying to learn something for themselves.

We can't help it, Joey said. It hurts.

That I know, but it seems to me there's such a thing as modulation. I believe a lad can overdo his howling if he ain't thoughtful of others. Just try to modulate that awful howl a little. I think you can do it.

He gave Joey a strapping of twenty and Joey tried his best not to howl so loud. After the strapping Joey's face was red and old man Dawson was very tired.

How was that? Joey said.

By far the most courteous you've managed yet.

I did my best.

I'm grateful to you, old man Dawson said.

He was tired and out of breath. I moved up to the chair in front of him that he furnished during these matters to help us suffer the stinging pain. I got in the right position and he said, Wait a minute, Aram. Give a man a chance to catch his breath. I'm not twenty-three years old. I'm *sixty*-three. Let me rest a minute.

All right, but I sure would like to get this over with.

So would I, but don't howl so loud. Folks passing by in the street are liable to think this is a veritable chamber of tortures. Does it really hurt that much?

You can ask Joey.

How about it, Joey? Aren't you lads exaggerating just a little? Perhaps to impress someone in your room? Some girl, perhaps?

We don't howl to impress anybody, Mr. Dawson. Howling makes us feel ashamed, doesn't it, Aram?

It's embarrassing to go back to our seats after howling that way. We'd rather not howl if we could help it.

Well, I'll not be unreasonable. I'll only ask you to try to modulate it a little.

I'll do my best, Mr. Dawson. Catch your breath?

Give me just a moment longer.

When he got his breath back he gave me twenty and I howled a little louder than Joey and then we went back to class. It was awfully embarrassing. Everybody was looking at us.

Well, Joey said to the class, what did you expect? You'd fall down and die if you *got* twenty. You wouldn't *howl a little*, you'd die.

That'll be enough out of you, Miss Flibety said.

Well, it's true, Joey said. They're all scared. A circus comes to town and what do they do? They come to school.

That'll be enough.

Who do they think they are, giving us dirty looks?

Miss Flibety lifted her hand, hushing Joey.

Now the circus was back in town, another year had gone by, it was April again, and we were on our way out to the grounds. Only this time it was worse than ever because they'd seen us at school and *knew* we were going out to the circus.

Do you think they'll send Stafford after us? I said.

Stafford was truant officer.

We can always run, Joey said. If he comes, I'll go one way, you go another. He can't chase *both* of us.

When we got out to the grounds a couple of the little tents were up, and the big one was going up. We stood around and watched. It was great the way they did it. Just a handful of guys who looked like tramps doing work you'd think no less than a hundred men could do. Doing it with style, too.

All of a sudden a man everybody called Red hollered at me and Joey.

Here, you Arabs, give us a hand.

Me and Joey ran over to him.

Yes sir, I said.

He was a small man with very broad shoulders and very big hands. You didn't feel that he was small, because he seemed so powerful and because he had so much thick red hair on his head. You thought he was practically a giant.

He handed me and Joey a rope. The rope was attached to some canvas that was lying on the ground.

This is easy, Red said. As the boys lift the pole and get it in place you keep pulling the rope, so the canvas will go up with the pole.

Yes sir, Joey said.

Everybody was busy when we saw Stafford.

We can't run now, I said.

Let him come, Joey said. We told Red we'd give him a hand and we're going to do it.

We'll tell him we'll go with him after we get the canvas up; then we'll run.

All right, Joey said.

Stafford was a big fellow in a business suit who had a beef-red face and looked as if he ought to be a lawyer or something. He came over and said, All right, you hooligans, come along with me.

We promised to give Red a hand, Joey said. We'll come just as soon as we get this canvas up.

We were pulling for all we were worth, slipping and falling. The men were all working hard. Red was hollering orders, and then the whole thing was over and we had done our part.

We didn't even get a chance to find out what Red was going to say to us, or if he was going to invite us to sit at the table for lunch, or what.

Joey busted loose and ran one way and I ran the other and Stafford came after *me*. I heard the circus men laughing and Red hollering, Run, boy, run. He can't catch *you*. He's soft. Give him a good run. He needs the exercise.

I could hear Stafford, too. He was very sore and he was cussing.

I got away, though, and stayed low until I saw him drive off in his Ford. Then I went back to the big tent and found Joey.

We'll get it this time, he said.

I guess it'll be Reform School.

No, it'll be thirty, and that's a lot of whacks even if he *is* sixty-three years old.

Thirty? That's liable to make me cry.

Me too, maybe, Joey said. Seems like ten can make you cry, then you hold off till it's eleven, then twelve, howling so you won't cry, and you think you'll start crying on the next one, but you don't. We haven't so far, anyway. Maybe we will when it's thirty, though.

Oh, well, that's tomorrow.

Red gave us some more work to do around the grounds and let us sit next to him at lunch.

It was beef stew and beans, all you could eat. We talked to some acrobats who were Spanish, and to a family of Italians who worked with horses. We saw both shows, the afternoon one and the evening one, and then we helped with the work, taking the circus to pieces again; then we went down to the trains, and then home. I got home real late. In the morning I was sleepy when I had to get up for school.

They were waiting for us. Miss Flibety didn't even let us sit down for the roll call. She just told us to go to the office. Old man Dawson was waiting for us, too. Stafford was there, too, and very angry.

I figured, Well, here's where we go to Reform School.

Here they are, Mr. Dawson said to Stafford. Take them away, if you like.

It was easy to tell they'd been talking for some time and hadn't been getting along too well.

In *this* school, old man Dawson said, I do any punishing that's got to be done. Nobody else. I can't stop you from taking them to Reform School, though.

Stafford didn't say anything. He just gave old man Dawson a very dirty look and left the office.

Well, lads, old man Dawson said. How was it?

We had lunch with them, Joey said.

Good. But now down to business. What offense is this, the sixteenth or the seventeenth?

It ain't that many, Joey said. Must be eleven or twelve.

Well, I'm sure of one thing. This is the time I'm supposed to make it thirty.

I think the next one is the one you're supposed to make thirty, Joey said.

No, we've lost track somewhere, but I'm sure this is the time it goes up to thirty. Who's going to be first?

Me.

All right, Aram. Take a good hold on the chair, brace yourself, and try to modulate your howl.

Yes sir. I'll do my best, but thirty's an awful lot.

Well, a funny thing happened. He gave me thirty all right and I howled all right, but it *was* a modulated howl. It was the most modulated howl I ever howled; because it was the *easiest* strapping I ever got. I counted them and there were thirty all right, but they didn't hurt, so I didn't cry, as I was afraid I might.

It was the same with Joey. We stood together waiting to be dismissed.

I'm awfully grateful to you boys, old man Dawson said, for modulating your howls so nicely this time. I don't want people to think I'm killing you.

We wanted to thank him for giving us such easy strappings, but we didn't know how. I think he knew the way we felt, though, because he kind of laughed when he told us to go back to class.

It was a proud and happy moment for both of us because we knew everything would be all right till the County Fair opened in September.

From *My Name Is Aram*. Dell Publishing Co., New York. © William Saroyan. Used by permission.

A HAT IN THE RING

Fred Bradna

When the circus played Washington, D.C., we occasionally had a visit from the President of the United States. Woodrow Wilson was a particularly ardent fan, and with great reluctance passed up Mr. Charlie Ringling's invitation, one year, to ride on an elephant. The President was game, but his advisers declined to permit a Democrat to ride on the symbol of Republicanism. The Secret Service forbade it too.

Wilson employed the circus on May 8, 1916, for political purposes. The nation was in ferment debating whether or not to enter World War I on the side of the Allies against the Central Powers. The President stood for peace. While everyone thought that he would be a candidate for re-election, he had not announced his intent. As I escorted him across the arena, from the performers' entrance to his reserved seats, to the music of "Hail to the Chief," he doffed his hat and threw it squarely into the middle of the center ring. The gesture was immediately interpreted by the crowd, who cheered lustily while newspaper reporters sprinted for the exits to telephone their journals that Wilson literally had thrown his hat into the ring.

When a President visited the circus, our normal routine was upset. First of all, Secret Service men snooped about the lot all morning, investigating shady characters, inquiring into the antecedents of employees, and otherwise ensuring the President's safety. On our part, we had to be sure not to start the performance until after the President arrived, even though he was a half hour late. But we could not relax, for the Secret Service insisted that there be no delay once the President was seated. Further precautionary efforts were required to hold the audience until the President had left.

The President drives, by custom, to the performers' entrance, alighting among the throng lined up for the spec. To much fanfare, I always escorted him to two rows of seats in Section E. The first row was for the President's party. The second row was filled with Secret Service operatives who thus guarded against the possibility that the Chief of State might be molested from behind. There was always great excitement on "President's Day."

I escorted four Chief Executives in my career. Wilson was by far the best audience. He gaped and applauded like a youngster, and got a big kick out of everything; as a result, everyone had fun. Warren G. Harding and Herbert Hoover acted as though they were sitting through a hundred-dollars-a-plate political dinner, applauding politely but unenthusiastically, self-conscious of the battery of cameramen. Calvin Coolidge was the worst. I watched him during an entire show and never saw his expression change. He might just as well have been an Indian chief, he was so deadpan. The performers knocked themselves out that day to give him a thrill or a laugh, but the President did not even blink. . . .

From *The Big Top* by Fred Bradna as told to Hartzell Spence. Simon and Schuster, New York, 1952. Used by permission.

HEMINGWAY SPEAKS TO THE POLAR BEAR

A. E. Hotchner

One of the few things about New York that Ernest [Hemingway] unreservedly enjoyed was the visits of the Ringling Brothers Circus. He felt that circus animals were not like other animals, that they were more intelligent and, because of their constant working alliance with man, had much more highly developed personalities.

The first time I went to the circus with him, he was so eager to see the animals he went to Madison Square Garden an hour before the doors were scheduled to open. We went below and made a tour of the cages. Ernest became fascinated with the gorilla; although the keeper was nervous as hell and warned him not to stand too close, Ernest wanted to make friends with the animal. He stood close to the cage and talked to the gorilla, in a staccato cadence and kept talking, and finally the gorilla, who appeared to be listening was so moved he picked up his plate of carrots and dumped it on top of his head; then he started to whimper; sure signs, the keeper said, of his affection.

By now all the keepers had assembled, anxious that Ernest try a few words with their charges, but he said that the only wild animal with whom he had any true talking rapport was the bear, whereupon the bear keeper cleared a path for him.

Ernest stopped in front of the polar-bear cage and closely watched its occupant swing back and forth across the small area. "He's very nasty, Mr. Hemingway," the bear keeper said. "I think you're better off talking to this brown bear, who has a good sense of humor."

"I should get through to him," Ernest said, staying with the polar bear, "but I haven't talked bear talk for some time and I may be rusty." The keeper smiled. Ernest edged in close to the bars. He began to speak to the bear in a soft, musical voice totally unlike his gorilla language, and the bear stopped pacing. Ernest kept on talking and the words, or I should say sounds, were unlike any I had ever heard. The bear backed up a little and grunted, and then it sat on its haunches and, looking straight at Ernest, it began to make a series of noises through its nose, which made it sound like an elderly gentleman with severe catarrh.

"I'll be damned!" the keeper said.

Ernest smiled at the bear and walked away, and the bear stared after him, bewildered. "It's Indian talk," Ernest said. "I'm part Indian. Bears like me. Always have."

> The circus is the only ageless delight that you can buy for money. Everything else is supposed to be bad for you but the circus is good for you. It is the only spectacle I know that, while you watch it, gives the quality of a truly happy dream.
> Ernest Hemingway, quoted in the *Saturday Evening Post,* April 10, 1965.

AUTHENTIC BLISS
William Lyon Phelps

Heaven lay about me in my infancy, and it took a circular shape. From the moment I entered the great tent until I emerged some hours later I was in Paradise. It was no illusion, no imaginary pleasure. It was authentic bliss, a delirium of delight. And now that I am over sixty I find I still love the circus. I do not go today for the pleasure of reminiscence, to see if I can recapture my childish enthusiasm; I go because I want to go, because the circus ring draws me, and it ought to, with centripetal force.

THE CLEANEST AMUSEMENT

Albert Parry

"My sister plays bridge. My brother plays golf. Me, I like to drive eight horses in the circus."

So said a pleasant, middle-aged, short-statured man each time he was asked by his fellow roustabouts of the Ringling Bros.-Barnum & Bailey Big Top as to why he didn't look for a better paying and less strenuous job.

For several seasons the little man reported for work in the spring just as the circus was ready to leave its winter quarters in Sarasota, Florida. His job was handling the team of eight strong horses which pulled the big top poles into position and helped break up the show for the trip to the next town. He was a master at his trade, but in addition to his neat clothes and nice manners he had a few other peculiarities. He always insisted on having the the same assistant just as a fine musician would have one certain accompanist and no other.

And then, one spring, the secret of the strange roustabout was out. This was the time when three of the eight horses became sick. The little driver had not as yet arrived for his season's work. His assistant was already on the job. The assistant sent a wire. That afternoon, in flew a private plane with the driver and a high-priced veterinary aboard. In a hired limousine he brought the horse doctor from the town of Sarasota to the circus camp. They stayed in the camp for several days, treating and nursing the animals until they were well again.

That is how the Big Top folk learned the identity of the little driver. He was a multi-millionaire whose name was a household word

the world over. His millions had come from a soap he packaged. But circus, not soap, was his true passion. His name? Circus folk pledged to the little man they would keep it secret. And secret it is to this day.

Other circus fans don't care who knows their real names and occupations as they leave hearth and shop for a day or week or month or even a whole season with the clowns, aerialists and bareback riders. In the spring of 1948 the Ringling Brothers staff knew that a visiting clown doing a one-night turn on their arena was Drew Pearson, the columnist. In Spokane anyone will tell you of Harper Joy, an investment banker, who each spring goes off on a circus tangent.

What prompts such men to cut loose their dignified moorings and don the circus roustabout's overalls or the clown's makeup? The answer is that the small boy is ever alive in every one of them, no matter how adult they seem to be in their regular occupations and relationships away from the circus. To a truly grownup person the circus is something sad—sad because it tells him more forcefully than many another thing can that his childhood is gone. He recalls that as a youngster he was awed and exhilarated no end by the daring, color, and fun of the circus. Now as an adult, in most cases, he cannot recapture that happy abandon of his mood, that complete absorption with the gay, brave world of these tents and rings. But some can and do transport themselves back into their youthful trance quite easily. For them, we shouldn't even use the word "recapture"; they never lost their boyish bond with the circus; they never lost their boyhood.

Some such addicts do not change their professions as they travel with the circus the width and length of America. Circus fans revere the memory of Dr. Neil Hoskins. He practiced medicine in Detroit, but each spring he closed his office to roam with a circus, relieving the show's regular physician. Once, during a tremendous storm, Dr. Hoskins proved himself a real hero by setting a roustabout's broken leg in a driving rain—while the Big Top was blowing over. . . .

In a class by themselves are the circus fans of Gainesville, Texas. They started out during the depression by giving an amateur circus show. Their aim was to raise enough money to lift their local Little Theater out of a financial hole. They finished up by having a homespun circus of their own. . . .

But outside Gainesville not all circus fans do or can become performers. Take, for instance, my friends Fred and Courtenay. Frederic W. Roedel is a jeweler in Utica, New York; Courtenay Barber, Jr., is a Chicago insurance man. But the circus is in their blood much more deeply. Mention the circus to them and their eyes light up, their breath comes hot and fast. If they could or dared, they too, would go off with a show at least for a season.

But since they cannot or dare not, they do their best by being non-participating fans. . . .

There are thousands upon thousands of such men (and a few women) in America today, of all ages and walks of life whose first and last love is the circus. They "catch" circus shows any time they can. They visit the back lot of each show to hobnob with the performers and handlers. They collect posters, tickets, photographs, newspaper and magazine clippings, books, costumes and accessories—anything and everything pertaining to the world of sawdust and spangles. The more gifted among them carve, build, glue and rig together models of circus rings, ornate calliopes and wagons, sideshows, and menagerie cages. They exhibit; they correspond; they swap.

As such fans meet on their excursions, they exchange gossip of their associations. There are four such associations in the United States, one in Great Britain, and one in France, and all six have bustling lives of their own.

This country's four organizations are the Circus Fans Association of America, the Circus Historical Society, the Circus Model Builders and Owners Association, and the Circus Saints and Sinners of America. Many American fans belong to all of the first three organizations. The fourth—Saints and Sinners —is more exclusive. You join it by invitation only.

In 1943, while the Big Show was in Akron, Ohio, one of its aerialists, Frank Sheppard, fell from a high trapeze and was badly injured. Carl Elwell, a bank employee in the city and a CFA member, was in the audience when Sheppard fell. He rushed to the back lot. "Don't worry," he told Sheppard's fellow actors "as long as he's in Akron, my wife and I will look after him." And the Elwells kept their word. For the four years or more that Sheppard was in the hospital they visited him at least once a week. . . .

"I like a fan that holds a ticket in his hand, and I like him even more when he gives the circus a hand!" says Fred Roedel to me. The businessman and the father of a family in him recedes for the moment. His smile is happy, childlike. And I tell him so.

"Childlike?" he echoes, and beams knowingly. "Sure, we fans are like happy children when it comes to the circus. And why not? You say we may idealize and overidealize the circus? Ah, but the circus is the only form of amusement that has never been censored. Because it needs no censoring! It's the cleanest amusement there is."

Condensed from *Kiwanis Magazine*, July 1949. Used by permission.

WHAT THIS CIRCUS NEEDS IS MORE AUTOMATION

Art Buchwald

I went to the Ringling Bros.-Barnum & Bailey Circus last week with my children and was shocked to discover that in the age of automation the circus was going along with old-fashioned, out-moded methods of operation.

As I sat there and watched the cast of over 100 people, not to mention the people behind the scenes, I couldn't help thinking what the circus really needed was a good managment consultant who could trim the manpower and make the show more efficient.

I can just hear him talking to John Ringling North.

"Now, Mr. North, I've made a study of your circus and you're in trouble, people-wise, that is."

"How do you mean?"

"Well, let's take the trapeze acts as an example. You've got six men and two women working two rings at the same time. I think you could cut this down to one ring, one woman, and one man."

"But you need a third man to catch the woman when she does a flip."

"You can install a computer which will be synchronized to the trapeze. It will be right where the woman artist wants it to be when she flies through the air. If it works well, you might even be able to do without the man."

"What else?"

"Well, I noticed, in your lion act, five of the lions are sitting around the cage while the sixth lion is performing. There really doesn't seem to be need for all six lions."

"But each lion has a different trick."

"You could teach one lion all the tricks. I did a time study on them and I discovered that for every minute they worked, the lions took three minutes doing nothing. This is a waste of lionpower."

"I don't want to argue with you, but one of the things that

makes that act is that the trainer is in there with six lions.
If he was only in there with one lion, there would be no danger as
far as the audience is concerned."

"We could play a tape over a loudspeaker during the act which
would make it sound as if there were 12 lions in the ring.
Now I want to talk to you about that Siberian tiger that
rides a horse."

"Don't tell me you want to get rid of the tiger?"

"No, I want to get rid of the horse. Why can't the tiger ride a
wooden horse? It seems to me people are more interested
in watching the tiger than the horse."

"But the whole idea is a live tiger is riding a live horse. If we
make it a wooden horse, the circus fans will object."

"They will at first, but they'll get used to it. Now about those
boxing bears. I think you only need one."

"How can you just have one bear fight?"

"What's the matter? Haven't you ever heard of shadow
boxing?"

"What other suggestions do you have?"

"You have too many juggling acts. We have a machine that
can juggle twice as many bowling pins in half the time. We
can speed up the whole operation and, at the same time, put a
lot more balls in the air."

"I suppose you want me to cut down on the clowns, too?"

"I was coming to that. My study shows you can easily get by
with two clowns."

"But how do you make the people laugh with just two clowns?"

"You install a laugh track over the loud speaker system. It
will sound as if you have 50 clowns."

"If it's all the same to you, I think I'll stick with what I've got
now."

"That's all right with me, Mr. North. But you'd better realize
we're living in a computer age, and if you keep using people
in your circus, you're going to lose your shirt."

Used by permission of Art Buchwald.

THE ROYAL FAMILY
Cyril Bertram Mills

In the summer of 1952 those few of us who knew the secret were
tingling with excitement, for it seemed very probable that Her
Majesty the Queen and His Royal Highness the Duke
of Edinburgh would attend a gala charity performance at Olympia.

In 1798 Philip Astley was calling his establishment the Royal
Amphitheatre because the Duke of York, in whose army he
had served, and the then Prince of Wales had honoured him with
their patronage, and in March 1887 Queen Victoria had
visited the first circus ever held at Olympia—but that had been a
private visit which took place one morning and Her Majesty
and some children of the Royal Family were the
only members of the audience.

Our [the Mills family] first connection with the Royal Family
was in 1926, when his Royal Highness, Edward, Prince of
Wales, made it known to my father that he and a party of friends
would like to see the circus, but it was to be a hush-hush affair.
I met the Prince, whose arrival was timed carefully to take place
a few minutes after the performance began, at a small door
which gave access to a stairway leading through unused passages
to the balcony. Thence there was a bridge leading to a totally
enclosed box at the back of the seating and by the time the party
was seated not a soul had spotted the Prince; as there was no
light in the box (the bulb had been removed) it was impossible
for people on the opposite side to recognize the occupants.

Ten minutes before the end of the show I conducted the Prince
and his friends back to the cars by the same route and they
departed unnoticed. There had not been a single reporter or
photographer and there was never a press reference to the visit.
It would have meant a great deal of prestige for us if there
had been an announcement, but we had managed to do just as the
Prince had wished and were rewarded when he made other
visits later. . . . He often went to Ascot to watch the training of

animals. His visits and those of his week-end guests prompted us to build and furnish a box and I think ours was the only training establishment to have one; it was certainly the only place to have a box of which the chief occupant was always the heir apparent. . . .

In 1935 . . . the Duke and Duchess of York made a private visit with their two small daughters the Princesses Elizabeth and Margaret. . . . I have always believed that it may have been during their first visit that the Princesses developed a liking for the circus, but it was not until they came to the tenting circus at Reading in 1946 that we were to see them again. That visit, and the one the next day by the Duchess of Kent and her children, began something which was to gather momentum for the rest of our days, for between 1946 and 1966 we were honoured by royal visits on nearly fifty occasions.

During my last season at Olympia, the Duke and Duchess of Kent brought their son, Prince George, who was only three and a half years of age, and while I was talking to them, I said I thought he was still too young to sit through anything that lasted two and a half hours. I do not like repeating anything said by a member of the Royal Family, but this time I must break my rule for the reply of the Duchess was so charming and so kind I shall never forget it. She just said: "Yes, he really is too young, but this is your last circus and we did not want him to grow up without having seen it."

Condensed from *Bertram Mills Circus—Its Story*. Hutchinson & Co. (Publishers), Ltd. London 1967. © C. B. Mills. Used by permission.

THE RUSSIAN AUDIENCE CHEERS

Robert J. Fleming

Reading, writing, and arithmetic have been basic to most people's education. But what about a circus school? In Russia's unique training ground for big-top entertainers, the pupils learn to juggle subjects from mathematics to the flying trapeze. It is one of the country's most highly regarded institutions.

The National School for Circus and Variety Arts in Moscow is housed in a building with a full circus ring topped by a dome for trapeze acts. A student body of 500, three out of four of them boys, get their basic secondary schooling along with circus training. They enroll at age eleven and graduate at seventeen to join the Union of Circus Actors of the Soviet Union. This agency then becomes their "manager," handling all casting and programming wherever they go in the world.

Almost every major Russian city has its permanent circus and the performers are regarded by the people as artists, not just entertainers. Moscow's national cemetery, reserved for heroes and artists, contains the grave of a famous circus clown. Seventy separate companies, whose clowns by tradition have always been permitted to spoof the Establishment, are currently operating, moving into big tops and public squares from the Far East to the Black Sea.

The Moscow circus school teems with students concentrating on their individual stunts, exercises and traditional lessons. A boy, thirteen, skillfully juggles six bowling pins. High above, a sixteen-year-old girl swings by her ankles from a trapeze.

Ballet movement plays an important role. In a special room a class of students clad in red tights goes slowly through body-control training exercises.

In the big ring, "upper classmen" are down to serious work. Under the dome a fifteen-year-old girl carefully maneuvers through a hoop while her instructor helps. Everyone is seriously training to go on the road.

At Bukhara in Soviet Asia, the town circus performed near the huge sandstone walls of the former emir's palace, a relic of past ages. A crowd quickly gathered as the show began setting up. Soon the throng was roaring with laughter and applause at a clown almost falling as he tenuously teetered across a high tightrope.

After a hectic day of parade-watching at the Tashkent fiftieth anniversary celebrations, the populace swarmed into a tent on a dusty vacant lot to enjoy the day's big attraction, the circus.

Like the human performers, the animals, too, are trained to perfection. The bear, that symbol of the Russian circus, is still the star and the audience cheers his stunts with obvious delight.

Such scenes are typical in this vast land where the circus retains its ancient thrill for all ages.

As much as any other institution, the circus is a vital part of the Russian way of life. Like nothing else it involves the ordinary person. He laughs and sings, sways to the motion of the trapeze and taps in time to the martial music. There is even an occasional fight in the stands when some excited patron refuses to get "down in front."

From *Pace Magazine*, March 1968. Used by permission.

THE QUICKENING

Elizabeth Blunn

It was merely by chance that I saw Bessie Makepeace come into the Happy Hours Club room that day. Although I hadn't seen Bessie for years, I recognized her immediately. It was a wonder! You would never have believed that scared little old lady in a rusty black coat could once have been the prettiest girl in school. Now the little wisps of once golden hair that stuck out from under her old black hat were frowzy grey; even her face was grey and drawn.

Older members of the Club ("older," that is, from the standpoint of membership; everyone at Happy Hours is what you, I am sure, would call "old") are supposed to greet the new-comers, but not a man or woman in that crowded room made a move to greet Bessie. A few snickered. I jumped up and rushed over to her.

Over coffee and cake I asked Bessie dozens of questions to keep her talking, as if we were again two school girls sharing confidences. And as it had done when we were girls, listening to Bessie filled me with melancholy. Her father had died when she was a little girl and the widowed mother had kept her only child jealously to herself. No one was ever asked to Bessie's house; even I never went there, though I was more her friend than any-one else. Bessie wasn't allowed to go to any of the young folks' social affairs, for fear (her mother would say) "something would happen." When we graduated from the

Academy, Bessie wanted to go away to college as I did, but her mother wouldn't permit her to leave home.

I used to feel Bessie wanted me to break through her isolation, but I was never able to do it. It isn't surprising that we drifted apart as the years passed. I was away most of the time teaching in the winter, traveling or studying in the summer. Now, however, I was sorry I had never bothered to get in touch with Bessie when I was visiting home. I wondered if she knew I had retired from teach-ing and had come back to live in the old house.

"Bessie, how are you?" I asked. "What have you been doing all these years?"

"Oh, I'm all right, Emma. It's just that I have such a cough—and I get so tired." She looked at me appealingly with her large round grey eyes that still were so astonishingly accented with thick dark lashes and brows. "After Mamma died I tried to stay on in the old house—she would have wanted me to. But it was so big. I didn't know what to do!"

It seemed to me Bessie was the scaredest, loneliest woman I had ever seen. "What did you do?" I asked as a matter-of-factly as I could.

Bessie set down her cup, "Mamma's lawyer helped me," she answered falteringly. He had advised her to sell the big, old home and move into a one-room apartment in a remodeled old-fashioned house.

Coming to Happy Hours was the best thing Bessie could have done, but I wondered how she had got up her courage to do it.

"Well, Mrs. Clark, one of the women at Church, comes here. She kept nagging at me, saying I might as well come because I don't do anything else."

It wasn't a very satisfactory reason for coming to the Club, but at least she was there and I was determined to keep her with us. She didn't think she would come back, but I would stop at her home on my way to the meeting and she couldn't very well refuse to come with me. After two or three weeks she came on her own. She didn't play any games, and she didn't dance, but a few people who just come to visit would sit by her and talk to her. Pretty soon you could see she was beginning to enjoy herself.

Then that Mrs. Brown stepped in. She's a regular she-devil, tall and skinny with no more shape than a hat rack. She dyes her hair vermilion, imagining it makes her look fifty although everyone knows she's practically seventy. She didn't favor Bessie with so much as a hello until the afternoon she saw Mr. Ames talking and laughing with Bessie. Mr. Ames was the old harridan's prey and she strode over to them in a hurry.

"How's your cough, Bessie? You look so thin and bad. It's no wonder you don't do anything. Isn't it pitiful, Mr. Ames?"

I could have choked her. Bessie's lips were twitching and her eyes were getting the old hurt look. She left. That was my day to be on the refreshment committee so I couldn't leave before five o'clock, but as soon as we got things tidied up I went straight to Bessie's house. I found her sitting in her mother's little old rocker staring out of the window at nothing.

I knew where she kept things in her little kitchen—a corner set off from the rest of the room by a folding screen—and before long I had supper well under way. Bessie, sad as she was, yielded to the tempting smell of frying bacon.

By the time we were through eating, Bessie was ready to talk about Happy Hours. "Really, Emma," she began, "Mrs. Brown, mean as she is, is right. I get scared if anyone speaks to me. I just don't belong."

"For Heaven's sakes, Bessie Makepeace, stop feeling sorry for yourself," I snapped. "You know perfectly well you 'belong' as much as anyone else! You could learn to play something. Then you wouldn't worry about people not wanting you," I said more calmly.

"Me play cards? I couldn't learn a card game."

"Why not?" I demanded, "Don't you want to?"

We argued a while longer, but in the end Bessie agreed to let me teach her Canasta. It wasn't long before she was a regular member of a sixsome. She didn't get over her shyness. Still, it was a wonderful thing to watch her playing in her group. Her eyes would shine, and she would laugh at the things people said. Sometimes she would venture a little joke herself. Her cough left her completely.

In February people began to talk about the circus. It is difficult to say why the circus means so much to these people. Perhaps it's nostalgia, but I think it's more than that. The marvelous, breathtaking, terrifying antics of the performers lift the older folks—floats them clear away from pains and arthritis and hardened arteries and cataracts—and raises them up in a glorious fantasy of beauty and strength. We talked about the clowns, the daredevil acrobats, the horses that danced to music and counted and even spelled out words; about the hot dogs, and popcorn, and double balloons; and rude Mrs. McCarthy who always insisted upon sitting in the front row.

Bessie Makepeace listened in a detached way to the circus talk. Some of the anecdotes amused her; others startled or perplexed her; but she never showed any real interest.

When the date for the circus was finally announced and the invitation officially received and accepted, the group became electric with excitement. "Are you going?" everyone asked everyone else. Of course everyone was going.

Bessie was asked the same questions as everyone else, but she never made a direct answer. The hunted look was coming back and she was coughing again. One morning as I thought about how upset she had become, I suddenly realized that she was afraid of the circus and wasn't going to go.

If someone else had decided to stay away from the circus I would simply have thought, "Too bad. You'll miss a good show." But with Bessie it was as if she had elected to commit suicide. Through some subtle machination of her subconscious the circus had become the summation of all her tormenting devils. Her timidity, her ignorances, her indecisions had gathered together and become the circus, and it was too big for her. It was behemoth. She was running away from it—and from all the little victories she had won.

When the realization hit me, I rushed over to her apartment. I was scarcely inside her door before I started to scold and plead.

"Bessie Makepeace, you certainly are going to that circus! Everyone goes. It's a wonderful thing!"

Bessie stood still while I raved on and she seemed to grow smaller, whiter, older. It occurred to me she might be going to faint, but I went on raging. The circus was the test. If it beat her, if she stayed away, she would go back—back—back—until she was again just frightened, sick, shadowy Bessie Makepeace. She was trembling all over but she didn't weep or faint. Her voice was so small I could scarcely hear her.

"Emma, I can't go. I never went to a circus, never. Crowds terrify me. It took all my courage to go to Happy Hours. Yes, I'm glad I did it. But I can't go to the circus. Last year, they say, a clown sat right down in Mrs. White's lap! The band plays so loud it seems as if the drums are right inside your head! There's the smell of popcorn. Everyone eats peanuts and cotton candy just like children. McClellans took their little grandson with them once and he got sick all over someone's lap. Dust fills the place so you can't breathe. I'd cough until I choked to death."

There was nothing left to say. I had said it all. My head was pounding. My heart was choking me. Then, all at once I felt exhausted. I did what I haven't done since I was a little girl; I began to cry. Now I was ashamed. I started to leave.

"Please, Emma," she said, "don't go. I'll go to your circus tomorrow."

We sat together. It was the best circus they ever had. Everyone said so. Bessie watched everything. I always like the elephant best, but Bessie's favorites were the trapeze artists, especially one. She was a very slight girl in crimson tights, and she swung hand over hand up a thick rope to a trapeze at the very top of the tent. Every now and then as she went up she would pause, support herself against the rope, and extend an arm in a graceful, languid wave. The orchestra played softly as she climbed and the lights all went out except for the great beam of a spotlight. For a while she swung playfully on the trapeze, waving and blowing kisses down to us. She started to spin, up—drop, up—drop, the music keeping us with her as she got faster. Up—drop, up—drop. The music stopped and a frenzied drum carried on until the spinning was so wild even the drum couldn't follow. She spun and spun and all you could see up there was a fiery spark in the path of the spotlight.

When it was over, Mr. and Mrs. Roberts drove us home. On the way Bessie asked us all to come up to her apartment for coffee.

"Won't you stop for a cup of coffee?" she said, just as easily as you might have. "Please do!" Her voice was singing.

I couldn't believe my ears.

From *Senior Citizen*, March 1963. Used by permission.

FRIEND OF THE GREAT ZACCHETTI

Mark Friedlander

Of course, many factors were involved. There was the excitement of pennants lancing the sky, the sawdust-scattered ring on which were fixed a thousand pair of eyes, and there was the magic of superb performances.

Such were the circumstances under which during those few summer days, less than a week, they became old friends. As for the *reasons,* the boy's presence recalled to the great Zacchetti an outlook he too had once known. In the acrobat the boy saw a hero in the flesh.

Yet there was something additional, subtler, present almost from the start. It had to do with life's purposes, the omens of which the man had learned to read in his forty-two years. Always these signs had come to him at the climaxes of his career.

So it was after the matinee on that first day when Ross made his way among the slanting guy lines to the rear of the great tent. There the oncoming night already cast its sad, beautiful tints over the scattered trailer caravan of transport equipment and living quarters. From the running board of the truck where he sat, the acrobat was gazing thoughtfully at the west.

Evening and the let-down after his act gripped him. Then he had looked up and there stood the boy—not one of a noisy group like most but quietly by himself.

"Well," Zacchetti inquired at the end of a pause. "What do you want, kid?"

"Nothing."

"Nothing? In my life I've seen a million kids and never did I know one that wanted nothing."

"What did they want?"

"Ha, that's good. First you comprehend," Zacchetti went on in mock enumeration like a clerk reading from a list. "First they wish free tickets. If that is your thought, dismiss it. Then they ask me to write my name. Number three, to get a job. Four, to feel my muscle. You want to feel? Here."

Zacchetti's arm stiffened but not like a schoolboy's. From shoulder to elbow it froze parallel with his torso. Ross touched the great fist of muscle swelling smoothly beneath the skin. When the acrobat moved his forearm, a tremendous tide swept across the hard chest. Abruptly he slapped his leg.

"And now you are satisfied? Yes," he said loudly. "So bye bye."

The boy sucked his lips in over his teeth. From his high forehead the brown hair tumbled over one eye. The sensitive mouth would change little when hurt, though the chin would set and the blue eyes seem deeper.

"What now?" Zacchetti demanded.

At that moment, he recalled later, it began to happen. The key entered the lock and something *outside* took over their lives.

When Ross raised his head to reply, their eyes met for an instant. Before his question was answered, the acrobat saw they were friends.

"I watched the one-arm swing. It was . . .

was great," Ross concluded, his tones conveying an appreciation of the word's inadequacy.

"Merci bien," Zacchetti said. He extended his hand, the wrist showing pale where the leather band had encircled it. "What's your name, kid?"

"Ross Bondy."

"You are with your parents?"

"Hilary and Bob are with me. They are my friends but I left them after the show."

"You and me we are friends, too."

"Sure. Aren't you only going to be here a week?"

"Until Saturday. Perhaps you come again."

"Well, I've spent my whole allowance," Ross confessed, adding hopefully, "Maybe I could make a loan from Dad."

"Pouf. Listen, tomorrow before the matinee I will tell them to let you in without paying. Now I think maybe your mama waits with supper. Bye bye."

"Thanks. See you tomorrow."

"Zacchetti to my friends."

"Thanks, Zacchetti."

The following day and the next they learned much concerning each other. The acrobat was filled with curiosity about everything that went on in the boy's home: how the family lived, how the children were brought up, what their father did, their future plans.

He himself, he explained, had run away from his brother in Milan when he was ten. He had starved in the streets of a dozen cities before the performer LaFond took him under his wing and taught him the act. It was more of what he had learned *since* that he spoke, however, and more of people than of things.

Ah, he had travelled! Men had to live together and yet apart. That was the secret. But for each was kinship to be found somewhere, not of blood but the heart. He had come upon it in the Australian rancher in Melbourne and the Negro stevedore at Caracas and Ross. That was fortunate, since a man would surely die without friends.

By the fourth day they had never been strangers. Sometimes they wandered into the deserted tent where Ross imagined the audiences sweeping down from the empty benches. They visited the superb nervous circus horses in their stalls or the elephants, swaying their trunks slowly from side to side.

Ross said, as if speaking his thoughts aloud, "Gosh, things are going to be different after you go."

"Perhaps. But let me show you what time is, Ross. We make believe that all clocks stop and by magic nothing changes." He snapped his fingers twice. "Maybe one second, maybe a thousand years pass. Yes, you see what time is, my friend? We do not worry about it."

Nevertheless to the man the future offered a lonelier prospect than ever. The tight inadequacy of his life opened to admit the boy. He was going to miss him. More and more he sensed the purpose, still obscure but unfolding, which had brought them together.

Later he smiled to himself at the remark of Van Huit, the ringmaster. He was well aware his performance had improved. For the first time in months he had done ninety turns. Perhaps youth was contagious.

But joking aside, it was for Ross he wished to excel. He desired to be magnificent so that when the boy grew up to be a doctor or a teacher or something he would think back to Zacchetti and aim at such splendor for himself. He wanted Ross to recognize its quality—a kind of wonderful pause in life, an absolute attainment for an instant—the perfect gesture that became breathless by its sheer perfection while all else fell away upon the junk heap of the ages. . . .

That evening a reporter from the local paper came to the circus with a photographer and the next day his picture and a story about him appeared. Ross brought the clipping. The boy's pride in it gave him real pleasure.

"Did LaFond honestly set the world's record?" Ross asked.

"Yes, that is true. One hundred fifty."

"Golly. What's the most you ever did?"

"One hundred and forty."

He remembered the occasion three years before when it had struck him of a sudden to try. He never knew why. Teeth clenched, his body had swung in great punishing circles until, within ten of the record, he had been beaten. What had Adam LaFond possessed that escaped him?

"Hilary says nobody could ever do that many," Ross was saying.

"Then your Hilary is a fool."

"He never believes anything."

"One must," Zacchetti said, laying a hand upon his shoulder. "Always you believe people should be kind and that God watches over us. Yes. Without it, life is nothing. I do not expect you should understand but it will come when you are older."

After a moment, Ross said, "I believe your act is the greatest in the whole world."

Zacchetti started to protest but checked himself, toning it down for the boy's sake.

"It's pretty good, even if not the best," he conceded.

On Friday afternoon, two boys of Ross's age approached where they sat talking.

"Beat it," Ross ordered when he saw them. "You don't belong here."

Instead they came closer and the one with the round face said, "I knew we'd find you."

"It's Hilary and Bob," Ross whispered. "I tried to duck out on them."

"Never mind," Zacchetti said.

"We trailed him easy, didn't we?" Hilary remarked. "Bob and me can trail anybody."

"You don't have to do everything I do. They're just a couple of old copycats." Ross was so angry he was almost in tears. "Wait until we get back."

"Did you like the performance?" Zacchetti intervened.

"Aw, pretty good. It was all right," Hilary acknowledged.

"Only pretty good, yes?" Zacchetti asked.

"We figured maybe you'd try and break the record or something," Bob explained, "after what was in the paper."

"Ninety, that isn't so good?" Zacchetti pursued.

They shrugged and looked away. Ross said, "They don't know anything. They don't know what they're talking about."

"I know more what I'm talking about than you," Hilary answered. "My uncle is in the Navy and he saw the atomic bomb explode. When he gets back, he's going to tell me about it too."

"A lot I care for your old atomic bomb," Ross said.

"It's the biggest thing in the world," Hilary went on. "It could blow up a million people if they wanted it to."

My God, Zacchetti thought, boys and atomic bombs. Soon perhaps they will be for sale in the toy stores for children to buy.

"Is it strong, this bomb?" he inquired.

"My goodness, don't you read the papers?" Bob exclaimed.

"But there are still some things it cannot do," Zacchetti added.

"What, for instance?" Hilary cried. "The atomic bomb could do anything."

"Why, just one, it could not make your mama love you. It could not ride one of our horses."

"Aw, that's not fair."

"But, yes. So far the thing that can do that deed is more powerful."

"What thing?" Hilary demanded with disbelief.

"Friendship, love, what you like to call it."

"Aw, that's Sunday school stuff."

"Nevertheless, it is so. For that I am very glad and I think Ross is too."

"You mean it could do anything, anything at all?"

"Oh, yes."

"If it's so wonderful then, maybe it could even help you break the record. Otherwise I guess it's all baloney."

So, Zacchetti thought to himself, the final tumbler of the lock fell into place. There was no more mystery. He understood now what he had sensed before. It was more than to have destiny depend on a child's challenge. It was more than Ross was watching him. Had he meant what he had said? Well, he had said it or it had been spoken for him and the three of them had taken him at his word. While they waited for his answer, the silence widened.

He looked at Hilary, feeling Ross's eyes on him.

"Yes, it could help me do that easy, kid."

His sudden knowledge gave him an odd sensation. He felt a kind of happiness he had not known for a long time. With this then he would give his friend Ross the strength the boy would need when he was older and had to face doubt.

"When will you show us?" Hilary said.

"You can come here tomorrow night."

"Okay."

"So run home now, you two, and we see about your bombs."

After Hilary and Bob left, he said to Ross smiling, "There are many Hilaries in the world. We will show them together, yes."

"We?" Ross repeated. "Gee, what can I do, Zacchetti? I wish I *could* help you."

"You can, my friend. No, I am very serious. This will be a hard thing. That is why without you I cannot succeed. While I am up there you must keep believing it. Do not stop. That will give me strength and there will be no doubt then about breaking the record. Let us shake hands and remember. Tomorrow afternoon I rest but you come at night with them and do as I say. Then the record goes pouf."

That afternoon he limited himself to seventy turns and later had Van Huit send a man to massage him. He said nothing, however, of what was on his mind. Lying in his bunk afterward he could distinguish the multitudes of small night sounds outside the trailer: the horses shook their heads, an elephant dragged his chain, light winds fluttered the tent, and cars passed at intervals along the highway.

His thoughts sank into the past. He heard LaFond cursing him a hundred times, a thousand, but always teaching him, or boasting of the command performance before the little princesses at which he had set the record. Suddenly, for the first time doubt assailed him. The other had been only twenty-nine, thirteen years younger. He felt himself perspiring.

His fear ebbed as abruptly as it had come when he thought of Ross, the steady blue eyes, and the serious, sensitive mouth. "Princesses," he exclaimed into the darkness. What was good enough for them was not sufficient for his friend and strangely with that thought he felt better and fell asleep.

Ross's uncle, Dr. Bondy, asked, "Say, how many times already have you kids seen this?"

"Hilary and me twice," Bob said. "I guess Ross was here every day."

"But tonight's special," Hilary added as they squeezed past a dozen pairs of knees to get to their seats. "Zacchetti thinks he's going to break the record."

"You be quiet," Ross commanded.

The boy had hardly spoken all evening, the doctor realized.

"You all right, Ross?" he inquired.

"Yes, Uncle Dick. Zacchetti is too going to break the record. Don't you think he could?"

"I don't know, son."

As soon as the lights were lowered, the clowns came tumbling after one another into the ring. After them was the human pyramid, followed by the dancers, who were succeeded in turn by the elephants. When, when, *when* will he come, wondered Ross. He sat perfectly still, his throat hurting, until at last he saw him dressed in white tights, standing motionless in the ring.

Immediately after Van Huit announced him, it was plain that Zacchetti had varied his routine. Instead of mounting the rope suspended from the top of the tent hand over hand as in the past, he gripped it with his legs.

At the same time he signaled to be raised and held a piece of paper out to the ringmaster who glanced up quickly. The ringmaster's face was grave as he spoke briefly to the band-leader and returned to the center of the ring.

"Ladies and gentlemen," he announced and the patent leather boots flashed beneath the spotlight as he strode. "Your attention, please. Within the next few minutes, the great Zacchetti will attempt to break the world's record for the giant one-arm swing, which now stands at one hundred and fifty. In view of this, we will omit his less spectacular but daring feats on the high bar."

The band resumed as everyone applauded. Ross watched Zacchetti transfer to the horizontal bar high above, balancing delicately and testing the strap around his waist. Beneath him hung a short length of rope ending in a silk loop into which he now thrust his hand. Then he left the bar and swayed slowly fifty feet above the ground. For an instant his legs extended straight out from his body. With a sudden tremor he had described a giant circle, his entire body a spoke about the loop.

Ross began to count. His chest was a well of pain and his neck hurt but he paid no atten-tion. Zacchetti had gathered momentum and the pinwheel motion became continuous and regular. Ten the boy counted. At forty he was afraid to think how many yet remained. The white blur continued and every tenth revolution was punctuated by a roll of the drums.

He found himself standing but it was as if it were someone else who shook off his uncle's restraining hand. He was shouting too and it was as if a strange voice came from his constricted throat.

As the acrobat passed one hundred, the music grew lower as though even the players were awed at the tireless performance. It was more than Ross had ever seen him do but still there was no end. The pain within the boy

grew but he took no more notice of it than of the tears that ran down his cheeks

At one hundred and forty Van Huit, who had been standing to one side of the ring, drew a shining nickel revolver from his pocket. Ross counted through blurred eyes from which his fist kept striking the tears away so he could see . . . 47, 48, 49, 150. The pistol went off.

Still the white figure swung, one, two, three, four times more before halting half way through the next swing and hanging while Zacchetti's feet and free hand groped weakly for the other rope, which the attendants lowered quickly to the ground.

Ross was aware of nothing, neither the roars of the crowd nor Van Huit's announcement as Zacchetti was helped backstage. What he had seen and felt he knew he could never forget. The tears still coursed down his face.

There were two more acts. At the end he felt his uncle's arm across his shoulders as the people around them rose to leave.

"Let's wait until the rest get out," his uncle said. "Are you all right?"

"Yes, Uncle Dick," answered Ross calmly. He felt different, older.

"You're sure? I didn't think it would upset you so."

"We have to go back and see him, Uncle Dick."

"Well, Ross, I don't know. It's late and. . . ."

"Please, Dr. Bondy," Hilary said.

"We have to," Ross went on. "He's my friend and I promised." He sounded very solemn.

Van Huit barred their way to the door of Zacchetti's trailer.

"Nobody can go in, please. We are waiting for the doctor."

"I'm a doctor."

The expression on Van Huit's face changed. "Come this way, please," he said.

Ross alone followed his uncle and the ring-master up the three steps. Inside Zacchetti lay

in his bunk, still in costume, his eyes closed.
The gasoline lantern overhead made all
the shadows soft and solid. Sitting on a stool
the doctor leaned over and put his ear to
the hard chest. Zacchetti opened his eyes.

"Hello," he said. "We did it, Ross."

"Yes."

"You liked it?"

"It was great. The greatest act I ever saw."

"Sure. You know, up there I could feel
you would help me."

Dr. Bondy sat up and Ross said, "This is
my uncle. He's a doctor."

"How do you do?" Dr. Bondy said.
Zacchetti acknowledged the introduction
with a nod and a smile.

"You'll be all right," the doctor said,
"But. . . ."

"I know," Zacchetti said. "No more *up
there*. Right?"

"Zacchetti," Ross began.

"My friend, it doesn't matter. Without it
was one maybe two years more. Like this,
they never forget. Huh?"

"No."

"It is late," the acrobat said holding his
hand out. "You go back with Hilary and Bob.
No more atomic bombs. We are friends,
yes? And you know what a thing we have done
together. That is the most important. So
good night."

The boy was unable to speak as they shook
hands. He turned and the doctor stood up
also but Zacchetti called him back.

"Please, doctor, one more moment. Van
Huit will show the boy out. Thank you."

When the two men were alone, Zacchetti
took a velvet box from beneath his pillow and
handed it over. "For Ross, please, tomorrow,
after I have gone. It is something my old
friend LaFond gave me. He received it
for breaking the record and I give it to the
boy."

"He'll be very proud," the doctor said.
"And what will you do?"

"Perhaps I will go to sea for a few years.
There is no need to worry, I assure you.
Doctor, you have seen much of life?"

"Every doctor does."

"So. And you have thought much of it
also?"

"Yes. I've done that too."

"Good. Then if you will, please tell this to
the boy. Not yet but sometime when he is
older. You comprehend. I must break the record because with my big mouth in front of
his friends I say if a man believes a thing
enough he can do it."

"So that was it."

"Yes, and now he sees he learned something of life." He paused shaking his
head slowly on the pillow. "Maybe you think I
teach him a lesson, Doctor? I say no. I've
the big mouth to talk and travel so much and
have seen the world. It is I who learn more
than the boy does. At forty-two years he
makes me see tonight what it is to have real
faith. You will tell him this one day please."

"I'll tell him," Dr. Bondy said. "And now
you'd better get some rest. Good night and
good luck."

"Thank you. Au revoir."

None of the boys spoke as Dr. Bondy drove
them home. It was the first time he'd ever
known that to happen.

The next morning Ross took the bus to the
circus grounds after breakfast. The workmen
had been busy through the night and there was
nothing left except the holes where the stakes
had been driven, some straw, and a sort of
a circle marking the ring

Standing where he thought Zacchetti's trailer
had been he looked at the sky. The wind
blew his thick hair and his fingers combed it
away from his eyes. Presently, he walked
in the direction from which he had come. He
didn't look back. His forehead was wrinkled.
He had much to think about.

From *Collier's*, May 10, 1947. Used by permission.

DAN RICE
ENTERTAINS CONGRESS

Maria Ward Brown

Congress adjourning to attend a circus! Dan Rice, in April, 1850, appeared in the circus ring at Washington as the "great jester and clown" to startle and delight the assembled statesmen.

The day had been set aside for Rice's benefit. Members of both houses of Congress, the heads of departments, the President and Cabinet, and scores of leading people in the social life of the Capitol received elaborate invitations printed on satin for the benefit performance. Nearly everybody accepted the invitation, and it was generally supposed that the bits of satin were free passes to the show.

Among the first to arrive at the tent was Henry Clay with a party of ladies. The satin invitations were presented as passes of admission.

"How many in the party?" sternly asked the doorkeeper, who had been drilled for his post.

"Twelve," answered Clay confidently.

"Twelve dollars!" exclaimed the doorkeeper. "Buy your tickets at the box-office." Dan Rice was behind the canvas looking through a peep-hole and enjoying the agitation of Mr. Clay, who, after fumbling in his pockets, was unable to find the necessary amounts. The practical joker had provided for such emergencies, and had nearby a well-known Washington tradesman with pockets stuffed with silver dollars. Henry Clay's embarrassment was relieved and his party passed in. He remarked, "I'll bet this is one of Dan's tricks." It was.

President Zach. Taylor was there; so were Daniel Webster, John C. Calhoun, Stephen A. Douglas, and scores of others. It was a great day for Dan. That he was a high-roller is evinced by the fact that he rattled off fifty original verses of "local hits," and everybody was scored, from the austere President down to the pages in Congress.

From *The Life of Dan Rice*, J. J. Little & Co., New York, 1901.

NOT TOO BIG A SACRIFICE

Arthur M. Schlesinger [Sr.]

From time to time one-ring circuses and dog-and-pony shows came
to Xenia, and on one unforgettable occasion in the summer of
1902 or 1903, Buffalo Bill's Wild West Show. In anticipation the
whole county grew excited, and to cash in on the expected
attendance the townsfolk set up along the sidewalk, booths heaped
with sandwiches and tubs of lemonade. Well, the great day
arrived with its exhibitions of sharpshooting, frontiersmen
in covered wagons beating off redskins, and other astounding
feats; but the weatherman had neglected to cooperate, and
a deluge of rain reduced the out-of-town patrons almost to zero.
That night sandwiches were a drug on the market. My father,
like many another thrifty parent, loaded up with a big supply,
and for days afterward the family ate them as the buns grew harder
and the butter more rancid. But we youngsters did not think
this too big a sacrifice for the marvels we had seen.

From *In Retrospect: The History of a Historian*. Harcourt, Brace & World, Inc.
New York 1963. Used by permission.

SURELY, PARADISE

John Masefield

Most of us, when young, have known the delight of going to the circus. To those with imagination it is a delight which does not lessen much with age, but remains unchanged, year after year. The old have been known to leave the circus-tent saying that thus, surely, Paradise will first appear to the entering soul, as a world of strangeness and beauty in which all the inhabitants have a loveliness, a skill, or a swiftness not before seen, and where even the oldest jokes take on new life. The young can seldom leave the circus-tent without the thought that this is life itself, real life, the heart and glow of life. . . . The middle-aged, coming from the circus, reflect that whatever their own wisdom, position, or power may be, yet here has been something for which one would give much. For what sage is there so wise that he would not give a finger to be able to do a "jump-up" or somersault upon the back of a ring-horse, or hold a thousand people spellbound, like the clown in the red and white?

Introduction to Edward Seago's *Circus Company—Life on the Road with the Travelling Show,* Putnam, London, 1933. Used by permission of Edward Seago.